New Directions in
the Philosophy of
Social Science

New Directions in the Philosophy of Social Science

Daniel Little

ROWMAN & LITTLEFIELD
INTERNATIONAL

London • New York

Published by Rowman & Littlefield International, Ltd.
Unit A, Whitacre Mews, 26-34 Stannary Street, London SE11 4AB
www.rowmaninternational.com

Rowman & Littlefield International, Ltd. is an affiliate of Rowman & Littlefield
4501 Forbes Boulevard, Suite 200, Lanham, Maryland 20706, USA
With additional offices in Boulder, New York, Toronto (Canada), and Plymouth (UK)
www.rowman.com

British Library Cataloguing in Publication Data
A catalogue record for this book is available from the British Library

ISBN: HB 978-1-7834-8739-4
      PB 978-1-7834-8740-0

Library of Congress Cataloging-in-Publication Data
Names: Little, Daniel, author.
Title: New directions in the philosophy of social science / Daniel Little.
Description: Lanham : Rowman & Littlefield International, 2016. | Includes
    bibliographical references and index.
Identifiers: LCCN 2016029098 (print) | LCCN 2016034324 (ebook) |
    ISBN 9781783487394 (cloth : alk. paper) | ISBN 9781783487400 (pbk. : alk. paper) |
    ISBN 9781783487417 (electronic)
Subjects: LCSH: Social sciences—Philosophy.
Classification: LCC H61 .L544 2016 (print) | LCC H61 (ebook) |
    DDC 300.1—dc23 LC record available at https://lccn.loc.gov/2016029098

Printed in the United States of America

Contents

List of Illustrations   vii

Foreword   ix

Introduction   xiii

1 A Better Social Ontology   1

2 Actor-centered Sociology   37

3 Social Things   73

4 Reduction and Emergence   115

5 Generativity and Complexity   147

6 Social Causation   183

7 Social Realism   221

Conclusion   259

References   263

Index   275

About the Author   279

List of Illustrations

FIGURES

Figure I.1   Themes in the philosophy of social science   xix
Figure 2.1   Map of sociological approaches   71
Figure 3.1   Levels of the social   88
Figure 3.2   A flat social ontology   89
Figure 4.1   Levels of the social   116
Figure 4.2   Coleman's boat (drawn after Hedström
               and Ylikoski 2010: 59)   119
Figure 4.3a   Supervenience of social facts   130
Figure 4.3b   Weak nonsupervenience of social facts   130
Figure 4.3c   Strong nonsupervenience of social facts   131
Figure 5.1   EpiDEM model of organizational recruitment   160
Figure 5.2   Scenario 1: occurrence of mobilization with no
               party members   162
Figure 5.3   Scenario 2: occurrence of mobilization with
               1% party members   162
Figure 6.1   Causal powers, causal mechanisms, and microfoundations 203
Figure 6.2   Meso-meso causal relations   209
Figure 6.3   Inter-level causal mechanism   213
Figure 7.1   Taxonomy of social science methods   243

TABLES

Table I.1   Sources in three debates   xix
Table 1.1   Michael Mann's concepts in analyzing fascism (2004)   31

Table 2.1   Central methodological assumptions   72
Table 5.1   Modifications to REBELLION code   161
Table 6.1   Examples of social mechanisms   193

Foreword

This book is one of the fruits of an experiment in philosophical writing that I began in 2007. I created *Understanding Society* as an online venue where I would be able to do a different kind of academic writing. It was to be a "blog"; but, more accurately, it was a venue for "open-source philosophy" where I could formulate my thinking about a series of ideas and topics about the social sciences and the nature of society without attempting to regiment my thoughts into a sequential argument consisting of "chapters" and "books." I described the work from the start as a "web-based, dynamic monograph on the philosophy of social science," and it has lived up to this description better than I ever could have hoped. To use a different point of reference, the blog became my laboratory notebook, representing the findings and progress of my thinking about a number of topics about the nature of society and social knowledge.

Here is how I described the project in 2007:

> This site addresses a series of topics in the philosophy of social science. What is involved in "understanding society"? The blog is an experiment in thinking, one idea at a time. Look at it as "open-source philosophy"—a web-based, dynamic monograph on the philosophy of social science and some foundational issues about the nature of the social world.

Today *Understanding Society* has lived up to these ambitions. There are over 1,050 posts, amounting to over a million words of philosophical discussion and reflection. The site has received over six million page views since 2010, and has welcomed visitors from every part of the world. The impact that *Understanding Society* has achieved is perhaps a sign of the increasing and positive role that digital media can play in the creation and dissemination of academic research.

The topics I have treated in *Understanding Society* have ranged widely. The most frequent topics are in the areas of social ontology and social epistemology: What is the nature of social reality, and how can social science better come to know and explain that reality? I have also treated topics ranging over a broad and diverse set of other issues: failures of democracy, the workings of race in the United States, the features underlying collective action, the nature of personal character, the relevance of quantum mechanics to the social world, the nature of historical explanation and historical change, and diverse approaches to theories of the actor. It is striking to me to realize how much I have learned as a philosopher through the activity of writing the blog, the books that I would not have otherwise read, and the positions that I would not have otherwise considered. Writing *Understanding Society* continues to stimulate me to read and think outside the confines of the specific tradition in which I work.

Here are the first words published in *Understanding Society* on November 2, 2007:

> I maintain that virtually all social entities are "plastic": their properties change significantly over time, as a result of the purposive and unintentional behavior of the socially constructed individuals who make up a society. Organizations, labor unions, universities, churches, and social identities all show a substantial degree of flexibility and fluidity over time, and this fact leads to a substantial degree of heterogeneity among groups of similar social organizations and institutions. This points to a general and important observation about the constitution of the social world: The properties of a social entity or practice can change over time; they are not rigid, fixed, or timeless. They are not bound into consistent and unchanging categories of entities, such as "bureaucratic state," "Islamic society," or "leftist labor organization." Molecules of water preserve their physical characteristics no matter what. But in contrast to natural substances such as gold or water, social things can change their properties indefinitely.

As you read this book you will see that this view has continued to reflect my best thinking about the distinctive nature of the social world.

New Directions in the Philosophy of Social Science is my effort to pull several of these threads together into a more sequential and cumulative form. I have presented many of the ideas raised in the blog at conferences and workshops in Europe, China, and the United States, and these opportunities for face-to-face discussion of the issues have been invaluable. There has been a great deal of useful interaction between the new sphere of online publication and debate and the more traditional academic forums of conferences and workshops, and I offer my appreciation to the dozens of young scholars whose innovative ideas and perspectives have proven so stimulating. For this book, I have selected the topics that seem to me to be the most fundamental to current efforts at reframing the philosophy of social science in ways that make it most responsive to the needs of good social science theory and research in the twenty-first century. This work has proven to be more difficult than I imagined. It turns out that a book requires a different level of generality than a "web-based, dynamic monograph." So, the work of synthesis and focus in preparing *New Directions* has been demanding.

Readers are invited to visit *Understanding Society* at www.understandingsociety.blogspot.com. The themes that are developed in this book will continue to be discussed in the pages of *Understanding Society*, and the discussions will continue.

① The importance of the social science
for understanding the world around us —
large macro-events war, civil wars
give an extended example

② The importance of individual level
processes — moral + personal identity —
what makes us who we are

Introduce us to   the payoff

③ Social science: war, religion, extremism

④ Phineas Gage — example — moral identity —
what makes us who we are

The downpayment

journey, boats
ships etc ← guidance
standards
✓ how we go about
doing stuff

Introduction

WHY "PHILOSOPHY OF SOCIAL SCIENCE"?

The subject of the philosophy of social science is important but poorly understood. The field considers the most foundational questions about the possibility of scientific knowledge about the social world. What are the scope and limits of scientific knowledge of society? What is involved in arriving at a scientific understanding of society? What are the most appropriate standards for judging proffered social explanations? A philosophy can guide us as we construct a field of knowledge, and it can serve as a set of regulative standards as we conduct and extend that field of knowledge. Philosophy has served both intellectual functions, as guide and as normative recommendations, in the past century.

The importance of the philosophy of social science derives from two things: first, the urgency and complexity of the challenges posed by the poorly understood social processes that surround us in twenty-first-century society, and second, the unsettled status of our understanding of the nature of the social world and the ways we can best describe and explain it. It is as if we were passengers on a technologically complex spacecraft whose propulsion and life-support systems we do not fully understand; and further, we have only a limited understanding of the systems of science and engineering on the basis of which these technologies were designed and maintained. We would have a very lively interest in learning the science that explains the workings of the technologies, and in learning the limitations and areas of uncertainty that the relevant sciences include. Likewise, it is crucial for us to come to a better and more well-grounded understanding of the social, political, and behavioral phenomena that constitute the modern social world. And, there are

i

e.g.

pick sci.fi. examples

large and unresolved philosophical questions about the logic of social science knowledge and theory on the basis of which to arrive at that understanding.

A better understanding of the nature and logic of the social sciences has great practical importance. Just think of the complexity and magnitude of the processes that have been under way in the past fifty years: rapid change in youth culture, ethnic hatred and conflict, full incorporation of most countries into the global economy, terrorism, the emergence of East Asia as a manufacturing super power, population movements, the reemergence of significant social inequalities within and across countries, deepening of inner-city poverty, new social networks created by the Internet, and so on. And, these processes are not well understood. We do not have comprehensive theories for which these contemporary processes are a special case—whether "modernization theory," "world systems theory," "rational choice theory," or "theory of exploitation."

In fact, it is a radical misunderstanding of the nature of the social, to imagine that there might be such theories. Rather, social change is a contingent, multi-threaded social congeries of behavior, institutions, and contingent events, and no single set of comprehensive theories can be expected to explain all these phenomena. These changes are as deep, rapid, and perplexing as those associated with the process of industrialization in nineteenth-century England—and consider how profoundly the experience of Manchester and Birmingham stimulated new sociological thinking in the hands of Engels, Tocqueville, Marx, Carlyle, and the other founders of modern Western sociology. So, the complexity and opacity of the contemporary social world demand a better understanding of the logic and methods of the social sciences.

Or, consider a more current example. Contemporary China is a vivid demonstration of the fact that sociology is not a "finished" science. The processes of change that are under way in both rural and urban settings in China are novel and contingent. Existing sociological theory does not provide a basis for conceptualizing these processes according to a few simple templates—modernization, urbanization, structural transformation, or demographic transition. Instead, a new sociology for China needs to engage in sustained descriptive inquiry, to untangle the many processes that are occurring simultaneously, and innovative theory formation, in order to find some explanatory order in the many empirical realities that China represents. The social reality of China is complex—many separate processes are simultaneously unfolding and interacting; and it is diverse—very different conditions and processes are occurring in different regions and sectors of Chinese society.

Consider one specific area of change, the wide and heterogeneous range of processes involved in the transformations of rural society. Here, we find the explosive growth of a periurban sector that is neither city nor village; the rapid expansion of businesses and factories; the creation of an entrepreneurial social segment; the migration of tens of millions of people from rural areas to cities and from poor areas to more affluent areas; the emergence of new social groups in local society; the push–pull relationships between central government and regional and local government; the shifting policy positions of the central government toward rural conditions; the occurrence of social movements and disturbances over issues of property, labor, environment, and corruption; the rise of ethnicity as a political factor; various permutations of clientelism as a mechanism of political control; and the social consequences of family planning policies (e.g. skewed sex ratios). These are all social processes involving policy makers, local officials, entrepreneurs, farmers, workers, business owners, activists, and other actors; they are processes that have their own dynamics and tempos; they are processes that interact with each other; and they aggregate to outcomes that are difficult or impossible to calculate on the basis of analysis of the processes themselves.

Sociologist C. K. Lee (2007) explores the sociology of industrial change and protest in China's labor institutions in an appropriately local way: What are the specific features of the Chinese economy, Chinese production, Chinese policy and law, and Chinese culture that produce two rather different patterns of protest and contention in two segments of the Chinese manufacturing economy (sunbelt and rustbelt)?

Lee emphasizes the contingency of these developments and their dependency on rather proximate social causal factors. She believes that the nature of the mobilizations and protests is affected by the way in which they are framed. Writing about Rustbelt protest: "My main concern.. . . is to analyze how the characteristics and limits of worker protests are linked to the mode of state regulation of labor and the social reproduction of labor power" (Lee 2007: 71). Elsewhere she makes the point that sunbelt protests have less mobilizational "staying power" because of the living situation of migrant workers: they return to their villages in times of distress, and their movement collapses. She distinguishes subtypes of Rustbelt protests by their underlying issue: nonpayment protests, neighborhood protests, bankruptcy protests. In other words, rather specific circumstances that set the context for life and work in the two regions and sectors have substantial effects on the nature of dissent and protest that results. She also highlights the nuance and heterogeneity of the social realities she studies. "What strikes an outside observer as a homogeneous group confronting common economic predicaments growing out of structural reform is experienced from within the group as fragmented interests, unequal treatment, and mutual suspicion" (Lee 2007: 84). So, she does not make the mistake of assuming homogeneity of "workers" or other social categories.

In short, a particular strength of her approach is that it emphasizes the contingency, variation, and internal heterogeneity in social processes that we should expect. "Theory" is a help but not a blueprint.

These points demonstrate that we cannot understand the current and future development of rural society in China based on existing theories of social change. Instead, we must analyze the current social realities, recognize their novelties, and perhaps discover some of the common causal processes that recur in other times and places. And, we should expect novelty; we should expect that China's future rural transformations will be significantly different from other great global examples (United States in the 1880s, Russia in the 1930s, France in the 1830s, etc.).

I said above that China demonstrates that sociology is not a finished science. But we can say something stronger than that: it demonstrates that the very notion of a comprehensive social science that lays the basis for systematizing and predicting social change is radically ill-conceived. This hope for a comprehensive theory of social change is chimerical; it does not correspond to the nature of the social world. It does not sufficiently recognize several crucial features of social phenomena: heterogeneity, causal complexity, contingency, path dependency, and plasticity. Instead of looking for a few general and comprehensive theories of social change, we should be looking for a much larger set of quasi-empirical theories of concrete social mechanisms. And, the generalizations that we will be able to reach will be modest ones having to do with the discovery of some similar processes that recur in a variety of circumstances and historical settings.

As Chinese universities and academies work to formulate new programs of research for sociology and the social sciences, it will be useful for Chinese researchers and theorists to consider many of the questions raised by the philosophy of social science. This may permit the development of a superior "China-centered" approach to social science research.

THE THRUST OF THIS BOOK

This book is not intended to provide an encyclopedic treatment of the philosophy of the social sciences. Instead, it pursues a fairly specific line of thought. First, it embraces the idea that _ontology matters_ in the social sciences. In chapter 1, I argue that we need to reflect carefully about the nature of the entities we think we find in the social world and how they are constituted. Once we begin to think more reflectively about the social world, we come to recognize characteristics that distinguish it strongly from the natural world. Social entities and processes are highly _heterogeneous_ in their composition and dynamics. There is a substantial degree of _plasticity_ in the social world. And, social outcomes—enduring structures, large-scale events like wars, famines, and revolutions—display a high degree of _contingency and path dependency_ in their composition and unfolding.

Second, the book works generally within the perspective of what I call below an *actor-centered* approach to the social sciences. The key idea worked out in chapter 2 is that social entities, processes, and forms of influence are ultimately rooted in individual actors. This is not to endorse methodological individualism, since I also argue that individuals are always enmeshed in ongoing social relationships and practices that are, for them, external and objective. So, we cannot separate sharply between "social" and "individual"; the social depends on individuals, and individuals depend on their formation and situation within a social setting. But it does mean that when a social scientist confronts a complex social process, he or she needs to always be thinking as well of the ways in which individuals embody this process and are influenced by this process. And, it suggests that there is a compositional character to social arrangements; they are built up through a process of lamination and composition from lower-level individual and social activities.

Third, the book acknowledges the reality of higher-level *social entities*—structures, normative systems, institutions, social movements. In chapter 3, I pay close attention to the implications of the actor-centeredness of the social world, but I try to give sense to the fact that social structures and institutions nonetheless have a degree of stability and causal force that allows us to regard them as entities, not merely accidental configurations. Here, we consider the social reality of norms, institutions, organizations, and structures, and the causal properties that these meso-level social factors possess.

Next, the book works in recognition of the fact that the social world is *complex* in both the ordinary and the specialist's sense of the term. This is the work of chapters 4 and 5. Chapter 4 considers the related ideas of reduction and emergence, and chapter 5 treats the ideas of generativity and complexity that emerge from current work in computational social science. The causes that interact in the social world imply a degree of unpredictability and incalculability that is very distant from the vision many people have of simple physical systems. The book looks carefully at the work currently being done by computational social scientists who attempt to simulate and model complex social phenomena—residential segregation, ethnic conflict, or interstate competition. Agent-based models and the mathematics of complexity both shed light on some of the difficult problems of explanation that social scientists face.

Next I look at the nature of *social causation* in some detail. I consider the central status that the discovery of causal mechanisms plays in good explanatory research, and I consider recent arguments to the effect that we need to discover the causal powers of things if we are to have coherent causal explanations. Both views—mechanisms and powers—reject the Humean idea that causation is constant conjunction, and I argue that they are compatible with each other rather than otherwise.

Finally, the book works on the assumption of a nondemanding kind of *scientific realism*. In chapter 7, it is argued that it is perfectly reasonable for sociologists and political scientists to attribute reality and objectivity to the social entities, structures, and practices that they study. Collaterally, I work on the assumption that the social world is as amenable to causal relations as the natural world; so it is entirely appropriate for social scientists to structure their work around ideas about causal powers, causal mechanisms, and forms of causal influence. The book advocates a version of *causal realism* for the social sciences.

Some philosophers have argued that causal explanation is inapt in the social realm, and that we need instead pay close attention to the nature and role of *meanings* within the social realm. These philosophers take the view that social meanings are crucial and poorly understood, and they advocate a hermeneutic approach to the study of the social world. Arguments offered in chapter 7 agree that meanings are important; in fact, the actor-centered approach I defend here focuses renewed attention on this question. But unlike the interpretive tradition in the philosophy of social science, I believe the facts about meanings and mental frameworks are completely compatible with, and necessary for, a satisfactory understanding of social causation. This is so because the substrate of social causation is human social action and interaction, and human action requires interpretation of the meanings and mental frameworks that guide actors' choices.

NEW PHILOSOPHY OF SOCIAL SCIENCE

The philosophy of social science today is a living field with several distinct areas of growth and dozens of talented contributors bringing fresh ideas and rigorous thinking.

The first diagram (Figure I.1) represents one way of thinking about current topics in the philosophy of social science, and Table I.1 provides a few examples of writers in each tradition. The three poles of Figure I.1 are analytical sociology, critical realism, and assemblage theory. It is often believed that these are fundamentally incompatible paradigms for understanding the social world and social explanation. Against this incompatibilist view, I believe that each perspective has something to add to a new and more adequate philosophy of the social world and the social sciences.

How do these topics intersect with each other? There are vehement differences in method, philosophical style, and substantive findings across the three frameworks. But there are also some interesting and surprising points of continuity.

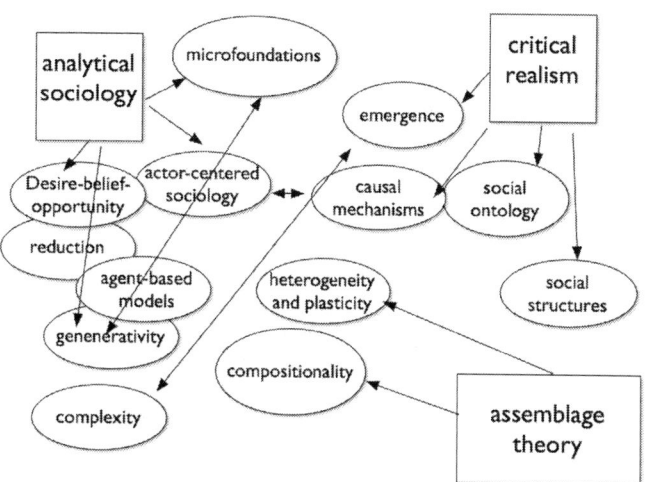

Figure I.1 Themes in the philosophy of social science.

Table I.1 Sources in three debates

Analytical sociology	Hedström, Peter. 2005. *Dissecting the Social: On the Principles of Analytical Sociology*. Cambridge; New York: Cambridge University Press.
	Schelling, Thomas C. 1978. *Micromotives and Macrobehavior*. New York: Norton.
	Elster, Jon. 2007. *Explaining Social Behavior: More Nuts and Bolts for the Social Sciences*. Cambridge; New York: Cambridge University Press.
Assemblage theory	Deleuze, Gilles, and Félix Guattari. 1987. *A Thousand Plateaus: Capitalism and Schizophrenia*. Minneapolis: University of Minnesota Press.
	DeLanda, Manuel. 2006. *A New Philosophy of Society: Assemblage Theory and Social Complexity*. London; New York: Continuum International Publishing Group.
	Latour, Bruno. 2005. *Reassembling the Social: An Introduction to Actor-network-theory, Clarendon Lectures in Management Studies*. Oxford; New York: Oxford University Press.
Critical realism	Bhaskar, Roy. 1975. *A Realist Theory of Science*. Leeds: Leeds Books.
	Archer, Margaret Scotford. 1995. *Realist Social Theory: The Morphogenetic Approach*. Cambridge; New York: Cambridge University Press.
	Kaidesoja, Tuukka. 2013. *Naturalizing Critical Realist Social Ontology, Ontological explorations*. London: Routledge.

Analytical sociology favors a broadly speaking reductive approach to social explanation, relying heavily on the diagram of Coleman's boat (Figure 4.1) to illustrate how social explanation should proceed, with macro-level facts to be explained by configurations of micro-level facts. It favors an enlightened version of methodological individualism, where social reality is constituted by purposive actors in constrained circumstances. It favors causal explanations couched in terms of causal mechanisms. And, it presents a philosophical style that gives priority to clarity and simplicity over extended and sometimes obscure philosophical theorizing.

Critical realism disagrees with almost all of these premises. It defends an antireductionist understanding of social structures, with structures being seen as possessing stable emergent causal powers. It rejects the idea of reducing social properties to the combined effects of individual actions, often favoring emergence over reduction. It does not accept the logic of Coleman's boat, because it recognizes the reality of type 4 causal relations from structure to structure. And, it is couched in terms of a philosophical system that many readers find unnecessarily obscure—Bhaskar's transcendental ontology.

Assemblage theory appears to be at odds with both these perspectives. The key idea is that social entities at every level of organization are *assemblages* of other units. The theory of assemblage rejects the idea of privileging individual humans as the bearers of social processes. It too arises out of a luxuriant and often obscure set of philosophical ideas. Assemblage theory is ambivalent about the idea of social explanation and causation, and sometimes appears to privilege description over explanation. And, it is also skeptical about the reality of social structures, favoring heterogeneous assemblages over enduring structures.

So, with all these differences, is there room for useful synthesis of these perspectives into innovative ideas about social ontology and explanation?

Start with a few resonances between assemblage theory and critical realism. Both are grounded in a philosophical system (Deleuze, Kant), and they both make use of philosophical arguments to arrive at substantive conclusions. Both take up ontological ideas as being key to an adequate philosophy of social science, and they both offer stringent critiques of received positivist ideas about the nature of the social world. The idea of assemblage itself may also be a point of contact, in that enduring structures might be thought of along the lines of relatively stable assemblages. But a point of contrast is pervasive: critical realism is realist, and assemblage theory is constructionist.

Are there points of contact between analytical sociology and assemblage theory? It would appear that there are not. The anti-philosophical bent of analytical sociology makes it difficult for scholars in this tradition to read and benefit from the writings of assemblage scholars. The model of explanation that is presupposed by analytical sociology—demonstration of how higher-level entities are given their properties by the intentional actions of individuals—is explicitly rejected by assemblage theory. And, the idea of *assemblage*—contingent conjunction of heterogeneous configurations of "actors" in the peculiarly non-individualist sense that this tradition adopts— seems to be a difficult one for analytical sociology to take seriously.

Finally, what about the relation between analytical sociology and critical realism? On the issue of causation, there is a degree of separation—analytical sociology favors causal mechanisms, preferably grounded in the level of individuals, whereas critical realism favors causal powers at all levels. The critical realist idea of emergent social properties is a difficult one to assimilate to the analytical sociology framework, since the latter group wants to understand higher-level structures as the compound effect of the constituents. But here there is perhaps room for a degree of accommodation, if critical realism scholars can be persuaded of the idea of relative explanatory autonomy advocated elsewhere here. Relative explanatory autonomy is a way of reconciling the ultimately individualist ontology of analytical sociology with the emergentism of critical realism.

So, the three frameworks have little overlap in method or substance. However, the philosophy of the social that is advocated in this book may be one way of finding commonality among the three poles. The weak microfoundationalism I defend captures at least a part of the analytical sociology position without demanding reduction. The scientific realism about social structures that I advocate creates a degree of affinity with critical realism and, in any case, affirms the central view of critical realism: that it is legitimate to attribute causal powers to concrete social structures. The views I have developed here about the heterogeneity and plasticity of social entities (and the implausibility of the idea of social kinds) creates a significant link to the assemblage theory that comes out of that tradition. And, the framework of methodological localism also provides a degree of consonance with the rejection of reification of social things by assemblage theory. So, perhaps the philosophy of social science developed here occupies the center of the diagram above, with linkages to each of the polar beacons. Significantly, there is discussion of each of the topics included in the diagram in what follows.

Chapter 1

A Better Social Ontology

The subject of social ontology has often been treated as an afterthought compared to epistemology and the theory of explanation in the philosophy of social science. But I believe that the social sciences need to be framed out of consideration of a better understanding of the nature of the social—a better social ontology—if we are to be more successful in understanding and explaining the processes of social change the twenty-first century presents. The social world has characteristics that fundamentally distinguish it from the natural world—heterogeneity, plasticity, and contingency, to name several. The social world is not a system of law-governed processes; it is instead a mix of different sorts of institutions, forms of human behavior, natural and environmental constraints, and contingent events. The entities that make up the social world at a given time and place have no particular ontological stability; they do not fall into "natural kinds"; and there is no reason to expect deep similarity across a number of ostensibly similar institutions—states, for example, or labor unions.

A central thrust here is this: it is important for social scientists to avoid the fallacy of "naturalism"—the idea that social science should resemble natural science and the idea that social entities have a similar constitution and ontology to natural entities.

Why are these ontological questions important to the philosophy of social science? And, how could they possibly contribute to better research and theory in the social sciences? One answer is that it is not really possible to investigate any domain without having a good idea of what sorts of things the domain consists of. So, attempting to arrive at perspicuous models of what the social world is made up of is a necessary step on the way to more specific forms of empirical and causal research.

A second answer derives from recognition of the harm that has been done to the cause of knowledge by misconceived ontologies in the history of science. This has been especially true in areas of knowledge adjoining human life and activity—radical behaviorism in psychology, naturalism and positivism in sociology, and what Andrew Abbott calls the "variables paradigm" in quantitative social science (Abbott 1998). Better science will result from a more propitious ontology, because we will not be in the situation of trying to force the social world into the wrong sorts of boxes.

Third, there are good reasons for thinking that reasoning about social ontology is possible. If ontological thinking about the social world were purely *apriori*, then we might justifiably be skeptical about our capacity to move from philosophy to the world. But we are participants and observers within social reality. We are participants in organizations, we find ourselves in the grips of ideologies and normative systems, and we are both wielders and subjects of power. So, theorizing about social reality of ontology is not wholly *apriori*; rather, it is more akin to a form of intelligent observation of real social processes in which we participate. Ontological thinking is really a form of empirically informed theorizing, at a fairly abstract level.

What do we see when we look at the social world afresh? Instead of imagining the social world in analogy with the law-governed world of natural phenomena, I suggest an approach to social science theorizing that emphasizes agency, contingency, and plasticity in the makeup of social facts. This perspective recognizes that there is a degree of pattern in social life—but emphasizes that these patterns fall far short of the regularities associated with laws of nature. It emphasizes contingency of social processes and outcomes. It insists upon the importance and legitimacy of eclectic use of social theories: the processes are heterogeneous, and therefore it is appropriate to appeal to different types of social theories as we explain social processes. It emphasizes the importance of path dependence in social outcomes. It suggests that the most justifiable scientific statements in the social sciences have to do with the discovery of concrete social-causal mechanisms through which some types of social outcomes come about.

And, finally, this approach highlights what I call "methodological localism": the view that the foundation of social processes, structures, and changes is the local, socially located, and socially constructed individual person (Little 2006). The individual is socially constructed, in that her modes of behavior, thought, and reasoning are created through a specific set of prior social interactions. And, her actions are socially situated, in the sense that they are responsive to the institutional setting in which she chooses to act. Purposive individuals, embodied with powers and constraints, pursue their goals in specific institutional settings; and patterns of social outcome often result. Ultimately the social world consists of nothing but compounds, aggregations, assemblages, and complex systems of these forms of socially situated agency.

NEW METAPHORS FOR THE SOCIAL

We need new metaphors in terms of which to think of the social world. The social world is not like the natural world. Nature is composed of things, forces, and geometries that have strong determining regularities whose interactions can be formulated with mathematical precision. There are problems of indeterminacy in physics, of course; but fundamentally we can rely on the material properties of steel, the magnetic properties of the sun, or the curvature of space-time to continue to work as expected. Nature constitutes a *system* of interactions. And, this is because, fundamentally, nature consists of atoms and forces—just as some of the pre-Socratic philosophers thought 2,500 years ago. (Some will object that this characterization overlooks quantum mechanics and the peculiar characteristics of the subatomic world. That is true, of course; but it is not relevant to our concerns about the nature of the social world. The social world is not affected by quantum physics, contrary to Alexander Wendt's arguments (Wendt 2015).)

The social world is different. It is not a *system*, but rather a patchwork, a mixture, an ensemble, a Rube Goldberg machine, a collage, or a jumble. Its properties arise from the activities, thoughts, motivations, emotions, and interactions of socially situated persons. Outcomes are influenced by a hodge-podge of obstacles and gradients that crop up more or less randomly—leading to substantial surprises relative to how we might have expected things to work out. Agents are not fully predictable or comprehensible; and their actions and interactions are indeterminate as well. We discover that people usually compare costs and benefits when they make choices, and we invent rational choice theory and microeconomics. But these are simply abstract models of one aspect of human behavior and choice, and it is rare indeed to find large social processes that are governed exclusively by this aspect of agency. We see large, somewhat stable social structures that persist over time—patterns of habitation and social exchange (cities), patterns of racial or ethnic discrimination, and rising and falling rates of violent crime—and we believe there are large social causes and influences that help to explain these dynamic configurations. But we should never imagine that social outcomes and patterns are the manifestation of an underlying abstract social order, analogous to laws of nature. Social causes are heterogeneous, probabilistic, agent driven, exception laden, and interconnected—with the result that we cannot hope to have a full model of the workings of a social system. We should not reify social entities and structures.

The heterogeneity and contingency associated with the social world sug-
gested by this set of ideas do not imply that social scientific research, knowledge, and explanation are unattainable. This new perspective implies, rather,
that we need to understand the limits on representation, abstraction, and
prediction that are implied by the fundamental nature of social things. Our
knowledge of any particular snapshot of social reality is inherently partial
and incomplete.

The Flea Market Analogy

Consider a provocative alternative metaphor for the social world: a large
urban flea market. The wares on sale on a particular Saturday are simply the
sum of the accidents of circumstance that led a collection of sellers to converge on that particular day. There are some interesting patterns that emerge
over time—in the spring, one finds more used lawnmowers, and in times of
dearth, one finds more family treasures. These regularities require explanation. But they do not derive from some governing "law of flea markets" that
might be discovered. Instead, the flea market and the larger society are, alike,
simply the aggregate result of large numbers of actions, motives, circumstances, and structures that turn kaleidoscopically and produce patterned but
non-lawlike outcomes.

Is the flea market a helpful analogy for understanding the social? Does
it serve to provide a different mental model in terms of which to consider
the nature of social phenomena? What it has going for it is heterogeneity
and contingency and an evident share of agent dependency. The people who
show up on a given Saturday are a contingent and largely disorganized mix of
humanity. And, the products that wind up on the jumble tables too are highly
disorderly and random. Each has its own unique story for how it got there.
There is no overall guiding design.

But there is also a degree of order underlying the apparent chaos of the
jumble tables. All is not random in a flea market. The participants, for
example: there are regular vendors, street people, police officers, health
inspectors, jugglers, and pickpockets—as well as regular shoppers, tourists,
school children, and occasional shoppers looking for a used toaster or a
single kitchen chair. In most cases, there are reasons they are there—and the
reasons are socially interesting. Moreover, the ethnographer of the flea market is likely enough to spot some seasonal or social patterns in the products
and people present in a certain month or time of year. So, we can discern
a blend of stochastic events and order. But the order that can be discerned
is the result of a large number of overlapping, independent conditions and
processes, not the manifestation of a few simple forces or a guiding system
of laws.

Both accident and order are characteristic of important segments of the larger social world as well. The helter-skelter of the flea market is in fact highly analogous to many aspects of social phenomena—army recruitment, patterns of crime, mortgage defaults, and urban development. But it is also true that there are other social phenomena that are not so accidental. So, the jumble sale is perhaps less good as an analogy for highly organized and managed social processes—a tight administrative hierarchy, an orchestrated campaign event, or a coordinated attack in battle.

This addresses the "accidental conjunction" part of the analogy. What about the "composite order" part of the analogy? This element too works pretty well for many examples of social phenomena. When students of the professions discover that there are interesting patterns of recruitment into accountancy or the officer corps, or discover that there are similarities in the organizations of pharmacists and psychotherapists—they also recognize that these patterns result from complex, intertwined patterns of strategic positioning, organizational learning, and economic circumstances (Abbott 1988). In other words, the patterns and regularities are themselves the result of multiple social mechanisms, motives, and processes. And, these processes are in no way analogous to laws of nature.

So, all considered, the analogy of the flea market works pretty well as a mental model for many aspects of what we should expect of social phenomena: a degree of accident and conjunction, a degree of emerging pattern and order that results from many independent but converging social processes, and an inescapable dimension of agent dependency that refutes any hope of discovering an underlying, law-governed system.

HETEROGENEITY OF THE SOCIAL

Let us now focus more closely on several important ontological features of the social world. I maintain that heterogeneity is a very basic characteristic of the domain of the social. And, I think this makes a big difference for how we should attempt to study the social world "scientifically." In what respects are social phenomena heterogeneous? And, why is this important?

Let's start with some semantics. A heterogeneous group of things is the contrary of a homogeneous group, and we can define homogeneity as "a group of fundamentally similar units or samples." A homogeneous body may consist of a group of units with identical properties, or it may be a smooth mixture of different things, consisting of a similar composition at many levels of scale. A fruitcake is nonhomogeneous, in that distinct volumes may include just cake or a mix of cake and dried cherries, or cake and the occasional walnut. The properties of fruitcake depend on which sample we encounter.

A well-mixed volume of oil and vinegar, by contrast, is homogeneous in a specific sense: the properties of each sample volume are the same as any other. The basic claim about the heterogeneity of the social comes down to this: at many levels of scale we continue to find a diversity of social things and processes at work. Society is more similar to fruitcake than cheesecake.

Heterogeneity makes a difference for social science methodology because one of the central goals of positivist science is to discover strong regularities among classes of phenomena, and regularities appear to presuppose homogeneity of the things over which the regularities are thought to obtain. So, to observe that social phenomena are deeply heterogeneous at many levels of scale is to cast fundamental doubt on the goal of discovering strong social regularities. The fact of heterogeneity refutes crude positivism as a guide to social research.

Consider some of the forms of heterogeneity that the social world illustrates.

First is the heterogeneity that can be discovered within social categories of things—cities, religions, electoral democracies, and social movements. Think of the diversity within Islam documented so well by Clifford Geertz (*Islam Observed: Religious Development in Morocco and Indonesia*; Geertz 1968); the diversity at multiple levels that exists among great cities like Beijing, New York, Geneva, and Rio (institutions, demography, ethnic groups, economic characteristics, administrative roles, economic functions); the institutional variety that exists in the electoral democracies of India, France, and Argentina; or the wild diversity across the social movements of the right, from Franco to Le Pen to Trump.

Second is the heterogeneity of social causes and influences. Social events are commonly the result of a variety of different kinds of causes that come together in highly contingent conjunctions. A revolution may be caused by a protracted drought, a harsh system of land tenure, a new ideology of peasant solidarity, a communications system that conveys messages to the rural poor, and an unexpected disagreement among the rulers—all coming together at a moment in time. And, this range of causal factors, in turn, shows up in the background of a very heterogeneous set of effects. A transportation network, for example, may play a causal role in the occurrence of an epidemic, the spread of radical ideas, and a long, slow process of urban settlement. The causes of an event are a mixed group of dissimilar influences with different dynamics and temporalities, and the effects of a given causal factor are also a mixed and dissimilar group. This feature of social causation leads us to describe social and historical causation as "conjunctural" (Steinmetz 1998, 2004; Little 2000).

Third is the heterogeneity that can be discovered across and within social groups. It is not the case that all Kansans think alike (Frank 2005)—and this is true for whatever descriptors we might choose in order to achieve greater homogeneity (evangelical Kansans, urban evangelical Kansans, . . .). There are always interesting gradients within any social group. Likewise, there is great variation in the nature of ordinary, lived experience—for middle-class French families celebrating *quatorze Juillet*, for Californians celebrating July 4, and for Brazilians enjoying *Dia da Independência* on September 7.

A fourth form of heterogeneity takes us within the agent herself, when we note the variety of motives, moral frameworks, emotions, and modes of agency on the basis of which people act. This is one of the weaknesses of doctrinaire rational choice theory or dogmatic Marxism, the analytical assumption of a single dimension of motivation and reasoning. Instead, it is apparent that one person acts for a variety of motives at a given time, persons shift their motives over time, and members of groups differ in terms of their motivational structure as well. So, there is heterogeneity of motives and agency within the agent and across agents involved in similar projects.

These dimensions of heterogeneity contribute to an important point for social scientists as they confront their research topics: the social world is an ensemble, a dynamic mixture, and an ongoing interaction of forces, agents, structures, and mentalities. Social outcomes emerge from this heterogeneous and dynamic mixture, and the quest for general laws is deeply quixotic.

Where does the heterogeneity principle take us? It suggests an explanatory strategy: instead of looking for laws of whole categories of events and things, rather than searching for simple answers to questions like "why do revolutions occur?" we should look to a "concatenation" strategy. That is, we might simply acknowledge the fact of molar heterogeneity and look instead for some of the different processes and mechanisms in play in a given item of interest, and then build up a theory of the whole as a concatenation of the particulars of the parts. This is precisely the strategy that McAdam, Tarrow, and Tilly take in *Dynamics of Contention* (McAdam, Tarrow, and Tilly 2001). We will take up the causal mechanisms approach in chapter 6.

Significantly, this strategy takes us to several fruitful ideas about social science method that already have some currency. First is the idea of looking for microfoundations for observed social processes (Little 1998). Here, the idea is that higher-level social processes, causes, and events need to be placed within the context of an account of the actor-level institutions and circumstances that convey those processes. Second is the method of causal mechanisms advocated by McAdam, Tarrow, and Tilly in *Dynamics of Contention* (McAdam, Tarrow, and Tilly 2001). Put simply, the approach recommends that we explain an outcome or social circumstance as the contingent result of the concatenation of a set of independent causal mechanisms (escalation, intra-group competition, repression, . . .). And, third is the theory of "assemblages," derived from some of the theories of Gilles Deleuze. Manuel DeLanda describes this theory in *A New Philosophy of Society: Assemblage Theory and Social Complexity* (DeLanda 2006), which we will discuss below.

This perspective aligns closely with some of the key insights of Nancy Cartwright in her writings on the philosophy of science. Her work particularly interesting for the new ways she offers of thinking about old ideas like "laws of nature" and the ways things work in the natural world. Much of what she writes about the entities and processes of the natural world is equally valid when applied to the social world. Especially interesting is her 1999 book, *The Dappled World: A Study of the Boundaries of Science* (Cartwright 1999). In *The Dappled World*, Cartwright focuses on the idea of the fundamental heterogeneity of the world. Here are the opening words of the book:

> This book supposes that, as appearances suggest, we live in a dappled world, a world rich in different things, with different natures, behaving in different ways. The laws that describe this world are a patchwork, not a pyramid. They do not take after the simple, elegant and abstract structure of a system of axioms and theorems. Rather they look like—and steadfastly stick to looking like—science as we know it: apportioned into disciplines, apparently arbitrarily grown up; governing different sets of properties at levels of abstraction; pockets of great precision; large parcels of qualitative maxims resisting precise formulation; erratic overlaps; here and there, once in a while, corners that line up, but mostly ragged edges; and always the cover of law just loosely attached to the jumbled world of material things. (1)

Cartwright is particularly interested in demolishing the quest for scientific unity—a single unifying theory that can be said to represent the whole of a field of natural or social phenomena. She firmly rejects the idealized notion that quantum mechanics deductively encompasses all areas of physics, or that rational choice theory encompasses all areas of the social sciences. Instead, she argues that the "patchwork" nature of the disciplines of the sciences—different definitions of domain, different ideas about methodology and proof—corresponds in a deep way to the patchwork nature of the world. So, methodology and ontology are intermingled.

In short, Cartwright's philosophy of science lends support for the important truth of the heterogeneity principle: that social outcomes are the aggregate result of multiple lower-level processes and institutions that give rise to them, and that social outcomes are contingent results of interaction and concatenation of these lower-level processes.

Composition of the Social

Heterogeneity suggests composition. Heterogeneous entities are composed of disparate components. Our social ontology therefore needs to reflect the insight that complex social happenings are almost invariably composed of multiple causal processes and components rather than existing as unitary systems. The phenomena of a great social whole—a city over a 50-year span, a period of sustained social upheaval or revolution (Iran in the 1970s–1980s), an international trading system—should be conceptualized as the sum of a large number of separate processes with intertwining linkages and often highly dissimilar tempos. We can provide analysis and theory for some of the component processes, and we can attempt to model the results of aggregating these processes. And, we can attempt to explain the patterns and exceptions that arise as the consequence of one or more of these processes. Some of the subordinate processes will be significantly amenable to theorizing and projection, and some will not. And, the totality of behavior will be more than the "sum" of the relatively limited number of processes that are amenable to theoretical analysis. This means that the behavior of the whole will often demonstrate contingency and unpredictability *modulo* the conditions and predictable workings of the known processes. (We take up this topic again in chapter 5 when we discuss complexity.)

This ontology of social things resulting from a "composition of heterogeneous processes" can be illustrated by a variety of examples. Consider the example of the development of a large city over time. The sorts of subordinate processes that urban historians can observe might include examples like the following:

- The habitation dynamics created by the nodes of a transportation system
- The dynamics of electoral competition governing the offices of mayor and city council
- The politics of land use policy and zoning permits
- Surges of immigration into the city
- The dynamics and outcomes of public education on the talent level of the population
- Economic development policies and tax incentives emanating from state government
- Dynamics of real estate system with respect to race
- Employment and poverty characteristics of surrounding region

Each of these processes can be investigated by specialists—public policy experts, sociologists of race and segregation, and urban politics experts. Each process contributes to features of the evolving urban environment. And, it is credible that there are consistent patterns of behavior and development within these various types of processes. This justifies a specialist's approach to specific types of causes of urban change, and rigorous social science can result. (The research included in the *New Blackwell Companion to the City* illustrates some of this range of disciplinary variety (Bridge and Watson 2011).)

Further, it should also be recognized that there are system interdependencies among these groups of factors. A rapidly changing demography (caused by economic factors in the hinterland) may have dramatic effects on electoral competition and, eventually, urban policy. So, it is not enough to understand the separate processes individually; we need to make an effort to discover these endogenous relations among them. (This feature of the social world is one feature that gives rise to the phenomenon of complexity in social dynamics. Chapter 5 returns to this topic.)

But over and above this complication of the causal interdependency of recognized factors, there is another and more pervasive complication as well. For any given complex social whole, it is almost always the case that there are likely to be additional causal processes that have not been separately analyzed or theorized. Our list of factors influencing the development of the city is plainly a partial one; but no amount of effort at extending the list will make it fully comprehensive. Or, in other words, social analysis and description is always incomplete and open. (This point is emphasized in Roy Bhaskar's philosophy of social science; he argues that the domain of the natural sciences is frequently a closed system, whereas the social world is an open field of dynamic interactions (Bhaskar 1982, 1989).)

The upshot is that a complex social whole exceeds the particular theories we have created for this kind of phenomenon at any given point in time. The social whole is composed of lower-level processes; but it is not exhausted by any specific list of underlying processes. Therefore, we should not imagine that the ideal result of investigation of urban phenomena is a comprehensive theory of the city; the goal is chimerical. Social science is always "incomplete," in the sense that there are always social processes relevant to social outcomes that have not been theorized.

Assemblage Theory and the Philosophy of Social Science

Assemblage theory is a philosophy of the social world that derives from Gilles Deleuze and Félix Guattari (1987). Manuel DeLanda provides an extensive and clear exposition of the theory (DeLanda 2006). DeLanda proceeds on the basis of the theme of anti-reification that was introduced above:

> Is there, for example, such a thing as society as a whole? Is the commitment to assert the existence of such an entity legitimate? And, is denying the reality of such an entity equivalent to a commitment to the existence of only individual persons and their families? The answer to all these questions is a definitive no, but several obstacles must be removed before justifying this negative response. (DeLanda 2006: 8)

So, we should not think of the social world in analogy with examples drawn from what we know about the natural world. We should not think of society as a "thing" or a unified system. The ontological properties of the natural and social realms are substantially different. This is the primary reason I find some of the basic ideas of assemblage theory appealing: because these theories and theorists deliberately question the naturalistic approach to the social world, and they attempt to advance strikingly different and original concepts for characterizing the social world. They emphasize heterogeneity and composition over uniformity and subsumption.

The most substantial idea in this body of work is the notion of "assemblage." Deleuze's theory of "assemblage" as a way of thinking about the social world is a genuinely novel one (Deleuze and Guattari 1987). Fundamentally the idea is that there does not exist a fixed and stable ontology for the social world that proceeds from "atoms" to "molecules" to "materials." Rather, social formations are assemblages of other complex configurations, and they, in turn, play roles in other, more extended configurations. What is appealing about this way of thinking about the social world is that it takes us away from the presuppositions we often bring about the social world as consisting of a range of discrete social objects or things. According to this static way of thinking, the state is a thing composed of other things; likewise, Islam is an extended social thing; likewise, Chicago; and so on. The assemblage approach suggests a different set of metaphors for the social world: mosaic, patchwork, heterogeneity, fluidity, and transitory configuration. And, this is a more realistic way of characterizing large extended social formation like states or regulatory agencies.

Here is DeLanda's effort at providing a preliminary description of assemblage:

> The concept of assemblage is defined along two dimensions. One dimension or axis defines the variable roles which an assemblage's components may play, from a purely material role at one extreme of the axis, to a purely expressive role at the other extreme. . . . The other dimension defines variable processes in which these components become involved and that either stabilize the identity of an assemblage, by increasing its degree of internal homogeneity or the degree of sharpness of its boundaries, or destabilize it. . . . The components of social assemblages playing a material role vary widely, but at the very least involve a set of human bodies properly oriented (physically or psychologically) towards each other. . . . Illustrating the components playing an expressive role needs some elaboration because in assemblage theory expressively cannot be reduced to language and symbols. (DeLanda 2006: 12)

DeLanda tries to explain "assemblage" by saying what it is not. First, assemblage theory is opposed to essentialism and reification (26ff.). DeLanda emphasizes that Deleuze's concept resists the "organismic" approach to conceptualizing the social, by which he means an approach that looks at the whole as an inextricable combination of interrelated parts. This implies that the parts are implicated in each other; the organismic perspective emphasizes the internal connectedness of a thing. (This approach has affinity to Bertell Ollman's philosophy of internal relations in *Alienation: Marx's Conception of Man in a Capitalist Society* (Ollman 1971).) DeLanda distinguishes between "interiority" and "exteriority" in conceptualizing the components of a thing. For assemblage theory, the relations among the parts are contingent, not necessary. And, crucially, parts can be extracted from one whole and inserted into another. "These relations imply, first of all, that a component part of an assemblage may be detached from it and plugged into a different assemblage in which its interactions are different. In other words, the exteriority of relations implies a certain autonomy for the terms they relate" (DeLanda 2006: 10–11). Another aspect of the theory, according to DeLanda, is the fact that it does not privilege one level of organization over another. "Micro" is not more fundamental than "macro"; instead, social reality is "multiscaled" (38), with assemblages occurring at every level.

Neither Deleuze nor DeLanda succeeds in making the concept of assemblage a very clear or analytically specific one. What does this mean in practical terms? As a first approximation, the core idea of assemblage is that social things (cities, structures, ideologies) are composed of an overlapping and contingent collection of a heterogeneous set of social activities and practices. The relations among these activities and practices are contingent, and the properties of the composite thing—the assemblage—are likewise a contingent and "emergent" sum of the properties of the component threads. The composite has no "essence"—just a contingent and changeable set of properties. Fundamentally, the idea is that there does not exist a fixed and stable ontology for the social world that proceeds from "atoms" to "molecules" to "materials." Rather, social formations are assemblages of other complex configurations, and they in turn play roles in other, more extended configurations.

Consider a simplified version of assemblage theory that might be useful for sociological theory while foregoing much of the metaphysical language characteristic of Deleuze's writings:

- Social entities are composed of components and lesser systems.
- The components of a social entity are heterogeneous.
- The components include both material factors and meaningful expressions.
- The components have their own characteristics and dynamics.
- The components may have very different temporal and spatial scales.
- The effects and interactions among components may be indeterminate because of complexity effects and probabilistic causal mechanisms.
- The behavior of the whole is difficult or impossible to calculate even given extensive knowledge of the dynamics of the components.

These statements all seem plausible, and that suggests that the theory of assemblage contributes a valuable perspective for social ontology.

What is the intellectual role of assemblage theory for sociology and for the philosophy of social science? Is assemblage theory a substantive social theory? Is it a guide to research and methodology? Or, is it an ontology? I think we do best to understand assemblage theory as a high-level and abstract ontological framework, an abstract description of the nature of the social world. It is, as DeLanda says, a "new philosophy of society." It highlights the pervasive fact of the heterogeneous nature of phenomena in the social world. But it is not a concrete sociological theory. It does not provide a substantive theory of what those component threads are; this is for concrete sociological theory to work out. Unlike rational choice theory, Marxist theory, or pragmatist action theory—each of which rests upon a substantive core set of ideas about the fundamentals of social action and structure—assemblage theory is neutral with respect to these topics.

So, assemblage theory is not a guide to the constituents of the social world. It is not similar to atomic theory or the Mendeleev table of the elements. However, I believe the theory is indeed methodologically helpful. Exploring assemblage theory is a potentially valuable activity for social scientists and philosophers. This is because the theory encourages us to study component systems and underlying social processes rather than looking for unified theories of large unified social objects. In this way it gives value and direction to multi-theoretical, interdisciplinary approaches.

Moreover, this approach encourages social scientists to arrive at partial explanations of social features by discerning the dynamics of some of the components. These accounts are necessarily incomplete, because they ignore many other constituents of the assembled whole. And, yet they are potentially explanatory, when the dynamics being studied have the ability to generate trans-assemblage characteristics (continuity, crisis).

So, assemblage theory is not a substantive social theory. It does not prescribe any specific ideas about the specific nature of the components, layers, laminations, or threads out of which social phenomena are composed. Instead, it offers a vision of how we should think of all such constructions in the social world. It reinforces the points made above based on other considerations: we should be skeptical about the appearance of unity and coherence in an extended social entity (e.g. the Department of Justice or the Muslim world) and look instead to discover some of the heterogeneous and independent processes that underlie the surface appearance. And, it gives ontological support for some of the theoretical inclinations of comparative historical sociology (Tilly 1984; Steinmetz 2007; Mann 1986): look for the diversity of social arrangements and the context-dependent conjunctural causes that underlie complex historical events.

PLASTICITY

Let us turn now to a third important ontological idea for the social sciences: plasticity. I maintain that virtually all social entities are "plastic": their properties change significantly over time, as a result of the purposive and unintentional behavior of the socially constructed individuals who make up a society. Organizations, labor unions, universities, churches, and social identities all show a substantial degree of flexibility and fluidity over time, and this fact leads to a substantial degree of heterogeneity among groups of similar social organizations and institutions. This points to a general and important observation about the constitution of the social world: the properties of a social entity or practice can change over time; they are not rigid, fixed, or timeless. They are not bound into consistent and unchanging categories of entities, such as "bureaucratic state," "Islamic society," or "leftist labor organization." Molecules of water preserve their physical characteristics no matter what. But in contrast to natural substances such as gold or water, social things can change their properties indefinitely.

This feature of social entities implies several things. First, it requires that we bring into our investigation a readiness to observe change within the entity we are observing—the institution, the social identity, and the organization. And, second, it implies that we should expect a degree of drift among institutions that are fairly similar at one point in time. Harvard, Princeton, and Yale may have been fairly similar universities in the 1950s, with similar missions and internal institutions. Over the intervening sixty years, however, there has been an accretion of modification and adaptation that has made them less similar.

This ontology emphasizes a deep plasticity and heterogeneity in social entities. Organizations and institutions change over time and place. Agents within these organizations change their characteristics through their own behavior, through their intentional efforts to modify them, and through the cumulative effect of agents and behavior over time and place. Social constructs are caused and implemented within a substrate of purposive and active agents whose behavior and mentality at a given time determine the features of the social entity. As individuals act, pursue their interests, notice new opportunities, and innovate, they simultaneously "reproduce" a given institution and also erode or change the institution. So, institutions are not fully homeostatic, preserving their own structure in the face of disturbances. This is not to say that institutions lack such homeostatic mechanisms altogether, only that we cannot presuppose that a given institution or organization will persist in its fundamental characteristics over extended time and space. (Kathleen Thelen's approach to the institutions through which different countries have solved the problem of training skilled workers is highly sensitive to the twin problems of stability and plasticity; Thelen 2004.)

A familiar example will illustrate the kinds of plasticity and variation under consideration here. Take the tenure process in American universities. We can see an overall similarity in processes, rules, and goals in the tenure processes at various institutions. Organization is to some extent influenced by function, and by the diffusion of "best practices," as institutions copy each other. But we also see substantial variation and drift in both process and content (criteria and processes for awarding tenure). For example, some universities have attempted to incorporate "community service" into tenure criteria. Different universities give a different balance of faculty review and provost and dean review. There are different cultures of seriousness in review by faculty committees and academic administrators. Different institutions define different institutional goals: enhance national reputation of the faculty (through research productivity), improve teaching, orient faculty to community service, and so on. There is a visible push-pull by stakeholders on these institutions: deans, provosts, and presidents; faculty governance units; and individual faculty. There have been changes in the past twenty years that have affected many institutions: post-tenure review, greater willingness to do reviews leading to removal, etc. So, university tenure processes display the variability and plasticity that this chapter argues to be inherent in all social institutions.

So far I have focused on institutions and organizations. But features of social consciousness and social identity are also variable across time, place, and group. The mechanisms through which social identities and mentalities are transmitted, transmuted, and maintained are varied; inculcation, imitation, and common circumstances are central among these. Moreover, the transmission of an identity is a bit like the transmission of a message through a telephone chain. Because of "noise" in the system, because of individual differences among the transmitters, because of conflicting interests over the content of the identity message, and because of multiple other influences on micro-identities, we should expect great variation within and across groups with regard to the particulars of their social identities. In fact, it appears that the plasticity of identities, norms, and mental frameworks is particularly great. The mechanisms of transmission invite variation across successive instances and generations. Local variations will take root in subpopulations. There are only limited mechanisms of homeostasis. And, individuals and groups have the ability to modify the content and meaning of these elements of social consciousness more or less indefinitely over time. Small variations in locally embodied content proliferate through imitation and parent-child transmission. (Recent work on realist approaches to racial and sexual identities by Paula Moya, Satya Mohanty, and others has shed new light on these topics; Moya and Hames-Garcia (2000).)

Finally, we might also say that individuals too are "plastic." The social psychology of the existing person is the product of the individual's earlier experiences, education, and training. So, this particular person—perhaps now a "rational maximizer with racial prejudice and a fear of flying"—has been constructed through a concrete set of experiences. But (a) this concrete temporal individual herself can be brought to change some basic motivational and psychological characteristics through additional experiences—perhaps diversity training and a positive experience with a person of another race; and (b) other individuals from a similar background can be brought to have a different set of motivational characteristics through different circumstances of development. So, the individual's basic characteristics of personality, belief, and motivation are plastic.

In each case, we find that institutions, practices, and social identities show a substantial degree of plasticity over time and place. And, this is what we should expect—fundamentally, because we can sketch out the social processes and mechanisms through which institutions and social identities are formed, maintained, and modified. Institutions are human products and are embodied in human actions and beliefs. Sometimes an institution is designed through a deliberative process; sometimes it results through a series of uncoordinated adaptations and appropriations by a number of participants. Institutions solve social problems; they coordinate individual activity, control resources, and allocate benefits and burdens. And, institutions either maintain their structure or change depending on the interests and actions of the participants. The participants in institutions interact with the particulars of the organization in ways that improve the effectiveness of the organization, or better serve a particular set of interests, or some combination of both. Leaders may determine that a modification of the institution would increase the capacity of the organization to deliver services, reduce costs, or improve their own ability to control activities within the organization. Participants may modify the organization in their own ways—through spontaneous local modifications of process; foot-dragging as a way of impeding the functioning of unpopular aspects of the organization; collaboration with other participants to modify the institution in directions more favorable to their interests; etc.

Social Continuity and Abrupt Change

There is a tendency for some mainstream social scientists to expect continuity in processes of social change. This poses an ontological question: what features of social causation and processes would either support or undermine the expectation of continuity? We can say quite a bit about the features of continuity and discontinuity in physical systems. Clearly, "nonlinearities" occur in some physical systems that lead to singularities and discontinuities, but many physical systems are safely linear and continuous all the way down. And, these mathematical features follow from the fundamental physical mechanisms that underlie physical systems. But what about the social world?

Take first the stability of large social and political institutions. Is there a reason to expect that major social and political institutions will retain their core features in face of disturbing influences? Consider, for example, the Securities and Exchange Commission as a financial regulatory institution; the European Union as a multinational legislative body; or a large health maintenance organization. How much continuity should we expect from those major institutional systems? Here, institutional sociologists have provided a number of important insights. First, institutions often change through the accumulation of a myriad of small adaptations in different locations within the institution. This is a process that is likely to give rise to slow, continuous, gradual change for the institution as a whole; and this is continuous behavior. Second, though, institutional sociologists have identified important internal forces that work actively to preserve the workings of the institution: the stakeholders who benefit from the current arrangements. Stakeholders are given incentives to actively reinforce and preserve the current institutional arrangements—the status quo. Both of these factors suggest that institutional change will often be slow, gradual, and continuous.

Consider next the ways in which attitudes and values change in a population. Here, it is plausible to observe that individuals change their attitudes and values slowly, through exposure to other individuals and behaviors. And, the attitudes and values of a new generation are usually transmitted through processes that are highly decentralized—again suggesting a slow and gradual process of change. So, this suggests that changes in attitudes and values might behave analogously to the spread of a pathogen through a population—with a slow and continuous spread of "contagion" resulting in a gradual change in population attitudes.

These are all reasons for expecting a degree of stability and continuity in social arrangements and social behavior. But before we conclude that the social world is a continuous place, consider this: we also have some glaring and important examples of how social phenomena might occur in a *dis*-continuous fashion. Critical mass phenomena, tipping points, and catastrophic failures are examples of groups of social phenomena where we should expect discontinuities. The behavior of a disease in a population may change dramatically once a certain percentage of the population is infected (critical mass); a new slang expression ("yada yada yada") may abruptly change its frequency of usage once a certain number of celebrities have adopted it (tipping point); a civic organization may be stretched to the breaking point by the addition of new unruly members and may suddenly collapse or mutate. (The hypothesis of punctuated equilibrium brings this sort of discontinuity into Darwinian theory of evolution.)

So, there are some good foundational reasons for expecting a degree of continuity in the social environment; but there are also convincing models of social behavior that lead to important instances of discontinuous outcomes. This all seems to lead to the slightly worrisome piece of advice: don't bet on the future when the stakes are high. Stock markets collapse; unexpected wars occur; and previously harmonious social groups fall into fratricidal violence. And, there is no foolproof way of determining whether a singularity is just around the corner.

One reason why social scientists expect social arrangements to be stable over time is the idea that institutions and practices are commonly in a state of "equilibrium." A system is in equilibrium with its environment when corrective processes exist that return the system to the equilibrium state when small disturbances occur. The temperature in an office building is subject to external influences that would result in change; but the thermostat provides cool or warm air as needed to bring the office temperature back to the equilibrium value. We may refer to these corrective processes as "homeostatic" processes. The assumption that social institutions are in equilibrium tacitly presupposes the existence of homeostatic forces in the social world. A social structure might be a self-correcting system that restores its equilibrium characteristics in the face of disturbing influences. However, review of the literature on institutions and institutional change suggests that mechanisms like these can sometimes be specified, but their existence cannot generally be assumed. When I say that social entities are plastic, I also mean to say that they are not generally determined within a dynamic equilibrium (as sociological functionalism maintains, perhaps), with powerful homeostatic mechanisms that correct for disturbing influences. There is no "essential" form to which the structure tends to return in equilibrium.

To what extent are social ensembles and processes involved in equilibrium conditions? The paradigm example of equilibrium reasoning in the social sciences arises in microeconomic theory. Supply and demand curves are postulated as being fixed, and the price of a good is the equilibrium position where the quantity produced at this price is equal to the quantity consumed at this price. If the price rises, demand for the good falls and the price falls; if the price falls below the equilibrium position, producers manufacture less of the good and consumers demand more of it, which induces a price rise. Likewise, mathematical game theory demonstrates the existence of equilibrium sets of strategies for all players in a game: given that players have adopted these strategies, none has an incentive to modify his or her strategy.

However, even in these simple examples there are circumstances that can make the equilibrium condition difficult to attain. If the supply and demand curves shift periodically, then the equilibrium price itself moves around. If the price and production response characteristics are too large in their effects, then the system may keep bouncing around the equilibrium price, from "too high" to "too low" without the capacity of fine-tuning production and consumption. The resulting behavior would look like a graph of the stock market rather than a stable, regular system returning to its "equilibrium" value. And, in the case of game theoretic equilibria, it is challenging to see how individual players in a nonzero sum n-person game will be able to adjust their strategies over time to find the equilibrium point.

So, if the conditions defining the terms of an equilibrium change too quickly, or if the feedback mechanisms that work to adjust the system value to current equilibrium conditions are too coarse, then we should not expect the system to arrive at an equilibrium state.

Is there any reason to think that institutional arrangements reach equilibrium in the technical sense? It is true that there are examples of homeostatic forces in social arrangements that work to restore the equilibrium; but these are more uncommon than social scientists might imagine. Perhaps a more common mechanism for stability of social arrangements over time is the one emphasized by Fligstein and McAdam (2012) and Crozier and Friedberg (1980): the persistence of an alignment of interest and power in various groups of stakeholders within the institution or practice. These theories are discussed more fully in chapter 3.

In fact, it seems that equilibria are relatively rare in the social world. The reasons for this are several: it is uncommon to be able to discover homeostatic mechanisms that adjust social variables; when quasi-homeostatic mechanisms exist, they are often too coarse to lead to equilibrium; and, most fundamentally, the constraints that constitute the boundary conditions for idealized equilibria among social variables are often themselves changing too rapidly to permit an equilibrium to emerge. Instead, social outcomes more often look like constrained random walks, in which social actions occur in a fairly uncoordinated way at the individual level and aggregate to singular social outcomes that are highly path dependent and contingent. Social outcomes are more often stochastic than being guided by homeostatic mechanisms.

We might postulate instead that institutions and practices maintain their characteristics over time only when there are powerful social actors who have an interest in maintaining these characteristics. And, when those interests or powers change, then we should expect the institutions and practices to change as well.

Slow Institutional Change

Let's look more closely at a particularly important kind of social entity, mid-level social institutions and organizations. What are the properties of change and stability that institutions display? Institutions are interlocking sets of rules and practices that shape specific sets of actors to behave this way rather than that. The institutions governing public comment on newly proposed regulations provide an interesting case in point. Citizens have interests with respect to new policies, and the rules and formal processes define the means through which they are permitted to express their concerns formally as part of the process. The specific ways through which comments are solicited and processed make a difference for the quality and effectiveness of citizen feedback on public regulatory regimes.

James Mahoney and Kathleen Thelen undertake to provide a basis for answering the question of gradual institutional change. Their volume, *Explaining Institutional Change: Ambiguity, Agency, and Power*, provides a simple but compelling answer: institutions change when position holders within them find circumstances in which they have both an opportunity and an incentive to change or reinterpret the rules in ways that serve their interests (Mahoney and Thelen 2010).

The issue of the internal processes of change within an institution is of interest here for several reasons. But central among them is the idea of plasticity. The basic idea of plasticity being explored here is that institutions and organizations are the product of various kinds of structured human action, and that they can change over time. So, we should not think of institutions as having fixed characteristics, or as though they were equilibrium systems that tend to return to their original states after perturbances. Mahoney and Thelen's work demonstrates some of the ways in which this plasticity emerges; they prove an account of the mechanisms of gradual institutional change. And, this approach makes plain the high degree of path dependency that institutions display.

Here is how Mahoney and Thelen frame their research problem:

> A growing body of work suggests that important changes often take place incrementally and through seemingly small adjustments that can, however, cumulate into significant institutional transformation. (preface)
> Once created, institutions often change in subtle and gradual ways over time. Although less dramatic than abrupt and wholesale transformations, these slow and piecemeal changes can be equally consequential for patterning human behavior and for shaping substantive political outcomes. (Mahoney and Thelen 2010: 1)

The theory Mahoney and Thelen offer of gradual institutional change is an actor-centered theory. Incremental change occurs as the result of the opportunistic and strategic choices made by a range of actors within the institution. In this respect it resembles the theories of organizations provided by Fligstein and McAdam (2012) and Crozier and Friedberg (1980). Consider these important observations:

We argue that institutional change often occurs precisely when problems of rule interpretation and enforcement open up space for actors to implement existing rules in new ways. (4)

But institutional outcomes need not reflect the goals of any particular group; they may be the unintended outcome of conflict among groups or the result of "ambiguous compromises" among actors who can coordinate on institutional means even if they differ on substantive goals. (8)

Institutions are generally thought of as "shaping" factors on human action and choice; individuals construct their actions and strategies within the context of the rules and norms of various institutions. But how do the rules of an organization actually constrain behavior? Mahoney and Thelen do not take compliance within an institution as a given; instead, they look for the interests and opportunities of various agents within the organization or institution that interlock to secure compliance. This parallels the idea of "governance units" in the Fligstein and McAdam theory of strategic action fields.

So, what happens when institutions change? Mahoney and Thelen categorize gradual change into four types: displacement, layering, drift, and conversion (Mahoney and Thelen 2010: 15–16). And, they argue that these categories are significant, given the different roles that actors and strategies play in each of them. (This categorization seems to have something in common with the way geneticists and ecologists might characterize different modalities of adaptation within a changing environment.) They provide a 2 × 2 table that predicts the kind of adaptation that will occur, depending on combinations of strong and weak veto possibilities and low and high levels of discretion in interpretation of rules. For example, they assert that strong veto associated with high discretion produces drift rather than layering or conversion. They offer a similar analysis of different types of change agents and attribute different kinds of strategies to the different categories of change agents.

Liquid Modernity?

Here, I have advocated for the idea that social institutions and arrangements are plastic and deformable, and I have reviewed some of the social factors that provide a degree of stability for them over time. Zygmunt Bauman takes an even more radical view with his idea of "liquid modernity" (Bauman 2000). This view emphasizes the fact of change within society; and it argues that change is occurring more and more rapidly in the "modern" world. Here is an observation by Bauman about the modern world:

Forms of modern life may differ in quite a few respects—but what unites them all is precisely their fragility, temporariness, vulnerability and inclination to constant change. To "be modern" means to modernize—compulsively, obsessively;

not so much just "to be," let alone to keep its identity intact, but forever "becoming," avoiding completion, staying underdefined. Each new structure which replaces the previous one as soon as it is declared old-fashioned and past its use-by date is only another momentary settlement—acknowledged as temporary and "until further notice." (Bauman 2000: viii)

This is an evocative paragraph, but it is important to be specific in reading what it does and does not assert. Plainly Bauman underscores the fact of change in modern social life. "Change is permanent." But Bauman makes no assertion here about discontinuity, randomness, or complete absence of "structure." Indeed, the quotation explicitly allows that there are structures—which implies that they persist over some period of time; and it observes, reasonably enough, that structures change and extinguish.

We know that the social world changes and that these changes extend to deep structures as well as more superficial characteristics. Department stores change owners, so the local Marshall Fields becomes a Macy's. More fundamentally, shopping patterns change and downtown department stores close for good in favor of suburban shopping malls. And, in the end Amazon eventually replaces them all. So, both superficial and deep-structure characteristics of the social world change over time for the consumer marketplace. Is this "liquid modernity" or is it "change overlaying structural persistence"?

The key to the answer lies in formulating a more nuanced understanding of the temporality of change. It is important not to assume all-or-nothing liquidity: either the social world is wholly labile, from moment to moment; or else there are "determinate" structures that are impervious to change. A better answer might be couched in terms of different temporal scales (along the lines of Paul Pierson's ideas (Pierson 2004)). Rather than taking social structures or cultural systems as "static," we are better off thinking of these structural components as having a tempo of change that is many times the tempo of actors' choices. An investor considers purchasing a property in a neighborhood. He or she determines the current market price of the property but also takes into account the fact that market conditions change over time. So, the real estate values of this neighborhood may rise or fall significantly in the medium term—say, thirty years. This is not "permanence," but it is enough temporal range to admit of confident action.

If we adopt this point of view, then the relevant opposition is not between abiding structure and changing circumstance, but rather between long-duration change and short-duration change. And, the work by institutional sociologists like Thelen and Pierson is specifically aimed at discovering the forces that lead to the stabilization of an institution or organization—for a while.

STEINMETZ ON GERMAN COLONIAL REGIMES

It is useful to consider a current work in sociology that illustrates some of the ontological imagination that this chapter calls for in a way that contributes to the effectiveness of the analysis. George Steinmetz offers a comparative sociology of colonialism in *The Devil's Handwriting: Precoloniality and the German Colonial State in Qingdao, Samoa, and Southwest Africa* (Steinmetz 2007). He wants to explain differences in the implementation of 'native policy" within German colonial regimes around the turn of the twentieth century. He finds that there are significant differences across three major instances of German colonialism (Samoa, Qingdao, Southwest Africa), and he wants to know why. (For example, the Namibia regime was much more violent than the Samoa or Qingdao examples.) This is a causal question, and Steinmetz uses a comparative method to probe for answers. He makes substantial and rigorous use of Bourdieu's concept of a field to formulate his analysis.

Here are the guiding research goals for Steinmetz's study.

> What I try to account for in this book—my "explanandum"—is colonial native policy. Four determining structures or causal mechanisms were especially important in each of these colonies: (1) precolonial ethnographic discourses or representations, (2) symbolic competition among colonial officials for recognition of their superior ethnographic acuity, (3) colonizers' cross-identification with imagos of the colonized, and (4) responses by the colonized, including resistance, collaboration, and everything in between. Two other mechanisms influenced colonial native policy to varying degrees: [5] "economic" dynamics related to capitalist profit seeking (plantation agriculture, mining, trade, and smaller-scale forms of business) and [6] the "political" pressures generated by the international system of states. (2)

Steinmetz proceeds in an explicitly comparativist fashion (three cases with salient similarities and differences); and, he proceeds with the language of causal mechanism as a key explanatory tool. The comparativist orientation implies an aim to identify causal differences across the cases that would account for the differences in outcomes in the cases. These structural factors perhaps account for the similarities rather than the differences across the cases. Steinmetz emphasizes repeatedly that general theories of colonialism cannot account for the wide variation that is found across these three cases. "The patterns of variation among these three colonies are as puzzling as is the sheer degree of heterogeneity" (19).

Consider the kinds of accounts Steinmetz offers for the four key mechanisms he cites. Consider first factor (2) above: the idea that the specifics of colonial rule depended a great deal on the circumstances of the professional and ideological "field" within which colonial administrators were recruited and served. The idea here is that the particular intellectual and professional environment established certain points of difference around which participants competed. These dividing lines set the terms of professional competition, and prospective colonial administrators as well as functioning administrators needed to establish their program for governance around a distinctive package of these assumptions.

This mechanism is a fairly clear one; and it provides a promising basis for explaining some of the otherwise puzzling aspects of colonial rule and native policy. It derives, fundamentally, from Bourdieu's theories of social capital. This mechanism is consistent with an actor-centered theory of explanation: actors (administrators or generals) are immersed in a policy environment in which conflicting ideas about success are debated; the actors seek to align their actions to the framework they judge to be most likely to prevail (and preserve their careers).

What about (3)? This falls in the category of what Steinmetz calls, "symbolic and imaginary identifications" (55). Here, Steinmetz turns away from conscious calculation and jockeying on the part of the colonial administrator in the direction of a nonrational psychology. Steinmetz draws on psychoanalytic theory and the theories of Lacan here. But it remains an actor-centered analysis. Steinmetz refers to elements of mentality as an explanation of the administrators' behavior, and their possession of this mentality needs its own explanation. But what proceeds from the assumption of this mentality is straightforward; it is a projection of behavior based on a theory of the mental framework of the actor.

The fourth factor in Steinmetz's analysis turns to the states of agency of the colonized. Here, he refers to strategies of response by the subject people to the facts of colonial rule, ranging from cooperation to resistance.

> Resistance is located on the opposite side from cooperation. Colonized peoples were able to modulate and revise native policies. By signing up as a native policeman one might be able to temper colonial abuses of power. More frontal forms of resistance could bring a regime of native policy to an abrupt halt and force the colonial state to seek a new approach. (66)

This aspect of the account is compatible with a microfoundations approach; it is straightforward to see how social mobilization theory can be fleshed out in ways that make it an agent-centered approach.

It should be noted that a great deal of Steinmetz's account is descriptive and empirical. He provides detailed accounts of the history and behavior of the colonial regimes in these three settings, and much of the value of the book indeed derives from the research underlying these descriptive accounts.

CONCEPTUAL FRAMEWORKS

So far we have concerned ourselves with the question of the nature of the things that exist in the social world. But this question is deeply entangled with the question, "what concepts do we use to describe the world?" Ontology and language are intimately intertwined. This requires that we confront the issue of the conceptual schemes in terms of which we analyze and describe the world. For the remainder of the chapter we will consider the nature of the concepts and conceptual schemes used in the social sciences.

Defining Concepts

What is involved in offering a definition of a complex social phenomenon such as "fascism," "rationality," "contentious politics," "social capital," or "civic engagement"? Is there any sense in which a definition can be said to be correct or incorrect, given the facts we find in the world? Are some definitions better than others? Does a definition correspond to the world in some way? Or, is a definition no more than a conventional stipulation about how we propose to use a specific word?

There are several fundamental questions that need answering when we consider the meaning of a term such as "fascism" or "contentious politics." What do we intend the term to refer to? How is the term used in ordinary language? What are the paradigm cases? What are the ordinary criteria of application of the term—the necessary and sufficient conditions, the rules of application? What characteristics do we mean to pick out in using the term? What is our proto-theory that guides our use and application of the concept?

From the semantic point of view, the use of a concept is to single out a family of objects or phenomena that can usefully be considered together for further analysis and explanation. "Metals" are a group of materials that have similar physical properties such as conductivity and ductility. And, it turns out that these phenomenologically similar materials also have important underlying physical properties in common, which explain the phenomenological properties. So, it is possible to provide a physical theory of metals that unifies and explains their observable similarities. The scientist's interest, then, is in the phenomena and not the concept or its definition.

In order to investigate specific social concepts further, we need to specify more exactly what it is that we are singling out. What is "civic engagement"? Does this concept single out a specific range of behaviors and motivations? Would we include a spontaneous gift to a fund for a family who lost their home to a fire "civic engagement?" What about membership in a college sorority? So, we have to say what we mean by the term; we have to indicate which bits of the world are encompassed by the term;

and perhaps we need to give some reason to expect that these phenomena are relevantly similar.

Several semantic acts are relevant in trying to do this work. "Ostension" is the most basic: pointing to the clear cases of civic engagement or fascism and saying, "By civic engagement I mean things like these and things relevantly similar to them." If we go this route then we put a large part of the burden of the semantics in the world and in the judgment of the observer: Is this next putative example of the category really similar to the paradigm examples?

But there is also an intensional part of the work: What do we *intend* to designate in pointing to this set of paradigm cases? Is it the motivation of the activity, the features of social connections involved in the activity, or the effects of the activity that are motivating the selection of cases? Is fascism a kind of ideology, a type of social movement, or a type of political organization? These questions aren't answered by the gesture of ostension; rather, the observer needs to specify something about the nature of the phenomena that are intended to be encapsulated by the concept.

Once we have stipulated the extension and criteria of application of the term, we can then take a further step and offer a theory of this stuff. It may be a theory in materials science intended to explain the workings of some common characteristics of this stuff—electrical or thermal conductivity, melting point, and hardness. Or, it may be a social theory of the origins and institutional tendencies of the stuff (fascism, social movements, civic engagement). Either way, the theory goes beyond semantics and makes substantive empirical statement about the world.

It is not the case that all scientific concepts are constructed through a process of abstraction from observable phenomena. A theoretical concept is one whose meaning exceeds the observable associations or criteria associated with the concept. It may postulate unobservable mechanisms or structures which are only indirectly connected to observable phenomena, or it may hypothesize distinctions and features that help to explain the gross behavior of the phenomena. The value of a theoretical concept is not measured by its fit with ordinary language usage or its direct applicability to the observable world; instead, a theoretical concept is useful if it helps the theorist to formulate hypotheses about the unobservable mechanisms that underlie a phenomenon and that help to provide some empirical order to the phenomena.

In order to support empirical research, theoretical concepts need somehow to be related to the world of observation and experience. An important activity is "operationalizing" a theoretical concept. This means specifying a set of observable or experimental characteristics that permit the investigator to apply the concept to the world. But the operational criteria associated with a concept do not exhaust its meaning, and different investigators may provide a different set of operational criteria for the same concept. And, a specific scheme of operationalization of a concept like "social capital" or "civic engagement" may itself be debated.

The idea of a "natural kind" arises in the natural sciences. (Ian Hacking provides an excellent account of the history of this concept; Hacking (1991).) Concepts like metal, acid, insect, and gene are linguistic elements that are thought to refer to a family or group of entities that share fundamental properties in common. Kinds are thought to exist in the world, not simply in conceptual schemes. So, having identified the kind, we can then attempt to arrive at a theory of the underlying nature of things like this. (It is an important question to consider whether there are any "social kinds"; in general, I think not.)

These reflections raise many of the intellectual problems associated with defining a field of empirical research in the social sciences. Research always forces us to single out some specific body of phenomena for study. This means specifying and conceptualizing the phenomena. And, eventually it means arriving at theories of how these sorts of things work. But there is a permanent gap between concept and the world that means that certain questions can't be answered: For example, what is fascism "really"? There are no social essences that definitions might be thought to identify. Instead, we can offer analysis and theory about specific fascist movements and regimes, based on this or that way of specifying the concept of fascism. But there is nothing in the world that dictates how we define fascism and classify, specify, and theorize historical examples of fascism. The semantic ideas of family resemblance, ideal type, and cluster concept work best for concepts in the social sciences.

Conceptual Schemes

It is sometimes said that conceptual schemes govern the construction of the world of experience that we confront. What is a conceptual scheme? It is an interrelated set of high-level, abstract concepts that allow us to break the empirically or historically given into a discrete set of cognitive boxes. We might think of it as our highest-level concept vocabulary, within which more specific descriptors are arranged. Our conceptual scheme gives us the mental resources needed to represent, describe, and explain the empirical reality we encounter. Color, shape, mass, position, and force might be examples of components of a conceptual scheme for the realm of ordinary empirical experience. Structure, group, ideology, and network might be components for the realm of ordinary sociological experience. A conceptual scheme is thought in some way to be "comprehensive": all the phenomena in a certain domain ought to find a place within the conceptual scheme.

What does grammar tell us about the nature of our representations of the world? Do the linguistic categories that we use fundamentally shape the way we organize our understanding of the world? Do different cultures or different linguistic communities possess different "conceptual schemes"? Are different conceptual schemes incommensurable or can we translate from one to the other? These questions come up in the context of any discussion of social ontology—what does the social realm consist of? "Thing" and "object" are ontological categories that perhaps don't work as well in the social realm. Perhaps, more fluid categories such as process, relation, or activity work better.

Peter Strawson offered a focused analysis of the everyday metaphysics involved in the ways we analyze and represent the world around us. He proposes in *Individuals* (Strawson 1963) that we can do "descriptive metaphysics" by examining the conceptual schemes we actually use. And, he argues that there are core conceptual categories that are universal. Here is Strawson's preliminary description of a conceptual scheme:

> We think of the world as containing particular things some of which are independent of ourselves; we think of the world's history as made up of particular episodes in which we ourselves may or may not have a part; and we think of these particular things and events as included in the topics of our common discourse, as things about which we can talk to each other. These are remarks about the way we think of the world, our conceptual scheme. A more recognizably philosophical, though no clearer, way of expressing them would be to say that our ontology comprises objective particulars. . . . Part of my aim is to exhibit some general and structural features of the conceptual scheme in terms of which we think about particular things. (Strawson 1963: 15)

It is sometimes thought that our conceptual systems are simultaneously contingent and deeply influential in determining how we analyze the world around us. Different conceptual systems lead to different and incommensurable representations of the world. Here is how Donald Davidson summarizes the conceptual-relativist view (Davidson 1974):

> Conceptual schemes, we are told, are ways of organizing experience; they are systems of categories that give form to the data of sensation; they are points of view from which individuals, cultures, or periods survey the passing scene. There may be no translating from one scheme to another, in which case the beliefs, desires, hopes and bits of knowledge that characterize one person have no true counterparts for the subscriber to another scheme. Reality itself is relative to a scheme: what counts as real in one system may not in another. (1974: 5)

But, ultimately, Davidson argues that conceptual relativism and incommensurability are unintelligible. They are claims that cannot be stated coherently. More positively, Davidson argues that we can understand each other's concepts and words by making use of a principle of charity: we interpret the other's speech, vocabulary, and syntax in such a way as to maximize the truth of statements he or she utters.

How might we begin to provide a "descriptive metaphysics" for sociological knowledge along the lines of what Strawson describes? It is clear, to begin, that sociological analysis generally involves a rich and intertwined set of concepts and ontological assumptions about social phenomena. Consider the range of approaches we might take in analyzing a complex historical phenomenon such as fascism: as a social movement, as a political psychology, as an expression of psychopathology, as an ensemble of ideological currents, as a set of political institutions, as a collection of social constituents, and so on, indefinitely.

What is the situation with respect to conceptual schemes in the field of social knowledge? Are there deeply divided conceptual beginnings for the analysis of the social realm? Or, can we be confident in the mutual comprehensibility across practitioners of Marxist sociology, Durkheimian sociology, and ethnomethodology? Is Davidson right at the level of sociological theory? Or, are there fundamental paradigmatic differences across theories that make mutual understanding impossible?

We can get some leverage on this question by asking whether we can provide concrete examples of candidates for alternative sets of social conceptual schemes. For example, are individualism and holism distinct conceptual schemes for social cognition? The first identifies human individuals as the fundamental "particular," whereas the second identifies the social whole (structure, morality, ideology, class, way of life) as the fundamental particular. The first requires that we define or specify higher-level social entities or conditions in terms of a compound of features of individuals; the second takes the social whole as irreducible and specifies individuals in terms of their relations to a set of social factors.

Here is another possible contrast—perhaps, materialism and idealism are distinct conceptual schemes within which to organize social experience. The materialist scheme identifies a set of circumstances of the human organism (needs), the natural and build environment, and the forms of social activity that transform the environment as fundamental to social analysis. The idealist scheme takes states of consciousness—ideas, ideologies, moralities, wants, preferences, and modes of reasoning—as fundamental to social analysis and undertakes to characterize social facts in these terms.

Or, consider a third possible example: structure and process. A structure is an enduring configuration of social characteristics and positions, reproducing a set of powers and constraints for individuals enmeshed in these social relations. A process is an ensemble of things in circumstances of change over time. Structures emphasize permanence and stability; processes emphasize change and impermanence. So, perhaps, the "structure" lens leads sociologists to a very different representation of the social world than the "process" lens.

These examples make it credible that there are in fact alternative conceptual beginnings from which we can analyze the social world. What does not seem to be true, however, is the idea that these beginnings are incommensurable. Instead, it seems persuasive that ideas and statements that originate in an ontology of social wholes can be effectively restated in an ontology that originates in a world of individuals; likewise, materialist and ideological approaches to the social world seem compatible and mutually constructive rather than contradictory and incommensurable. The dichotomies considered here are not exclusive or incompatible. In fact, any adequate explanation of a social process or outcome is likely to need to refer to both sets of categories. And, this implies something very similar to the position Strawson and Davidson arrive at: the idea of intertranslatability and mutual comprehension across these large conceptual divides.

Consider an example from historical sociology. What conceptual choices do we need to make when we consider the swirling, fluid complexity of politics, culture, and struggle in Europe in the 1930s? We might place ideological and cultural change at the center; we might focus on the artistic and literary creations of the period; we might emphasize power or social class; we might give primary emphasis to economic change; or we might be drawn particularly to differences in behavior and regime across countries and regions of Europe. Each represents a different way of conceptualizing the historical reality of the 1930s in Europe.

Michael Mann is an insightful historical sociologist, who sought to understand and explain the rise of fascism in Europe in *Fascists* (Mann 2004). He was struck by the heterogeneity of fascist movements across the face of Europe; and he was forced to single out some features for primary study. Consider the main concepts Mann uses in his description and analysis of European in fascism Table 1.1.

These specific concepts could be related to a fairly short list of higher-level social concepts or what we might call social "categories": individuals and their characteristics, social groups, structures, ideologies, events, and influence terms (power, prestige, status). But many of the concepts on the list drawn from Mann's work involve a conceptual combination of other social concepts. Capitalism is a set of structures, a set of social movements, and a set of ideologies. Racism depends upon both structure and ideology. Modernity is an ideological-cultural formation, a technological-scientific stage, and a socioeconomic formation. So, the relation between the higher-level category system and mid-level sociological concepts is not one of subsumption but rather one of assembly, combination, or construction.

Table 1.1 Michael Mann's concepts in analyzing fascism (2004)

fascism [to be defined as "the pursuit of a transcendent and cleansing nation-statism through paramilitarism"]	social constituency [groups characterized by status, class, occupation]
socialism	modernity
fascist followers and activists	paramilitarism
power organizations	authoritarian regime
social movement	democratic regime
nation-state	capitalism [as an industrial social whole]
nationalism	social power [ideological, economic, military, political]
ideology	individualism, racism, ethnic purity ideology [as components of ideology]
individuals	major events and crises—World War I, the Great Depression
religious institutions and ideologies	

ARE THERE SOCIAL KINDS?

I will close this chapter with a discussion of the idea of social kinds. A natural kind concept is a concept that identifies a set of natural phenomena that share a common nature—metals, liquids, crystals. Philosophers of science sometimes define the idea of a natural kind as "a group of things that share a fundamental set of causal properties." And, we expect there to be important regularities or similarities across all instances of a natural kind term, deriving from the common features all instances share. Examples might be "gold," "metal," and "protein molecule" (Hacking 1991).

Examples of what might have been thought to be social kinds might include concepts such as these: proletariat, underclass resentment, revolutionary situation, racism; liberal representative states; fascism; feudalism; and bureaucratic state. But close examination shows that these are not kinds in the strong sense that philosophers of the natural sciences have in mind. Rather, they are plastic, variable, opportunistic, individually specific instantiations across a variety of human contexts. We need to be able to identify some topics of interest, so we need language and concepts; but we must avoid reifying the concepts and thinking they refer to some underlying discoverable essence. Think of how Chuck Tilly conceptualizes riot, rebellion, and resistance in terms of "contentious politics." Rightly, he avoids the idea that there is one common thing underlying all these instances across time, history, and place; his goal is to identify a medium-range body of causal mechanisms that bundle together in various contexts to give rise to one signature of contention or another.

Do some of the large noun concepts that are used in the social sciences succeed in identifying groups of things with sufficient stability and similarity that we might call a social kind? Consider some examples: feudalism, city, peasant, market economy, bureaucratic state, bureaucratic-clientelist regime, disaffected youth, riot, rebellion, revolution, civil war, credit system, totalitarian regime, and fascism. Do these typical concepts used in the social sciences succeed in identifying a social analog to natural kinds and a range of entities or processes that share a common structure or causal nature, which might be referred to as "social kinds"? And, if not, is it possible to be realist about the social world but antirealist with respect to "social kinds"?

This question ultimately concerns the relationship between general concepts and the items in the world that they encompass; or in other words, it has to do with the logic of classification. What is the basis of classification of items into groups? And, how do classifications fit into scientific inquiry and theory? First, what different types of classification are there?

Essential: The items may share a common defining characteristic (e.g. "liquid," "metal").

- Etiological: The items may share a common cause (e.g. "viral illness").
- Structural: The items may share a common underlying structure (e.g. "protein," "elm").
- Functional: The items may share a common function (e.g. "weapon," "school").

Nonessential: The items may lack necessary and sufficient conditions but share some overlapping characteristics.

- Symptomatic: The items may share a set of observable characteristics or symptoms (e.g. "pneumonia," "schizophrenia").
- Cluster: the items may share some among a list of characteristics (e.g. "game," "leader").

Now let's consider some social science terms and see where they fall in this scheme: riot, civil war, bicameral legislature, ethnic group, democracy, charismatic leader, financial city, and working-class organization.

Several of these concepts are symptom or cluster concepts: riot, democracy. Several others are etiological or structural: civil war, bicameral legislature, financial city. One combines structural with functional criteria: bicameral legislature.

Suppose we have identified a set of things as being "democracies." They share some among a set of features that are associated with democracy, but there is no set of features shared by all instances. What kinds of social science inquiry can we do? First, we can do comparisons within the group of democracies we have identified; we can look for similarities and differences across the group. And second, we can ask whether membership in this group is associated with membership in some other group beyond what chance would predict. In other words, we can consider whether there are true statements like "all democracies are X" or "most democracies are Y."

Similar issues arise in medicine. It is not the case that "all pneumonias respond to penicillin," for the reason that there are two causal and structural kinds of pneumonia, and only one of these involves organisms treatable with penicillin. The causal heterogeneity of this group means that strong generalizations are difficult or impossible here.

The concepts of riot, revolution, and democracy are similarly heterogeneous, both causally and structurally. So, we should expect only weak generalizations across this group and other social characteristics. On the other hand, the tools of social comparison are most valuable here. We can discover through additional comparative work within the category, whether there are similar structural and causal processes at work among instances of this concept.

It should be noted that there are other ways in which concept terms can function, without being kind terms. A cluster term is one for which the standards of application involve an open-ended group of characteristics, no subset of which are shared by all elements of the class. An ideal-type term is one that provides a specific model of something, and then classifies entities within the class depending on their similarity to some aspects of the model. And, a kind term is one that is supposed to classify entities as being similar on the basis of some deep set of characteristics that they share, ideally a common underlying causal structure. A concept is treated nominalistically if we understand that it is to some degree an arbitrary grouping of entities. A concept is treated realistically if we believe that the concept corresponds to an ontologically real class of entities in the world. (Weber's discussions of the logic of ideal-type concepts are very relevant to this topic; Weber (1949).)

None of the concepts mentioned above appears to be a plausible candidate for a kind term. The concept of "riot" covers a wide range of disturbances, with significant and causally important differences across the class. So, the items in the class of "riots" do not share an underlying causal nature. Likewise "fascist regime." We can give several different definitions of fascism. But all will encompass regimes that had substantial differences from each other: Nazi Germany, fascist Italy and Franco's Spain, and Romanian fascism. Each of these regimes had structural and cultural characteristics that importantly differentiated it from the others. So, we might consider whether explanation needs to occur at a lower level—not "why fascism"? but rather, "why the Iron Guard in Romania," "why this or that feature of Italian fascism," and "why this particular feature of Spanish state-military relations in Franco's fascism?" Here, the point is that there are no general or comprehensive explanations of the emergence and development of fascism in all the places it occurred and no common causes that were always or usually instrumental, but rather that each national history needs to be treated in its own terms.

Concepts are of course essential to social knowledge. The heart of social inquiry has to do with coming up with concepts that allow us to better understand social reality: for example, racism, patterns of behavior, free market, class consciousness, and ethnic identities. Theory formation in the social sciences largely consists of the task of constructing concepts and categories that capture groups of social phenomena for the purpose of analysis. But even the most successful social concepts do not identify groups of phenomena that should be called a "social kind." High-level social concepts that serve to pick out groups of social phenomena—states, riots, property systems—generally do not refer to causally homogeneous bodies of social phenomena; instead, each of these is composed of individual social formations with their own history and circumstances. There is no uniform causal constitution that underlies all states or riots. The philosophical notions of "family resemblance" and "cluster concepts" serve better to characterize these high-level social concepts than does "natural kind." And, it seems preferable to treat these concepts nominalistically rather than realistically.

There is another important obstacle to the plausibility of social kinds: the point about the plasticity of social entities that was argued above. The group of states that fall under the concept of "fascism" is a heterogeneous collection—that is, the point of the preceding paragraph. But there is a deeper problem as well: none of these states was itself a quasi-permanent set of institutional structures. Instead, the states of Germany, Spain, Portugal, and Italy changed over time, with the result that statements made about the early version of Spanish fascism may be false when applied to later versions of Spanish fascism.

This approach has specific implications for the conduct of the social sciences. For example, political science and the study of different types of states—we can identify common mechanisms, sub-institutions, building blocks, etc., that recur in different political systems. And, we can offer causal explanations of specific states in particular historical circumstances—for example, the Brazilian state in the 1990s. But we cannot produce strong generalizations about "states" or even particular kinds of states—for example, "developing states." Or, at least, the generalizations we find are weak and exception laden. Rather, we must build up our explanations from the component mechanisms and institutions found in the particular cases.

MULTIDISCIPLINARY STUDIES OF THE CITY

The arguments presented in this chapter suggest the value of asking new questions about the nature of the social world. We should understand social arrangements as substantially more contingent, heterogeneous, and plastic than we are often inclined to do. Are there any examples of social research today that conforms to these ideas?

A good source of examples of social science inquiry that seems to reflect these ideas is in area studies (Asian studies, Latin American studies, urban studies, environmental studies). In each of these areas, the problems that are identified for research are not confined to a single field of the social sciences—political science, economics, or sociology—but are instead defined by the large, messy topics that seem to be particularly important. In these fields, scholars come together in transdisciplinary organizations (e.g. the Association for Asian Studies and the Latin American Studies Association), and genuinely valuable collaborations across disciplinary lines ensue.

Urban studies is a particularly relevant example for the topics considered in this book. The general focus of urban studies is the city. But notice how heterogeneous every aspect of "the city" is. Regional and cultural differences mean that Mumbai functions differently from Liverpool. Cities embody an indefinite range of heterogeneous forces and configurations within them—ethnicity, poverty and wealth, functional differentiation, transportation networks, food preferences and systems of provision, and so on. And, cities are differentiated in terms of their involvement in the global system of communication and transportation (as Saskia Sassen demonstrates (Sassen 2001)). Cities are assemblages.

This substantive and disciplinary heterogeneity is illustrated in the range of research and methodology presented in handbooks of urban research. A good recent example is *The New Blackwell Companion to the City* (Bridge and Watson 2011). The sixty-five essays included in the volume are organized into major topics: city materialities, city mobilities, city affect, city publics and cultures, city divisions and differences, and city politics and planning. And, cities across the globe are considered in the various essays, so there is a good deal of geographical diversity reflected in this body of research. So, one might imagine that this collection represents a comprehensive snapshot of the current state of knowledge of cities and their dynamics. But this would be incorrect. The volume has its own perspective that governs the curation of the contributions. The collection reflects a generally postcolonial orientation toward the content; there is virtually no representation of mainstream economic or sociological research on the city; and the orientation of most of the contributions is present-ist rather than historical. These are not defects in the volume. Rather, the observation simply underlines one of the key points of this chapter: that there is enormous contingency and heterogeneity in any social subject, and the conceptual and methodological assumptions that we bring to social research are themselves heterogeneous and contingent.

Chapter 2

Actor-centered Sociology

ACTOR-CENTERED SOCIOLOGY

Key to the philosophy of social science offered here is the importance of what I've referred to as "actor-centered" sociology. Here is an elliptical description of three aspects of what I mean by this idea. First, it reflects a view of social ontology. The social world is constituted by the meaningful and oriented actions and mental frameworks of socially situated individuals and nothing else. Social things are composed, constituted, and given reality by the activities and interactions of individual actors—perhaps 2, perhaps 300 million. This does not mean social structures and forces do not exist. But it does mean that they gain their properties and powers through the activities and thoughts of social actors. Second, it puts forward a constraint on theorizing: Our social theories need to be compatible with the ontology, and we need to be confident that the social entities and forces that we postulate depend upon microfoundations at the level of social actors (whether or not we can specify those microfoundations). Third, "actor-centered sociology" represents a heuristic about where to focus at least some of our research energy and attention: at the ordinary processes and relations through which social activity take place, the ordinary people who bring them about, and the ordinary concatenations through which the effects of action and interaction aggregate to higher levels of social organization.

This view can be spelled out in a number of observations:

a. The premise of actor-centered sociology means that sociological theory needs to recognize and incorporate the idea that all social facts and structures derive from the activities and interactions of socially constructed individual actors. It is meta-theoretically improper to bring forward hypotheses about social structures that cannot be appropriately related to the actions and interactions of individuals. Or, in other words, it means that claims about social structures need to be compatible with there being *microfoundations* for the properties and powers attributed to social structures.

b. The meta-theory of actor-centered sociology requires that all social theories, at whatever level, need a theory of the actor. Economics and ethnomethodology differ in the level of specificity they offer for their theories of the actor; but both have such a theory. They both put forward fundamental ideas about how actors think and the mental processes that influence their actions.

c. Actor-centered sociology suggests that careful study of local social behaviors and mechanisms is a worthwhile exercise for sociological research. Ethnomethodology, micro-sociology, and the careful, place-based investigations offered by Goffman and Garfinkel move from the wings to the stage itself.

d. This framework implies that we may be able to explain at least some higher-level social facts by showing how they emerge as a result of the workings of actors and their structured interactions. This is the aggregation-dynamics methodology. Or, in terms discussed in chapter 4, it is the micro-to-macro link of Coleman's boat.

e. The actor-based sociology approach implies that the regularities that may exist at the level of macro-social phenomena are bound to be weak and exception laden. Heterogeneity within and across actors—across history and across social settings—implies that there are multiple sets of attainable outcomes from a given starting point. Would fascist organizations flourish in Italy after World War I? The answer was indeterminate in 1914. There were numerous groups of social actors with important differences in their states of agency, and these groups in turn were influenced by organizations of varying characteristics. So, it would be impossible to say in advance with confidence either that fascism was likely to emerge or that it was unlikely to emerge.

f. The actor-centered approach suggests that we can do better sociology by being more attentive to subtle differences in agency in specific groups and times. George Steinmetz's careful attention to the processes of formation through which colonial administrators took shape in nineteenth-century Germany illustrates the value of paying attention to the historical particulars of various groups of actors, and the historically specific circumstances in which their frames of agency were created (Steinmetz 2007). It implies that context and historical processes are crucial to sociological explanation. This in turn provides support for the methods associated with comparative historical sociology.

g. The actor-centered approach highlights the importance of careful analysis of the mechanisms of communication and interaction through which individuals influence each other and through which their actions aggregate to higher-level social outcomes and structures. Social networks, competitive markets, mass communications systems, and civic associations all represent important inter-actor linkages that have massively important consequences for aggregate social outcomes.

h. Finally, the actor-centered approach has some of the advantages of the spotlight in a circus. The idea of actor-centered sociology points the spotlight to the parts of the arena where the action is happening: to the formation of the actor, to the concrete setting of the actor, to the interactions that occur among actors, to the aggregative processes that lead to larger outcomes, and to the causal properties that those larger structures come to have.

THE BIG PICTURE

It seems self-evident, barely worth remarking, that social outcomes are the result of the actions of numbers of ordinary human beings, doing things for their own particular reasons—finding solutions to the challenges of life that confront them, taking care of themselves and their families, making mistakes, acting out their passions, hatreds, and loves, interacting with neighbors and strangers, taking risks, acting prudently, and following impulse or dream. And, out of these ordinary origins come great social outcomes—migrations, revolutions, demographic transitions, famines, economic crises, and the rise and fall of regions and cities. Sometimes a small number of individuals or groups have inordinate influence on the shape of events—Mussolini, Kant, Gramsci, Fidel; the Abolitionists, the Tea Party, the United Mine Workers. But even here it is still individuals, in relation and communication with other individuals, whose small and local actions sometimes aggregate to large social changes.

This description makes the individualistic impulse of social science disciplines like political science, economics, and historical demography seem intuitive. These disciplines basically ask a common question: What are the individual purposes and plans that work to shape a subset of social phenomena? Why did the Great Migration take place from the South to northern cities in the 1930s? Because vast numbers of poor rural black people gained information about better opportunities in northern cities and set out to improve their lives. Why do prices fall for goods whose manufacturing technology has become more efficient? Because rational producers compete for market share from rational consumers on the basis of price. We can explain the macro-level outcomes as the result of reasoning about the desires, beliefs, and opportunities of the agents involved.

But this same description also makes us consider how large "structural" factors come into social process and change. How do economic conditions, political institutions, social attitudes, and systems of race, class, and gender influence social outcomes? Once again, it is evident that individuals frame their worlds and make their choices within environments that are largely independent of their wills and their specific mental frameworks. They confront systems of labor allocation that work in a certain way when it comes to race, class origins, gender, and educational background. They operate within political institutions that offer them opportunities and limitations. They function in social environments where other actors have certain beliefs and attitudes about race, gender, and class.

These structural conditions confront real social actors as *facts* that they understand well enough and that set constraints around their choices. So, it is entirely understandable and legitimate that sociologists want to consider those structural factors in the abstract and to uncover how they work in detail. They want to abstract from the individuals who make up the structures. At the same time, these higher-level social realities are themselves embodied in the thoughts and actions of other individual actors. There is an iterative reality to the relation between structure and agency—a reality that Margaret Archer attempts to capture with her concept of *morphogenesis* (discussed further in chapter 7). The social world is highly dynamic and situational; we may want to abstract from this dynamism and characterize a moment as consisting of fixed structures and agents acting within them, but in the next frame we find yesterday's agent becoming through her actions a part of tomorrow's structure. So, static analysis creates an unrealistic rigidity for what is in actuality a highly fluid process.

There is a further complexity raised by the action-centered picture sketched above. Actors are deeply and inextricably socially constituted by the concrete historical and social circumstances in which they develop. We must attend to the *making* of social individuals through concrete and historically actual processes of formation and socialization. Actors are social from infancy forward, and their cognitive, affective, and practical mental frameworks are created and formed through their various social interactions. So, their practical agency as adults—their motives, frames, beliefs, and values—is itself a socially created product of the ideological and practical circumstances within which they developed. We cannot "reduce" social change to pre-social or nonsocial individuals. There is no starting de novo in the social world or in history.

THEORIES OF THE ACTOR

The basic idea in this chapter is that social phenomena are constituted by the actions of individuals, oriented by their own subjectivities and mental frameworks. It is recognized, of course, that the subjectivity of the actor doesn't come full blown into his or her mind at adulthood; rather, we recognize that individuals are "socialized"; their thought processes and mental frameworks are developed through myriad social relationships and institutions. So, the actor is a socially constituted individual.

If we take the approach to social explanation that demands that we understand how complex social processes and assemblages relate to the actions and thoughts of individuals, then it is logical that we would want to develop a theory of the actor. We would like to have a justifiable set of ideas about how individuals perceive the social world, how they think about their own lives and commitments, and how they move from thought to action. But we have many alternatives available as we grapple with this task.

A theory of the actor is an organized set of ideas about what individuals are doing when they engage in interactions in the world, and what we think at the highest level of generality about why they behave as they do. Individuals within social interactions constitute the social world; they do things; and they do things for reasons that we would like to understand. A theory of the actor ought to give us a basic vocabulary for describing behavior in the social world. And, it ought to provide some framing hypotheses about the causes or motivations of behavior.

An important aspect of action theory is the idea of *intensionality* and mental representation. This is the conception of the individual as possessing consciousness, purposes, and a mental orientation to the world. He or she "understands" the events that surround him or her—that is, the individual forms a mental representation of the swirling set of actions and events that surround him or her. And, the individual places himself or herself within this representation by conceptualizing wants, aversions, aspirations, and intentions concerning what might be achieved through intentional behavior.

This description may seem obvious. Or, it may seem to reflect a set of assumptions about how to parse the social world that are substantive, consequential, and debatable. They are consequential because they push our sociological researches in a particular direction: Who are the actors that make up a social ensemble? What are they doing? Why are they doing these things? They are debatable because they privilege the actor over the action, the individual over the interaction. They push us in the direction of a social ontology that is individualistic and perhaps reductionist. Andrew Abbott proposes, in contrast, that we begin with the interaction, the flow of moves and responses (2007). Charles Tilly suggests that we start with the relationships and turn to the individual actors only later in the analysis (1995). And, Neil Gross suggests starting with the creativity inherent in any complex flow of human activities and interactions (Gross 2009).

A THEORY OF THE ACTOR

Let us begin by asking, what work should a theory of the actor do? Here are a set of questions that a theory of the actor ought to consider:

1. How does the actor represent the world of action—the physical and social environment? Here, we need a vocabulary of mental frameworks, representational schemes, stereotypes, and paradigms.
2. How do these schemes become actualized within the actor's mental system? This is the developmental and socialization question.
3. What motivates the actor? What sorts of things does the actor seek to accomplish through action?
4. Here, too, there is a developmental question: How are these motives instilled in the actor through a social process of learning?
5. What mental forces lead to action? Here, we are considering things like deliberative processes, heuristic reasoning, emotional attachments, habits, and internally realized practices.
6. How do the results of action become incorporated into the actor's mental system? Here, we are thinking about memory, representation of the meanings of outcomes, regret, satisfaction, or happiness.
7. How do the results of past experiences inform the mental processes leading to subsequent actions? Here, we are considering the ways that memory and emotional representations of the past may motivate different patterns of action in the future.

It is plain that people act as a result of a great variety of mental influences: instincts, emotions, impulses, loyalties, norms, as well as reasons, intentions, and plans. A subset of this cacophony is "rational-intentional action": actions that are the result of deliberation about ends and means, and choice among the set of available options for action. How does this subsystem of action fit into the larger swirl of psychological causes within the actor's mental system? One picture that philosophers of action have used is the idea of "higher" and "lower" faculties of motivation and choice. This is an Aristotelian model of practical reason. The higher system is the rational process of deliberation; the lower system is the range of emotions and impulses; and the point of the picture is that the rational component should govern the workings of the lower faculties.

How does this construction work as an empirical theory of human behavior (even if an idealized and simplified one)? It could prove faulty in several different ways: the emotions could turn out to be the more important cause, with rational deliberation a weak and tardy late arrival. Or, it could turn out that the system of action is a more integrated process in which "emotion" and "deliberation" play a more equal and interactive role. Or, it could turn out that these two realms really can't be separated at all, and reason and emotion are comingled. We might find that it is possible to deliberate and reason about emotions, and it is possible for some emotions to push the deliberative process one way rather than another. And, most radically, it could be argued that these categories of introspection and folk psychology don't explain behavior at all; instead, we need a more scientific and nonmentalistic foundation for explanation of behavior.

There are a few basic facts about action that constrain any proposed theory:

1. Actions are influenced by the goals that people have, so deliberation must be a part of the story. Whatever else we observe, it is certainly true that people are sometimes goal directed and calculating.
2. We can provide clear and important examples of actions provoked by emotion or passion, so means-end rationality is not the whole story.
3. People often give reasons for actions that motivate their actions, but that are not framed as "means-end" reasoning (e.g. acting out of fairness). So, there are instances of action that are reasoned but not utility maximizing.

What these points seem to demonstrate is that the mental system underlying behavior and choice is complex, and our current understanding is incomplete.

The Actor's Mental Framework

Let's look more closely at agency and acting. We think we know quite a bit about being an "agent." It is to be an intervener in the world: a being capable of changing things around him or her through physical action; a subjectivity (consciousness, feelings, thoughts, desires); a user of language for thought and for communication. We also think we are well prepared when it comes to recognizing the diversity of the subjectivities on which agents act and live. We are familiar with important cultural differences; we know that people have different sets of values and commitments; we know that people from different backgrounds see and experience the world differently. Perhaps even, like Benjamin Whorf, we may think that different language systems and grammars give their users fundamentally different categories in term of which to analyze the world.

Think of the range of vocabulary that is relevant to our discourse about the kinds of examples of social action we confront in ordinary life: decision, belief, desire, emotion, fear, habit, norm, obligation, reason, impulse, weakness of will. . . . These terms and others constitute something like a mental ontology, a set of concepts that we attribute to the agent as he or she acts. And, some of them bring presuppositions that are debatable. Take "decision," for example. Did the thief "decide" to break into the car? Or, was the action an impulse, prior to thought and deliberation?

So, we seem to know a lot. But, in fact, this is the part of the social sciences and humanities that is the least developed and the least adequate to the complexity of the facts. What we lack most basically is a usable meta-framework in the context of which to characterize and analyze the workings of these features of agency.

We are not even clear about what to call these personally realized features of subjectivity and vision. Are they mentalities? Conceptual frameworks? Value systems? Worldviews? Depth grammars of social cognition? There are some meta-frameworks that might be considered at the outset. The idea of a scientific paradigm or research program is one; here, philosophers of science have tried to get concrete about the specific presuppositions and concepts in terms of which the community of physicists understands theory and the laboratory bench. The idea of a cultural tradition is likewise a fairly concrete idea, where anthropologists try to use the statements, speeches, and artifacts of a community to help decode the subjectivity that underlies. A third meta-framework is Charles Tilly's concept of a "repertoire of contention"—a set of examples and models of contention that exist in the consciousness of the people of a particular time and place (Tilly 1986).

One reason for this under-development is the intangibility of these sorts of characteristics. They are features of the subjectivity of the individual; they are unobservable; they are difficult or impossible for the agent herself to articulate. So, it is easier for the social sciences to proceed on the basis of highly schematic "models" of the agent—for example, the rational choice model of preferences and beliefs, or the traditionalist's model of roles and norms. But these models aren't adequate. Worse, they lead us to paraphrase features of novel agency into the stylized forms of the model. They erase the differences.

The topic is important, because, ultimately, all social phenomena are the result of agents acting for their own reasons, and we need to understand the varieties of their thought processes. So, the social sciences need detailed understandings of the varieties of human subjectivity and agency. We need to understand in concrete detail what it means to say that the subject is socially constructed, and through what concrete social mechanisms this construction takes place. We need to know how differences in culture produce systemically different worldviews or mental frameworks. And, we need to be able to investigate these differences in detail and rigorously.

A few concrete examples are helpful:

• How did French and Chinese legal systems think differently about "property"? How did these differences influence differences in judgment between French and Chinese officials?

- How does the idea of an after-life influence worldview, action, and behavior for believing Christians and Muslims?
- In what ways do Balinese people have a nonindividualistic conception of the individual person?
- Is it true that Japanese workers have a deeper affinity with team and group than American workers?
- Was the "Greatest Generation" really different in significant ways by having to do with values and social perceptions than the next generation?

There are research vehicles through which to conduct this kind of research—ethnography, careful study of texts, literary analysis, interviews in depth about political perceptions, the methods of phenomenological sociology, and perhaps the tools of cognitive and personality psychologists. A good example is Robert Darnton's reconstruction of the specific and surprising mentality of the eighteenth-century printer's apprentices in the *The Great Cat Massacre: And Other Episodes in French Cultural History* (Darnton 1984). And, his interpretation is based on rigorous analysis of varied documents and practices. It is good historical research and good discovery of subjectivity. This topic is important in many areas of the social sciences, but none more so than in comparative research across civilizations. When we consider economic and political institutions in Europe and Asia, as Bin Wong does in *China Transformed: Historical Change and the Limits of European Experience* (Wong 1997), the fact of massive differences in starting points, presuppositions, fixed values, and moral perceptions of the populations involved loom enormous. But without more refined tools for analyzing these differences, it is difficult to treat them in a satisfying way.

Before we are likely to make a lot of progress on framing a research agenda around "mentality," we need a better and more commonly understood vision of the goal of the study. And, this means trying to formulate a meta-theory of subjectivity and agency, into which our findings about value systems, cognitive frameworks, moral ideas, and the like can be fitted.

Purposive Rationality

There are various different approaches to existing efforts to answer questions like these. Here are some of the questions we would like to answer about the human actor in concrete circumstances of action.

- What motivated the action?
- What was the actor thinking?
- What was the actor feeling?
- What beliefs were highlighted in the actor's conscious thoughts?

- What memories played a role in the actor's decision?
- What rules of thumb did the actor make use of?
- What emotional stream occurred?
- How did the actor process emotions?
- What scripts were salient?
- What unconscious biases and impulses were operative?

Our ordinary "folk psychology" provides a range of simple theories available of the agent's mentality.

- Desire-belief-opportunity => action
- Emotion => dynamics of psychology => action
- Habit and practice => context => performance
- Environment scan => rules of thumb => action

And, we might incorporate all these factors into a large composite model: desires, beliefs, habits, emotions, past experience, and moral conviction all play a role. But the key point is this: we need to have richer modes of representation of consciousness and agency than we currently have. Philosophers have sometimes made efforts at this problem, but it seems that novelists like James Joyce or Henry James do as good a job of conceptualizing these processes as any philosopher has done.

Aristotle guides much philosophical thinking on these questions by offering an orderly theory of the practical agent in *The Nicomachean Ethics* (Aristotle 1987). His theory is centered on the idea of deliberative rationality, but he leaves a place for the emotions in action as well (to be controlled by the faculty of reason). Deliberation, in Aristotle's view, amounts to reflecting on one's goals and arranging them into a hierarchy, and then choosing actions that permit the achievement of one's highest goals.

Formal rational choice theory provides a related set of answers to several of these questions. Actors have preferences and beliefs; their preferences are well ordered; they assign probabilities and utilities to outcomes (the results of actions); and they choose a given action to maximize the satisfaction of their preferences.

One of the reasons that rational choice theory is appealing to social scientists is that it is an actor-centered approach to social explanation: explain the social outcome on the basis of an analysis of the beliefs, intentions, and circumstances of the individual agents who make up the social setting. What rational choice theory adds to this description is a specification of the decision-making processes that are attributed to the individual agent—typically, that the agent has a consistent set of preferences among accessible alternatives and that he or she chooses in such a way as to maximize the satisfaction of this set of preferences. This can be paraphrased as a "utility-maximizing" model of decision-making. Many objections have been offered against rational choice theory as a basis for social explanation—for example, it overlooks social motivations, it presupposes egoism, it oversimplifies the logic of practical reasoning, and it fails to correspond to typical human behavior. (See Green and Shapiro, *Pathologies of Rational Choice Theory: A Critique of Applications in Political Science*, for a developed set of critiques (Green and Shapiro 1994).)

Two points are worth underlining here. First, rational choice theory has a major theoretical advantage precisely because it is an actor-centered framework. Rational choice theory is one possible way of articulating a set of hypotheses about how individuals reason and act. This is a major advantage in comparison to explanatory frameworks that essentially assume programmed behavior on the part of participants in a social event. Moreover, the assumption of preference-satisfaction lines up pretty well with a somewhat broader conception of human action in terms of goal directedness and purposiveness. If we believe that individuals have goals and purposes that underlie their choices and actions, then it is an appealing simplification to represent their actions as the outcome of deliberation about goals, strategies, and circumstances. In other words, rational choice theory can be seen as a specification of a philosophical idea of human action that is at least as old as Aristotle: the idea of individuals as deliberative, purposive agents. And, this is in fact a credible and empirically defensible theory of action.

But a second point is equally important: rational choice theory and its model of utility maximization is only one out of a range of possible specifications of the idea of deliberation and purposiveness. There are important alternative specifications that can be offered. For example, we might say, along with Kant, that individuals possess a set of moral rules as well as a set of specific goals, and that they deliberate among possible choices of action on the basis of both considerations. How do the various possible actions conform to the moral rules? And, how do they do from the point of view of accomplishing my goals? This process of reasoning is "deontological"—that is, it cannot be subsumed under a simple model of maximizing rationality. It is, nonetheless, an intelligible interpretation of what rational human decision-making involves. (Mark Johnson's *Moral Imagination: Implications of Cognitive Science for Ethics* is interesting in its effort to bring cognitive science into dialogue with ethical theory (Johnson 1994).)

Another possible interpretation of the basic idea of deliberativeness that diverges from rational choice theory is one that illustrates some themes that Amartya Sen (1987), James Scott (1976), and Doug McAdam (1999) have emphasized: that real human social behavior is a complex mix of commitments, loyalties, emotions, solidarities—as well as purposes and goals.

So, a theory of action that isolates "goal-directedness" and its associated framework of utility maximizing is one that already overlooks a set of motivational factors that are crucial to explaining real social behavior. It is as if we imagined modeling wine-tasting judgments by experts but "erased" their sense of smell. Given that smell is a crucial ingredient of the experience of tasting wine, our reduced theory won't do a very good job of explaining discrimination across samples by the experts.

Instead, when we undertake to explain an individual's action in the context of a spontaneous rent strike, we need to ask a series of questions: What does he or she expect to get out of the action? What loyalties does he or she have to the organization or other participants? What principles does he or she endorse that are relevant to the context of proposed action? What forms of social identity does he or she embody, and how are these strands relevant to the decision to participate or not? How do the emotions created by the words and actions of others influence one's behavior?

What makes rational choice theory useful in spite of these complexities of actual motivation is the fact that there are many important situations of choice where other sources and structures of motivation are of minimal importance. When a person chooses a new toaster, it is likely enough that solidarity, emotion, principle, and identity drop away, and the choice is based on perceived value and price. So, the market in toasters behaves pretty much as neoclassical economics predicts. But the market for shoes is probably more complicated: emotion, status, style, identity, and a preference for "fair-trade" products may influence one person to buy the more expensive and less functional pair of shoes, while another person will go for the good buy. Likewise, the decision to join American Association of Retired People (AARP) is likely to be a fairly simple calculation—what are the side benefits of membership, how much importance do I attribute to being part of an organization that represents the public good of people over fifty, and how much can I gain from there being a successful AARP? This is simple in comparison to the situation of a rent strike or a street demonstration, where one's face-to-face relations with other potential participants may have a very large impact on the decision to participate or not.

So, we might say that rational choice theory represents a special case of the more general category of deliberative action, which is itself a subcategory of intentional action. And, rational choice theory will be most successful in generating explanations in social circumstances where the other sources of social motivation are largely silent—for example, anonymous market transactions, isolated decisions about participation or nonparticipation in collective action, and decisions about portfolio investments.

What we really need is a more developed and adequate theory of social agency—a better account of how the various factors mentioned above fit together into one scheme of deliberation and decision-making. This might be called a full theory of practical rationality. And, it would be a more general specification of the situation of agent-based social action than rational choice is able to provide.

So, the traditional rational-intentional theory of action remains a partial view. In addition to rational-intentional action and its variants, we can think of a range of other varieties that have little in common with this goal-directed model: expressive action, role-driven action, dramaturgical action, emotional action, . . . (Bourdieu's conception of *habitus* falls in this general domain; Bourdieu (1977).) Here, we have a number of paradigms of action that we can observe in everyday life, which provide an intelligible understanding of "what is she doing, and why?" and that appear to have a fundamentally different structure from the rational-intentional model. These actions express or enact rather than aim; or if they have an aim, it is to create a certain effect in the viewer.

If we take the view that social outcomes are ultimately the result of the actions of individuals, then we plainly need to have a more nuanced and satisfactory framework of analysis within which to understand "action." Rational choice theory is one such framework; Aristotelian theory of deliberation is a somewhat broader framework. But it is plain that the origins, motives, dynamics, and meanings of individual actions are broader and more heterogeneous than these rational-intentional theories would suggest. Purposive action is an important part of the story of social action—but it is only a part.

Embeddedness

An important critic of the narrow conception of self-interested rationality from within sociology is Mark Granovetter. Granovetter formulated this set of criticisms in his important 1985 article "Economic Action and Social Structure: The Problem of Embeddedness" (Granovetter 1985). He used the concept of *embeddedness* as a way of capturing the idea that the actions individuals choose are importantly refracted by the social relations within which they function. Granovetter's contribution is an important one to consider as we try to further clarify the issues involved. The large distinction at issue here is the contrast between rational actor models of the social world, in which the actor makes choices within a thin set of context-independent decision rules, and social actor models, in which the actor is largely driven by a context-defined set of scripts as he or she makes choices. The contrast is sometimes illustrated by contrasting neoclassical economic models of the market with substantivist models along the lines of Karl Polanyi's *The Great Transformation: The Political and Economic Origins of Our Time* (Polanyi 1957), and it links to the debate in economic anthropology between formalists and substantivists. Here is how Granovetter puts the fundamental question:

How behavior and institutions are affected by social relations is one of the classic questions of social theory. (Granovetter 1985: 481)

He argues that neither of the polar positions is tenable. The formalist approach errs in taking too a-social view of the actor:

Classical and neoclassical economics operates, in contrast, with an atomized, undersocialized conception of human action, continuing in the utilitarian tradition. . . . In classical and neoclassical economics, therefore, the fact that actors may have social relations with one another has been treated, if at all, as a frictional drag that impedes competitive markets. (Granovetter 1985: 483, 484)

But the extreme alternative isn't appealing either:

More recent comments by economists on "social influences" construe these as processes in which actors acquire customs, habits, or norms that are followed mechanically and automatically, irrespective of their bearing on rational choice. (Granovetter 1985: 485)

So, action doesn't reduce to abstract optimizing rationality, and it doesn't reduce to inflexible cultural or normative scripts either. Instead, Granovetter proposes an approach to this topic that reframes the issue around a more fluid and relational conception of the actor. Like the pragmatist theories of the actor (Abbott, Gross, Joas), he explores the idea that the actor's choices emerge from a flow of interactions and shifting relations with others. The actor is not an atomized agent, but rather a participant in a flow of actions and interactions. At the same time, Granovetter insists that this approach does not deny purposiveness and agency to the actor. The actor reacts and responds to the social relations surrounding him or her; but actions are constructed and refracted through the consciousness, beliefs, and purposes of the individual.

The idea of embeddedness is crucial for Granovetter's argument; but it isn't explicitly defined in this piece. The idea of an "embedded" individual is contrasted to the idea of an atomized actor; this implies that the individual's choices and actions are generated, in part anyway, by the actions and expected behavior of other actors. It is a relational concept; the embedded actor exists in a set of relationships with other actors whose choices affect his or her own choices as well. And, this in turn implies that the choices actors make are not wholly determined by facts internal to their spheres of individual deliberation and beliefs; instead, actions are importantly influenced by the observed and expected behavior of others.

Their attempts at purposive action are instead embedded in concrete, ongoing systems of social relations. (Granovetter 1985: 487)

Some of Granovetter's discussion crystallizes around the social reality of *trust* within a system of economic actors. Trust is an inherently relational social category; it depends upon the past and present actions and interactions within a group of actors, on the basis of which the actors choose courses of action that depend on expectations about the future cooperative actions of the other actors. Trust for Granovetter is therefore a feature of social relations and social networks:

> The embeddedness argument stresses instead the role of concrete personal relations and structures (or "networks") of such relations in generating trust and discouraging malfeasance. (490)

And, trust is relevant to cooperation in all its variants—benevolent and malicious as well. As Granovetter points out, a conspiracy to defraud a business requires a group of trusting confederates. So, it is an important sociological question to investigate how those bonds of trust among thieves are created and sustained. This line of thought, and the theory of the actor that it suggests, is an important contribution to how we can understand social behavior in a wide range of contexts. The key premise is that individuals choose their actions in consideration of the likely choices of others, and this means that their concrete social relations are critical to their actions. How frequently do a set of actors interact? Has there been a history of successful cooperation among these actors in the past? Are there rivalries among the actors that might work to reduce trust? These are all situational and historical facts about the location and social relations of the individual. And, they imply that very similar individuals, confronting very similar circumstances of choice, may arrive at very different patterns of social action dependent on their histories of interaction with each other.

It seems that this theory of the actor would be amenable to empirical investigation. The methodologies of experimental economics could be adapted to study of the relational intelligence that Granovetter describes here. Recent research by Ernst Fehr and Klaus Schmidt explore related empirical questions about decision-making in the context of problems involving fairness and reciprocity, and Fehr, Cohn, and Marechal explore the mentality created by the institutional setting of financial institutions for the professionals who work in them (Cohn, Fehr, and Marechal 2014; Fehr and Schmidt 1999).

Performance and Habit

Let us now turn to substantial alternatives to the rational choice model of agency. Ethnographic thinkers such as Clifford Geertz or Erving Goffman take a different tack altogether; they give a lot of attention to questions 1 and 2, given under section "A Theory of the Actor"; they provide "thick" descriptions of the motives and meanings of the actors (3); and they indicate a diverse set of answers to question 5. Other anthropologists have favored a "performative" understanding of agency. The actor is understood as carrying out a culturally prescribed script in response to stereotyped social settings.

Here, I will focus for a moment on the idea of action as a performance—a series of behaviors meaningfully orchestrated by the actor out of consideration of an expected "script." Here, we interpret actions as falling into scripts and roles, created by the culture's history and constituting the actor's behaviors as a performance. The agent is postulated to possess a stock of mini scripts and role expectations that are then invoked into a "syntax" of performance in specific social settings. The idea here is that social groups—cultures—have created for themselves a set of schemes of ways of behaving that individuals internalize and play out as social settings arise. There is the role of the doctor, the salesman, the librarian, the clown, and the general, and the individuals who assume those roles know the scripts. So, when they interact in social settings relevant to their roles, their behaviors reflect the role and the script. The scripts become part of the furniture of "behavioral cognition"—the routines the players string together in ordinary and extraordinary social settings. (Note the parallel with Erving Goffman's treatment of everyday behavior. Goffman is discussed more fully later in the chapter.) And, perhaps, the script governs the social actor so deeply that his or her behavior no longer has its own individual meaning or intention.

What does this framework imply about the actor's state of mind in performing an action? How much agency do actors maintain under this theory? And, to what extent is the actor's conduct his own, deriving from his or her own authentic self rather than from an externally created role? Consider, as an example, a fire captain's behaviors and speeches during his management of the fire company's handling of a major fire. Let's amplify the story a bit. The captain and the members of the company have a well-rehearsed set of procedures for various scenarios encountered in fighting a fire—"victim trapped in bedroom," "elderly person inside," "possible toxic materials on site," or "roof collapse imminent." As these contingencies arise, captain and company play out the prescribed actions. Second, though, there is probably a prescribed style of command that influences the captain's manner and conduct: be calm, give sufficient attention to the company's safety, keep control of the press and crowd on-site, and don't fall into a screaming, cursing rage when things go badly.

So, there are fairly tangible ways in which the behaviors of the commander and the company are in fact governed by scripts and roles. The dramaturgical interpretation makes sense here. The actions of these participants are not invented de novo on the scene of the fire; rather, they derive from earlier practice of roles and, more intangibly, carrying out of a certain conception of behavior of a commander under stress. We don't get actions here that derive from unadorned actors, considering a range of choices and choosing the best in the circumstances.

But neither do we get the opposite extreme—robots playing out their scripts without intelligence or adaptation to circumstance. Instead, each of the players in this story retains his or her own assessment of what is currently going on and what deviations of script may be demanded. The captain retains the ability and the responsibility to break with procedures when there is an imminent reason to do so; and this degree of autonomy extends down the line of command to the junior firefighter. So, the routines and scripts guide rather than generate the behavior.

So, the performative interpretation of social action is not inherently inconsistent with the idea of intelligent, purposive action or of embedded action. Instead, we can think of the actor in this case—captain or junior firefighter— as involving in a complicated series of behaviors that reflect both deliberation and internalized script. This interpretation is similar to Pierre Bourdieu's position on the subject of *habitus* in *Outline of a Theory of Practice* (1977). Conduct that is guided by norms (in this case, scripts and roles) can nonetheless also be intelligent and strategic. Seen in this light, the dramaturgical interpretation supplements the purposive theory of action rather than replaces it. Here is how Bourdieu describes action and habitus in *Outline of a Theory of Practice* (1977):

> The habitus, the durably installed generative principle of regulated improvisations, produces practices which tend to reproduce the regularities immanent in the objective conditions of the production of their generative principle, while adjusting to the demands inscribed as objective potentialities in the situation, as defined by the cognitive and motivating structures making up the habitus. (78)
>
> In practice, it is the habitus, history turned into nature, i.e. denied as such, which accomplishes practically the relating of these two systems of relations, in and through the production of practice. (78)

This concept offers a more fluid conception of thinking-experiencing-doing than is characteristic of a more Aristotelian conception. There is a suggestion of a sort of tacit knowledge underlying activity, with action looking as much like the smooth, intelligent motions of a soccer player as a deliberative chess master. It is a less epistemic view of the human condition—less a concoction of explicit beliefs and reasonings than a smooth coordination of tacit understandings and movements in the situation. It is less about deliberation and decision and more about intelligent doing.

This interpretation is born out of a cryptic passage a page or so later:

If witticisms surprise their author no less than their audience, and impress as much by their retrospective necessity as by their novelty, the reason is that the trouvaille appears as the simple unearthing, at once accidental and irresistible, of a buried possibility. It is because subjects do not, strictly speaking, know what they are doing that what they do has more meaning than they know. (79)

There are many uncertainties about how to think about this most intimate of human facts—the ways our thoughts process our needs and movements. And, it seems to me that the choice of ontology surrounding action—the concepts and entities we use—is important and difficult and worthy of careful attention.

It is challenging to get the balance right, though, between the compulsion of a set of norms or scripts and the practical freedom the actor maintains at every point to act differently than the prescription. It seems unavoidable that the kinds of scripts, roles, and norms mentioned here have some binding power over the agent in actual social life. Much of the time the behavior simply plays out the script, with no homunculus reconsidering the action from the point of view of other possible choices. And, often the role or norm is psychologically compelling to the extent that the actor can't realistically consider breaking it.

NORMS AND TRUST

Let's turn now to a related topic, the workings of norms and commitments within the actor's mental scheme. What is a norm? How do norms influence behavior? The question arises for two separate reasons. First, we are interested in knowing why people behave as they do (agency). And, second, we are interested in knowing how large social factors (moral and cognitive frameworks, for example) exert influence over individuals (social causation).

Here are a number of key empirical and conceptual questions that are raised by norms.

- What is a norm?
- How are social norms embodied in behavior and structure?
- How do individuals internalize norms?
- How do norms influence behavior?
- Why do individuals conform their behavior to a set of local norms?
- What factors stabilize a norm system over time?
- What social factors influence change in a norm system?

Before we can go much further into this issue, we need to have a fairly clear idea of what we mean by a norm. We might define a norm as

- a socially embodied and individually perceived imperative that such-and-so an action must be performed in such-and-so a fashion.

We can now separate out several other types of questions: First, what induces individuals to conform to the imperative? How do individuals come to have the psychological dispositions to conform to the norm? Second, how is the norm embodied in social relations and behavior? And, third, what are the social mechanisms or processes that created the imperative within the given social group? What mechanisms serve to sustain it over time?

To the first question, there seem to be only three possible answers, and each is in fact socially and psychologically possible. The imperative may be internalized into the motivational space of the individual, so he or she chooses to act according to the imperative (or is habituated to acting in such a way). There may be an effective and well-known system of sanctions that attach to violations of the norms, so the individual has an incentive to comply. These sanctions may be formal or informal. The sanction may be as benign as being laughed at for wearing a Hawaiian shirt to a black tie ball (I'll never do that again!), or as severe as being ostracized for looking like a New Yorker in a cowboy bar. Or, third, there may be benefits from conformance that make conformance a choice that is in the actor's rational self-interest. (Every time one demonstrates that he or she can choose the right fork for dessert, the likelihood of being invited to another formal dinner increases.) Each of these would make sense of the fact that an individual conforms his or her behavior to the requirements of a norm.

Now consider the question of the ways in which norms influence behavior. It would seem that there are only a few mechanisms through which norms could possibly influence individual and collective behavior, largely distinguished by being external and internal.

First, it may be that there is an effective mechanism of social education through which each individual develops or activates an internally regulative system of norms or rules. This process can be described as "moral education." The most superficial observation of social behavior indicates that this is so, and social psychologists and sociologists have some ideas about how these systems work. But the bottom line appears fairly clear: individuals who are reared in normal human settings eventually possess action-behavior systems that embody a set of personal norms that influence their conduct. We might draw the analogy to the example of language learning: a normal human child is exposed to the linguistic behavior of others, and arrives at a psychologically realized grammar that guides his or her own language production.

Second, a norm might be embodied in the attitudes, judgment, and behavior of others in such a way that their actions and reactions create incentives and disincentives for the actor. For example, others may possess a set of norms concerning civility in public discourse, and they may punish or reward others according to whether their words are consistent with these norms. In this case, the agent conforms to the requirements of the norm out of a calculation of costs and benefits of performance.

Third, it might be the case that there are some norms of interpersonal behavior that are hardwired. Some norms might have a biological, evolutionary basis. This is the line of thought that sociobiologists have explored with varying levels of success. The emotional responses that adults have to infants and children probably fall in this category—though it is a conceptually interesting question to consider whether these emotional responses are "norms" or simply features of the affective system. This is relevant to the work that Allan Gibbard does in *Wise Choices, Apt Feelings: A Theory of Normative Judgment* (Gibbard 1990). Gibbard's fundamental insight is that there must be an evolutionary basis for the "norm-acquisition system"—the features of human psychology that permit them to acquire certain kinds of moral motives (altruism, friendship, fairness).

So, what can we say about norms? It seems unmistakable that human beings act on the basis of deliberation, norm, impulse, and emotion. So, our theory of practical rationality and action must make a place for the workings of norms. Second, norms are transmitted to individuals through concrete social processes—family experiences, schooling, religious institutions, etc. Our theories of social life must incorporate an account of the processes of normative education through which individuals come to possess a particular normative structure. These experiences are the counterpart to the exposure to language on the part of the infant. And, third, norms are socially enforced through the actions of others. So, norms are socially embodied—in the institutions of enforcement, the institutions and practices of moral education, and the practical cognition of the individuals who make up the society.

Cooperation

Now consider another important feature of agency that has large implications for social life, the willingness to cooperate. Why do people cooperate? What motivates individuals to come together to share labor and resources in pursuit of a common good from which they cannot be excluded—fighting fires, hunting marauding tigers, and cleaning up a public beach? Standard rational choice theory, and its application to problems of individual rationality in group settings, implies that cooperation should be unstable in the face of free riding. This was Mancur Olson's central conclusion in his classic book *The Logic of Collective Action: Public Goods and the Theory of Groups* (1965). Roughly, his conclusion was that cooperation would be possible only if there were excludable side benefits for participants, selective coercion to enforce cooperation, or privatization of the gains of collective action. Otherwise, it is prisoners' dilemmas all the way down. However, we know from many social contexts that individuals do in fact succeed in establishing cooperative relationships without any of these supporting conditions. So, what are we missing when we consider social action from the narrow perspective of rational choice theory?

A part of the answer to this puzzle involves the role of norms in action. Here, the criticism is that the rational choice approach, by attending solely to calculations of self-interest, is blind to the workings of normative frameworks; but in fact norms are powerful factors underlying behavior in most traditional contexts. This perspective finds expression in the moral economy literature within peasant studies—for example, James Scott's *The Moral Economy of the Peasant: Rebellion and Subsistence in Southeast Asia* (1976). (This debate is sometimes referred to as one between formalists and substantivists. Karl Polanyi is another good example of the substantivist perspective (*The Great Transformation*, 1957), while Sam Popkin (*The Rational Peasant: The Political Economy of Rural Society in Vietnam* (Popkin 1979)) and Theodore Schultz (*Transforming Traditional Agriculture* (Schultz 1964)) fall on the side of the formalists.)

According to the substantivist moral-economy perspective, traditional societies are communities: tightly cohesive groups of persons sharing a distinctive set of values in stable, continuing relations to one another (Taylor 1982). The central threats to security and welfare are well known to such groups—excessive or deficient rainfall, attacks by bandits, predatory tax policies by the central government, etc. And, village societies have evolved schemes of shared values and cooperative practices and institutions that are well adapted to handling these problems of risk and welfare in ways which protect the subsistence needs of all villagers adequately in all but the most extreme circumstances. The substantivists thus maintain that traditions and norms are fundamental social factors and that individual behavior is almost always modulated through powerful traditional motivational constraints. One consequence of this modulation is that many societies do not display a sharp distinction between group interest and individual interest that is predicted by collective action theory. (An important theoretical defense of this conclusion can be found in the work of Elinor Ostrom and her fellow researchers in their treatment of "common property resource regimes" (Ostrom 1990).)

There are, of course, well-known social and behavioral processes that may tend to undermine the working of a given set of norms. Normative systems are inherently ambiguous and subject to revision over time. Consequently, we should expect that opportunistic agents will find ways of adapting given social norms more comfortably to the pursuit of self-interest. Consider the requirement that elites should provide for the subsistence needs of the poor

in times of dearth. There are some grounds for supposing that such a requirement is in the long-term interest of elites—for example, by promoting social
stability and establishing bonds of reciprocity with other members of an
interdependent society. But it seems reasonable to expect that elites—already
by their superior economic position able to exercise political and social power
as well—will find ways of limiting the effect of such norms on their behavior. So, it is insufficient to simply postulate a set of governing norms; we
need to identify the mechanisms at the group and individual levels that make
them behaviorally relevant and stable. But, significantly, some theorists have
tried to show that rational self-interest may actually reinforce certain kinds
of norms of fairness and reciprocity; thus Robert Axelrod's analysis of the
dynamics of reciprocity demonstrates that cooperation is rational in relation
to a variety of circumstances of face-to-face cooperation in *The Evolution of
Cooperation* (1984).

Trust

Chuck Tilly had a fascination with the mechanisms of social interaction at all
levels. His book *Trust and Rule* (2005) picks up on one particular feature of
social organization that is often instrumental in political and social episodes,
including especially in the everyday workings of predation and defense. This
is the idea of a trust network: a group of people connected by similar ties and
interests whose "collective enterprise is at risk to the malfeasance, mistakes,
and failures of individual members" (Tilly 2005: 41). Here is a definition:

> Trust networks, then, consist of ramified interpersonal connections, consisting
> mainly of strong ties, within which people set valued, consequential, long-term
> resources and enterprises at risk to the malfeasance, mistakes, or failures of
> others. (Tilly 2005: 12)

A band of pirates, a group of tax resisters, or a village of nonconformists in
a period of religious persecution fall in the category of trust networks. The
stakes are high for all participants. On the other hand, the American Medical
Association (AMA), the League of Women Voters, and the pickpockets who
work the Gare St Lazare train station do not represent trust networks, though
they have the properties of social action networks more generally. There is
little real risk for any particular physician even if other members of the AMA
don't play their parts in a lobbying campaign. The willingness of members
of the extended group to commit their own actions to a risky common effort
depends on their level of trust in other members—trust that they will make
their own contributions to the collective enterprise and trust that they will
not betray their comrades. (French historian Marc Bloch belonged to a trust

network, the French Resistance, that led to his death in 1944 by the Gestapo;
Fink (1989).) The general idea is that there are numerous examples of networks of people who share substantial interests in common, and who have a
high level of trust in one another that permits them to undertake risky joint
activities. Here is a more complete statement of Tilly's conception:

> How will we recognize a trust network when we encounter or enter one? First,
> we will notice a number of people who are connected, directly or indirectly, by
> similar ties; they form a network. Second, we will see that the sheer existence of
> such a tie gives one member significant claims on the attention or aid of another;
> the network consists of strong ties. Third, we will discover that members of the
> network are collectively carrying on major long-term enterprises such as pro-
> creation, long-distance trade, workers' mutual aid or practice of an underground
> religion. Finally, we will learn that the configuration of ties within the network
> sets the collective enterprise at risk to the malfeasance, mistakes, and failures of
> individual members. (Tilly 2005: 4)

Trust networks are particularly relevant in the context of efforts at violent
extraction and domination—both on the side of predators and prey. Predators—bandits, pirates, and gangs—need to establish strong ties within their
organizations in order to be able to effectively coerce their targets and to
escape repression by others. And, prey—farmers in ranch country, rural Jews
in Poland, or home owners in central Newark—are advantaged by the existence of strong ties of family, religion, or ethnicity through which they can
maintain the collective strategies that provide some degree of protection. But
Tilly makes the interesting point that the workings of trust networks cross
over both contentious and noncontentious activities. Here is a general statement that frames much of Tilly's discussion in the book:

> Noncontentious politics still make up the bulk of all political interaction, since
> it includes tax collection, census taking, military service, diffusion of political
> information, processing of government-mediated benefits, internal organizational
> activity of constituted political actors, and related processes that go on most of
> the time without discontinuous, public, collective claim making. Trust networks
> and their segments get involved in noncontentious politics more regularly—and
> usually more consequently—than in contentious politics. (Tilly 2005: 5)

The idea of a trust network represents a different way of getting a handle on
the contrast between self-interested agency and group-oriented agency, which
in turn corresponds to "economistic" and "sociological" approaches to social
behavior. Is it interests or norms that guide social behavior? By introducing
the idea of a trust network, Tilly is able to find a position someplace else on
the spectrum—neither purely self-interested behavior nor routine normative

conformance. Instead, agents within trust networks behave as purposive, goal-directed actors; but they have commitments and resources that people in other social settings lack, and they are thereby enabled to achieve forms of collective action that are impossible elsewhere. We might say that Tilly is offering an account of the microfoundations of collective action, or of a certain kind of collective action. In line with Tilly's lifelong interest in taxation and state building, the idea of resource extraction plays a central role in his analysis of trust networks. A central theme is the struggle between the tax-collecting state and the elusive, tax-evading trust networks that exist in civil society. "Rulers have usually coveted the resources embedded in such networks, have often treated them as obstacles to effective rule, yet have never succeeded in annihilating them and have usually worked out accommodations producing enough resources and compliance to sustain their regimes" (6).

So, what kind of analysis is Tilly offering here? What is the use of this concept from the point of view of the social sciences, beyond the metaphor and analytical specifics? Are there concrete historical or sociological hypotheses in play? Does this concept provide a better basis for explaining some puzzling outcomes than existing theories? Or, possibly, is the concept of a trust network another example of a part of the sociologist's toolkit: an ideal-typical description of a real social mechanism whose workings can be discerned in a variety of contexts?

Tilly is relatively explicit about several of these questions. To start, he does not believe that "trust networks" constitute a homogeneous social kind. We cannot offer a general account of the essential features of a trust network (9). We can do a certain amount of classification within the group of social configurations that we call "trust networks." So, "trust networks" are socially real, and we can use ordinary methods of social and historical inquiry to map out some of their properties.

Further, he believes, we can state some mid-level regularities, such as the following, about trust networks and political regimes:

- Trust networks survive and hold off predators when they generate enough resources to reproduce themselves.
- Trust networks are absorbed into systems of rule when existing autonomous trust networks disintegrate or cease to provide substantial benefits.
- Variations in the kinds of trust networks that exist help explain the variety of the consolidation of rule that occurs in given settings (50).
- Trust networks that mark, maintain, and monitor sharp boundaries between insiders and outsiders generally operate more effectively than others (57).
- Trust networks most commonly defend themselves from predation by adopting some combination of the strategies of concealment, clientage, and dissimulation (83).

Actors by Cohort

So far we have emphasized that individuals are socially constructed in the frameworks that guide their behavior. Here, I will show that there are important generational differences in the action frameworks and beliefs that individuals acquire. What difference does it make to a person's personality, values, agency, or interpretive schemes that she was born in 1950 rather than 1930 or 1970? How does a person's place in time and in a stream of historical events influence the formation of his or her consciousness?

If we thought of people as being pretty much uniform in their motivations and understandings of the world, then we wouldn't be particularly interested in the micro-circumstances that defined the developmental environment of a cohort; these circumstances would have been expected to lead to pretty much the same kinds of actors. We don't think it is useful to analyze ants or cattle into age cohorts. If, on the other hand, we think that a person's political and social identity, the ways in which she values a range of social and personal outcomes, and the ways in which she organizes her thinking about the world—these basic features of cognition, valuation, and motivation—are significantly influenced by the environment in which development and maturation take place, then we are forced to consider the importance of cohorts.

The ideas of the "Great Generation," the "Children of the Depression," or the "Sixties Generation" have a certain amount of resonance for us. We think of the typical members of these cohorts as having fairly important features of personality, memory, and motivation that are different from members of other cohorts. Americans born in the 1920s were thrown into social environments that were very different from those of people born twenty years earlier or later. And, their political consciousness and behavior seem to reflect these differences.

But here is the difficult question raised by these considerations: How should sociologists attempt to incorporate the possibility of cohort differences in behavior and outlook? Here is one possible way of conceptualizing cohort differences with respect to a personality characteristic—let's say "propensity to trust leaders." Suppose we have conducted a survey that operationalizes this characteristic so that the trust propensity of each individual can be measured. We might postulate that every individual has some degree of trust, but that different cohort groups have different mean values and different distributions around the mean.

Suppose there are three generations in our study. The first is the "Greatest Generation," born between 1915 and 1924. The second is the baby-boom generation—people born between 1945 and 1954. And, the third is the "me-generation," born between 1955 and 1964. We might speculate that growing up in the 1960s, with a highly divisive war in Vietnam under way, a government that suffered a serious credibility gap and a youth culture that preached the slogan, "trust no one over 30!" would have led to a political psychology that was less inclined to trust government than generations born earlier or later. So, the third cohort has a low level of trust as a group. The social necessity of sticking together as a country, fighting a major world war, and working our way out of the Great Depression might explain the high degree of unanimity of trust found in the first cohort. And, the second generation is all over the map, ranging from a significant number of people with extremely low trust to an equal group of extremely high trust. We might imagine that the circumstances of maturation and development following the turbulent 1960s imposed little structure on this feature of political identity, resulting in a very wide distribution of levels of trust.

It is also important to consider some of the factors that vary across time that might have important influences on the development of different cohorts. Circumstances like war, famine, or economic crisis represent one family of influences that are often markedly different across age cohorts. Ideologies and value systems also change from decade to decade. The turn to a more conservative kind of Christianity in the United States in the 1990s certainly influenced a significant number of young people coming of age during those decades, and the value system of nationalism and patriotism of the 1940s and 1950s influenced the young people of those decades. Moreover, institutions change significantly over time as well. Schools change, the operations and culture of the military change, and the internal workings of religious institutions change. So, the institutions in which children and young adults gain their perspectives, motives, and allegiances are often significantly different from one decade to another. And, presumably, all these factors are involved in the formation of the consciousness and identity of the young people who experience them. Difference in settings (events, ideologies, institutions) lead to differences in psychology across cohorts.

Andrew Abbott raised some of these questions in his presidential address to the Social Science History Association in 2004 (Abbott 2005). The title he chose is illuminating—"The Historicality of Individuals." And, the central point here could be put in the same terms: it is important for us to attempt to understand processes of social and historical change, through the shifting characteristics of the age-specific populations that make these processes up. The historicality of individuals adds up to the sociological importance of cohorts.

SOCIAL KNOWLEDGE AT THE MICRO LEVEL

The upshot of the discussion to this point is messy but important. People engage in their social worlds on the basis of a dense set of abilities and cognitive frameworks that permit them to make sense of the interactions they encounter and to shape their behavior in ways that work for their purposes in the setting. People are creative, adaptive social actors, and this means that they engage with their social worlds on the basis of active, cognitive sense-making processes. These frameworks are rich and textured, and they plainly result from a long process of social learning on the part of the actor-in-formation.

The kinds of things that are encompassed here include the following:

* Manners and stylized patterns of interaction
* Frameworks for recognizing and interpreting the cues presented by others
* Background knowledge about local social hierarchy
* Rules of thumb for dealing with new action scenarios
* Strategies for communicating and signifying socially important meanings to others

Some people are better at each of these modes of social interaction than others. Some are better at recognizing the cues of behavior or comportment of others—this stranger is safe, that one is menacing. Some are more adept at piecing together an action plan appropriate to the present circumstances. Some are more sensitive to the social expectations of a situation than others—the social dolt who neglects to offer a polite greeting before asking for assistance from a shop clerk in Brittany. And, these differences have consequences; the person who is chronically insensitive or brusque in rural France is likely to find he or she receives minimal assistance from strangers when needed.

This fact about social interaction raises several kinds of questions for sociologists. First, mapping out the "grammar" of these micro norms of interaction and social knowledge is itself an interesting task. Much of the work of Erving Goffman takes this form of investigation—for example, *Behavior in Public Places: Notes on the Social Organization of Gatherings* (Goffman 1963). One might describe this as discovery of a social grammar in a particular setting—a set of rules of interaction that can be discerned in ordinary social behavior.

Second, it is certainly an interesting question to ask what cognitive and emotional capacities are required for an individual to become adept in a familiar environment (one's home village) or an unfamiliar context (a visit to Hong Kong by the middle-aged French farmer, let's say). This is analogous to Chomsky's most fundamental question: What mental capacities are required in order to acquire a human-language syntax?

Cultural Sociology

The term "cultural sociology" is sometimes used to try to capture those research efforts that try to probe the meanings and mental frameworks that people bring to their social interactions. We can postulate that human beings are processors of meanings and interpretations and that their frameworks take shape as a result of the range of experiences and interactions they have had to date. This means that their frameworks are deeply social, created and constructed by the social settings and experiences the individuals have had. And, we can further postulate that social action is deeply inflected by the specifics of the mental and emotional frameworks through which actors structure and interpret the worlds they confront. At least a part of the disciplinary matrix of cultural sociology might be understood as the field of inquiry that tries to probe those frameworks as they are embodied in specific collectivities—working-class people, women, African Americans, American Muslims, or college professors, for example. (Erving Goffman and Harold Garfinkel might be viewed as progenitors of this aspect of the sociology discipline.)

Wendy Griswold addresses part of this viewpoint on sociological research in her very good overview of the field in *Cultures and Societies in a Changing World* (Griswold 2013).

> Most sociologists now view people as meaning makers as well as rational actors, symbol users as well as class representatives, and storytellers as well as points in a demographic trend. Moreover, sociology largely has escaped its former either/or way of thinking. The discipline now seeks to understand how people's meaning making shapes their rational action, how their class position molds their stories—in short, how social structure and culture mutually influence one another. (Griswold 2013: xiii)

So, how have sociologists attempted to investigate these kinds of subjective realities? Here is how Al Young describes his research goals *in The Minds of Marginalized Black Men: Making Sense of Mobility, Opportunity, and Future Life Chances* (Young 2004):

> I wanted to get a sense of whether poor black men looked beyond their immediate surroundings and circumstances when thinking about the future. Hence, the story told here is about how these men think about themselves as members of a larger social world—not just their communities and neighborhoods, but American society. (lc 134)
>
> Part 2, "Lifeworlds," explores the men's own accounts of their past and contemporary circumstances. It is here that the experiences and situations that have positioned them as poor, urban-based black men are explored. Chapter 2 provides a vision of the social contexts that circumscribe these men's lives and shape the comments and opinions that they shared with me. (lc 195)

In order to answer these questions, Young conducted several-dozen interviews with young black men on the south side of Chicago, and his interpretation and analysis of the results is highly illuminating.

Or, take as another example the highly interesting work of sociologist Michele Lamont in *Money, Morals, and Manners: The Culture of the French and the American Upper-Middle Class* (Lamont 1992). Here, Lamont studies the mentalities of high-status white men in the United States and France. Her question is a fairly simple one: How do these men formulate their judgments of success and failure in themselves and others? What features do they admire in others and which do they dislike? She conducts interviews with 160 men in four cities in France and the United States and makes a sustained effort to discern the profiles of culture and value that she finds among these individuals.

> I compare competing definitions of what it means to be a 'worthy person' by analyzing symbolic boundaries, i.e., by looking at implicit definitions of purity present in the labels interviewees use to describe, abstractly and concretely, people with whom they don't want to associate, people to whom they consider themselves to be superior and inferior, and people who arouse hostility, indifference, and sympathy. Hence, the study analyzes the relative importance attached to religion, honesty, low moral standards, cosmopolitanism, high culture, money, power, and the likes, by Hoosiers, New Yorkers, Parisians, and Clermontois. (Lamont 1992: xvii)

This kind of research is inherently interesting because of the light it sheds for readers about the lives and experiences of others. Reading Al Young or Michele Lamont offers the reader a window into the experience and meaning frameworks of people whose lives and experiences have been substantially different from our own; it helps us understand the ways in which these various individuals and members of groups understand themselves and their social worlds. All by itself this is a valuable kind of research.

But this kind of research becomes especially interesting if we find that the mental frameworks and systems of meanings that actors bring with them actually make substantial differences to their social actions and the choices that they make. In this case, we can actually begin to create explanations and interpretations of social outcomes that interest us a great deal.

A key issue with this kind of inquiry is methodological. How should we investigate and observe the subjective characteristics of thought and feeling that this work entails? What are appropriate standards of validity on the basis of which to assess assertions in this area? Sociologists like Alford Young and Michele Lamont have often chosen a methodology that centers on open-ended unstructured interviews. What these sociologists add to the approach of talented documentary journalists is an effort to analyze and generalize from the interviews they collect in order to arrive at mid-level statements about the mentality and symbolic frameworks of this group or that. And, both Young and Lamont succeed in providing portraits of their subjects that are highly insightful and sociologically plausible—we can understand the mechanisms through which these frameworks take hold, and we can see some of the meso-level consequences that follow from them in specific social settings.

The processes of learning through which these kinds of skills and knowledge frameworks are acquired are certainly of great interest for sociologists. How does one learn how to behave in one's home setting; in one's work setting; or in an unfamiliar social context? What is the process of observation and adaptation through which one becomes an expert denizen of a particular social context? How much is endogenous to a given community, and how much is constructed from broader cultural avenues (e.g. film and television)? Did gangsters make *Goodfellas*, or did *Goodfellas* make gangsters?

Several recent books provide very interesting analyses of these kinds of questions. One is Diego Gambetta's *Codes of the Underworld: How Criminals Communicate* (Gambetta 2009). Gambetta's central issue is communications and signaling. Given the illegality of their activities, how do organized crime groups communicate their "sales" approach to their clients, victims, and the public? How does the Sicilian mafia communicate its effectiveness and menace as a source of protection for shopkeepers? How does it keep lesser groups of criminals out of this racket or that? How does it avoid adulteration of the brand?

At a more micro level, how do "made" men learn how to act as gangsters? How do they learn how to dress, how to talk, and how to swagger? Gambetta suggests seriously that they do so in important measure through movies and television depiction of gangsters—*The Godfather* and the *Sopranos* were highly influential on gangster dress and behavior, Gambetta maintains. (Tony Soprano made one serious sartorial error in the *Sopranos*, wearing shorts to a barbecue. The producers were informed by mafia insiders this would never happen.) And, Gambetta believes there is a fairly clear explanation of this fact, the workings of convention as a way of stabilizing behavior and communicating one's identity. If one wants to say, "I'm a gangster" without confessing to a crime, what better way than wearing the sunglasses and open collars of the Corleone family in *The Godfather*? And, the influence goes in both directions; according to Gambetta, Michael Caan (Sonny Corleone) spent an inordinate amount of time with gangster Carmine Persico during the filming of *The Godfather*.

Gambetta goes into a fair level of detail in describing and explaining the use of nicknames within the mafia. He rejects group-level functional explanations; rather, he wants to know what situations and interests lead individual criminals to continue to make use of nicknames for some of their associates. Based on the records of the "maxi trial" in Palermo in 1986–1987, he argues that nicknames are more common among foot soldiers and killers in the mafia than in other occupational groups and that they are also more common in urban settings than rural settings. He argues that nicknames persist among gangsters for several reasons. They permit insiders to accurately identify individuals with otherwise indistinguishable birth certificate names. They confuse the police and prosecutors, allowing individual gangsters to slip from one identity to another in evading arrest or conviction. And, sometimes they serve a within-group purpose as well—allowing a little bit of cautious fun at the expense of one another with the use of ridiculous nicknames.

Another interesting recent contribution to micro-sociology is Peter Bearman's *Doormen* (Bearman 2005). Bearman is interested in making sense of the ways that doormen have professionalized their actions by mediating between the private worlds of their tenants and the public world of the street. Here is how he describes his research at the thirty-thousand-foot level:

> Here, through the window of observed behavior, we observe that the real springs for social action rest in a nest of workable social theories, bags of tricks, and larger network processes. These theories, tricks, and processes appear to be social facts, that is, things that are not changeable by the will of a single individual—either the researcher or the research subject. (257)

Bearman makes a point of moving back and forth between fieldwork and social models. He wants to make sense of the social phenomenology he observes—how the job market for doormen works, how informal networks of knowledge sharing facilitate movement of young men into open doormen jobs (rather than waiting for years in queues for those same jobs), how weak ties play a crucial role in this world, and the ways in which these mechanisms prolong the workings of race- and ethnicity-based inequalities. And, he makes expert use of the results of various areas of social modeling theory to explicate features of doorman activity—for example, the queuing of tasks and responses to tenants' requests (chapter 3).

The situation of the doorman is unusual, Bearman finds, compared to many other semi-skilled service occupations. The doorman provides a buffer between the tenant's world of privacy and privilege and the polluted world of the hustle-bustle street. He argues that the situation of the doorman is an unusual one, in that the doorman gains a high degree of personal knowledge about his tenants and uses that knowledge to provide personalized service to them.

Bearman makes a great deal of the fact that there is a wide social separation between doorman and tenant, even as there is a quasi-intimate relation between them based on the personal knowledge the doorman has of the tenant. The doorman knows an enormous amount about the life of the tenant, while the tenant knows almost nothing of the doorman's private life in Queens or Staten Island.

One of the striking things about Bearman's book is the skill with which he diagnoses the *semantics* of the behaviors and spaces that he considers.

What does the lobby of the residential building signify? In what ways do different residence styles signify different attitudes and qualities for their tenants? What does the routine, meaningless small chat between resident and doorman mean? What does the doorman's uniform signify, for himself, for the tenant, and for the visitor? (According to one of the informant doormen quoted by Bearman, the uniform makes him socially invisible as a human being.) This emphasis on social meanings is crucial and welcome; it is an acknowledgment for sociology of the insight that Geertz brought to ethnography, that the social world is a web of meanings that need to be deciphered if we are to understand the behavior of people within these settings (Geertz 1971).

Both these books are interesting because of what they bring to an actor-centered view of the social world. Both books are specifically interested in examining the social meanings invested in various modes of speech, dress, or comportment. We urgently need to have more nuanced theories of the actor, beyond stylized accounts of beliefs, desires, and opportunities. And, studies like these provide a very welcome contribution to the task of formulating such a sociology.

Erving Goffman

Erving Goffman is one of the sociologists who has given the greatest attention to the role of social norms in ordinary social interaction. One of his central themes is a focus on face-to-face interaction. This is the central topic in his book, *Interaction Ritual—Essays on Face-to-Face Behavior* (Goffman 1967). So, *Interaction Ritual* is a good way to gain some concrete exposure to how some sociologists think about the internalized norms and practices that are important to social action.

Goffman's central concern in this book is how ordinary social interactions develop. How do the participants shape their contributions in such a way as to lead to a satisfactory exchange? The ideas of "line" and "face" are the central concepts in this volume. "Line" is the performative strategy the individual has within the interaction. "Face" is the way in which the individual perceives himself, and the way he perceives others in the interaction to perceive him. Maintaining face invokes pride and honor, while losing face invokes shame and embarrassment. So, a great deal of the effort extended by the actor in social interactions has to do with maintaining face—what Goffman refers to as "face-work." Here are several key descriptions of the role of face-work in ordinary social interactions:

> By face-work I mean to designate the actions taken by a person to make whatever he is doing consistent with face. (Goffman 1967: 12)

The members of every social circle may be expected to have some knowledge of face-work and some experience in its use. In our society, this kind of capacity is sometimes called tact, savoir-faire, diplomacy, or social skill. (13)

A person may be said to have, or be in, or maintain face when the line he effectively takes presents an image of him that is internally consistent, that is supported by judgment and evidence conveyed by other participants, and that is confirmed by evidence conveyed through and personal agencies in the situation. (6–7)

So, Goffman's view is that the vast majority of face-to-face social interactions are driven by the logic of the participants' conceptions of "face" and the "lines" that they assume for the interaction. Moreover, Goffman holds that in many circumstances, the lines available for the person in the circumstance are defined by convention and are relatively few. This entails that most interactional behavior is scripted and conventional as well. This line of thought emphasizes the coercive role played by social expectations in face-to-face encounters. And, it dovetails with the view Goffman often expresses of action as performative and self as dramaturgical.

The concept of self is a part of our theory of the actor. What is the self? Goffman too addresses the topic of self:

So far I have implicitly been using a double definition of self: the self as an image pieced together from the expressive implications of the full flow of events in an undertaking; and the self as a kind of player in a ritual game who copes honorably or dishonorably, diplomatically or undiplomatically, with the judgmental contingencies of the situation. (31)

Fundamentally, Goffman's view inclines against the notion of a primeval or authentic self; instead, the self is a construct dictated by society and adopted and projected by the individual.

Universal human nature is not a very human thing. By acquiring it, the person becomes a kind of construct, build up not from inner psychic propensities but from moral rules that are impressed upon him from without. (45)

Moreover, Goffman highlights the scope of self-deception and manipulation that is a part of his conception of the actor:

Whatever his position in society, the person insulates himself by blindnesses, half-truths, illusions, and rationalizations. He makes an "adjustment" by convincing himself, with the tactful support of his intimate circle, that he is what he wants to be and that he would not do to gain his ends what the others have done to gain theirs. (43)

A very interesting part of the book is the concluding essay, "Where the Action Is." Here, Goffman considers people making choices that are neither prudent nor norm guided. He considers hapless bank robbers, a black journalist mistreated by a highway patrolman in Indiana, and other individuals making risky choices contrary to the prescribed scripts. In this setting, "action" is an opportunity for risky choice, counter-normative choice, throwing fate to the wind. And, Goffman thinks there is something inherently attractive about this kind of risk-taking behavior.

Here, Goffman seems to be breaking his own rules—the theoretical ones, anyway. He seems to be allowing that action is sometimes *not* guided by prescriptive rules of interaction, and that there are human impulses toward risk-taking that make this kind of behavior relatively persistent in society. But this seems to point to a whole category of action that is otherwise overlooked in Goffman's work—the actions of heroes, outlaws, counterculture activists, saints, and ordinary men and women of integrity. In each case, these actors are choosing lines of conduct that break the norms and that proceed from their own conceptions of what they should do (or want to do).

Each of the micro-sociologists considered here contribute to actor-centered sociology in very substantive ways. They help to create a more complete conception of the actor, because they leave room for spontaneity and creativity in action, as well as a degree of independence from coercive norms of behavior.

SIMILARITY SPACE OF ACTOR THEORIES

It is apparent that within the actor-centered field of social research itself there are large differences. The diagram (Figure 2.1) attempts to indicate some of those differences. Rational choice theory and game theory attempt to understand social outcomes as the result of the strategies and calculations of rational actors. Actor-centered sociology and pragmatist theory attempt to uncover a deep understanding of the actor's frameworks and modes of action. Analytical sociology attempts to work out the logic of Coleman's boat by showing how macro-level social factors influence the behavior of individuals and how macro factors result from the interactions of individuals at the micro level. And, agent-based models provide computational systems for representing the complex forms of interaction that occur among individuals leading to social outcomes.

All four approaches appear to pursue much the same basic strategy: derive social outcomes from what we know about the action models and composition of the individuals who make up a social setting. It is tempting to see these as four different formulations to the same basic approach. But this would be a mistake. The scientific distance between Hedström and Goffman, or Goffman

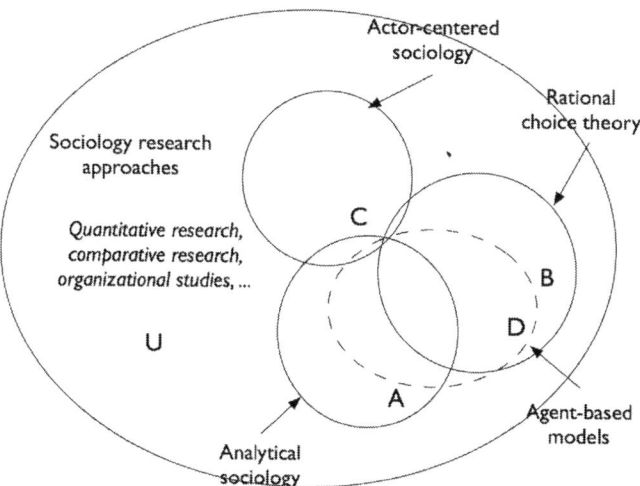

Figure 2.1   Map of sociological approaches.

and Becker, is great. Rational choice theory, analytical sociology, and actor-centered sociology bring different assumptions to the study of actors and different assumptions about what a social explanation requires. They are different research paradigms and give rise to qualitatively different kinds of research products. And, agent-based model is a tool that can be deployed in each of these frameworks but is most suited to analytical sociology and rational choice theory.

Figure 2.1 implies that the agent-centered approaches have more in common with each other than any of them do with other important strands of social science research methodologies. Can we codify these intuitions in some way? And, can we sort out the logical and pragmatic relations that exist among these approaches?

Table 2.1 represents some of the central methodological and ontological assumptions of each of these research frameworks.

How can we think about the relations that exist across these research approaches? Several possibilities exist. Figure 2.1 represents the space of research approaches to sociological topics in terms of a Venn diagram. **U** is the universe of research approaches. **A**, **B**, **C**, and **D** are the research approaches that fall within the rubrics of "analytical sociology," "rational choice theory," "actor-centered sociology," and "agent-based models." The overlaps in the sets are intended to represent the intersection between the selected groups: actor-centered approaches that use the assumptions of rational choice theory, analytical sociology approaches that make use of actor-centered assumptions, research efforts in the three sets that make use of agent-based models, etc.

Table 2.1   Central methodological assumptions

Actor-centered Sociology	Analytical Sociology	Rational Choice Theory
Social outcomes derive from the actions of socially constituted actors in relations with each other	Explain outcomes as the aggregate result of the actions and interactions of purposive individuals	Individuals behave as economically rational agents. Explain outcomes as the aggregate result of these actions
Attention to "thick" theories of the actor	Desire-belief-opportunity framework for actors (DBO)	Narrow economic rationality: consistent preferences and maximization of utilities
Actors are formed and shaped by the social relations in which they develop	Causal models; commitment to the causal mechanisms approach	Equilibrium models; commitment to mathematical solutions for well-defined problems of choice.
Narrative accounts of the development of social outcomes give actions of the actors	Primacy of Coleman's boat: explanation occurs from micro to macro and macro to micro	Game theory is used to represent interactions among rational agents
Agnostic about microfoundations	Commitment to requirement of microfoundations	Commitment to requirement of microfoundations

It should be noted that not all sociologists accept the actor-centered approach. Some (like Andrew Abbott (2007) and Margaret Somers (1998)) prefer what they refer to as a "relational" understanding of the basis of social activity. It is not so much the actor as the action; it is not the internal state of the individual agent so much as the swirl of interactions with others that determine the course of a social activity. This is part of Abbott's objection to the idea that sociology should aim to uncover social mechanisms. But quantitative and structuralist sociologists too would reject the importance of theories of the actor, arguing that the substantive findings of their research take the form of statistical findings across populations or theoretical discoveries about abstract social structures. So, the actor-centered approach is a distinctive one.

Chapter 3

Social Things

WHAT EXISTS IN THE SOCIAL REALM?

Let us shift now to a more traditional question of ontology, the nature of entities. There are substantive disagreements at this level of social ontology. What sorts of social things exist? Does the "proletariat" exist as a social entity? There are certainly workers; but is there a "working class"? Did "feudalism" exist as an extended social structure? What about the world trading system? What is needed in order to attribute existence to a social agglomeration?

In chapter 1, we argued that social entities are composed of socially constituted individuals. So, the lineaments of composition are important. We can recognize a wide range of ways in which individuals are composed into larger social entities: agglomeration, adherence, mutual recognition, coercion, contractual relationships, marketing, recruitment, incentive systems, and so forth. Here, we would like to look more closely at the nature of higher-level social entities and forces that emerge from these various forms of aggregation.

We might want to say that things exist when they have enough persistence over time to admit of re-identification and study from one time to another. Persistence involves some degree of stability in a core set of properties. A cloud shaped like a cat has a set of visible characteristics at a given moment; but these characteristics disappear quickly, and this collection of water droplets quickly morphs into a different configuration in a short time. So, we are inclined not to call the cat-shaped cloud an entity. On the other hand, "the Black Forest" exists because we can locate its approximate boundaries and composition over several centuries. The forest is an agglomeration of trees in a geographical space; but we might reasonably judge that the forest has properties that we can investigate that are not simply properties of individual trees (density and canopy temperature, for example). The forest undergoes change over time; the mix of types of trees may shift from one decade to another, the density of plants changes, and the human uses of forest products change. And, we can ask questions like: "How has the ecology of the Black Forest changed in the twentieth century?" So, it seems reasonable enough that we can refer to the forest as a geographical or ecological entity. We can also classify individual forests into *types* of forests: temperate rain forest, tropical rain forest, coniferous forest, etc. And, we can ask ecological questions about the properties and processes that are characteristic of the various types of forests.

So, what characteristics should a putative social entity possess in order to fall within the working ontology of the social sciences? Here are a few possible candidates of ontological features that might be associated with thinghood in the social realm:

- Persistence of basic characteristics over time—spatiotemporal continuity and social analogs such as nucleated population with persistent shared norms and identities
- An internal structural-functional organization
- Social cohesion among the individuals who constitute the entity deriving from their social orientation to the entity (labor union, religious community, ethnic group)
- Some sort of regulative social process that maintains the thing's identity over time, either internal or external
- An account of the particular material-social mechanisms through which the identity and persistence of the entity are maintained

According to these sorts of criteria, we might say that social things like these examples exist:

- United Auto Workers Union
- General Motors Corporation
- First Presbyterian Church of Dearborn
- Missouri Synod of the Presbyterian Church
- Kylie Minogue Facebook fan club
- 18th Street gang of Los Angeles
- Michigan Legislature
- Internal Revenue Service
- University of Wisconsin
- 1950s-era German apprentice system for electrical workers
- Social practice of *zakat* in Malaysia

At a higher level of abstraction, we might say that these kinds of social entities exist: organizations, both formal and informal; networks of individuals oriented to each other and a social goal; social groups unified by features of consciousness or existential circumstance; bureaucracies of the state; enduring social practices; normative and cultural systems regulating behavior; institutions possessing internal organization, rules, and purposes.

Part of the difficulty of this topic is the distinction between things and kinds of things. We might agree that the Chicago Police Department exists as a social entity. But we may remain uncertain as to whether "police departments" or "state coercive apparatuses" exist as higher-order categories of social things. And, perhaps, this is a confusion; perhaps, the issue of existence applies only to individual entities, not kinds or classes of entities. On this approach, we would stipulate the minimum characteristics of existence we would want to require of individual social entities and then be "nominalistic" about the higher-level categories or concepts into which we classify these singular individuals. On this approach, general concepts do not refer to real things; rather, they serve to group together a number of particular individuals who satisfy the conditions of the concept.

In considering the ontology of the social world, it is important to be attentive to the fallacy of reification: the error of thinking that the fact that we can formulate an abstract noun (proletariat, fascism) allows us to infer that it exists as a persistent, recurring social entity. So, when we identify a given social entity as an X, we need to regard it as an open question, "What do X's have in common?" We can avoid the fallacy of reification by focusing on the composition and internal structure of the enduring social entities to which we attempt to refer. It is the underlying composition of the entity rather than its location within a classificatory system that provides an explanatory foundation for the behavior of the entity.

METHODOLOGICAL LOCALISM

I offer a social ontology that I refer to as *methodological localism* (ML) (Little 2006). This theory of social entities affirms that there are large social structures and facts that influence social outcomes. But it insists that these structures are only possible insofar as they are embodied in the actions, interactions, and mental states of socially constructed individuals. There is no action at a distance in the social realm. The "molecule" of all social life is the *socially constructed and socially situated individual*, who lives, acts, and develops within a *set of local social relationships, institutions, norms, and rules*. Social action takes place within spaces that are themselves socially structured by the actions and purposes of others—by property, by prejudice, by law and custom, and by systems of knowledge. So, our account needs to identify the local social environments through which action is structured and projected: the interpersonal networks, the systems of rules, and the social institutions. The social thus has to do with the behaviorally, cognitively, and materially embodied reality of social institutions.

This account begins with the *socially constituted person*. As we saw in chapter 2, human beings are subjective, purposive, and relational agents. They interact with other persons in ways that involve competition and cooperation. They form relationships, enmities, alliances, and networks; they compose institutions and organizations. They create material embodiments that reflect and affect human intentionality. They acquire beliefs, norms, practices, and worldviews, and they socialize their children, their friends, and others with whom they interact. Some of the products of human social interaction are short lived and local (indigenous fishing practices); others are of long duration but local (oral traditions, stories, and jokes); and yet others are built up into social organizations of great geographical scope and extended duration (states, trade routes, knowledge systems). But always we have individual agents interacting with other agents, making use of resources (material and social), and pursuing their goals, desires, and impulses.

At the level of the socially constituted individual, we need to ask two sorts of questions: First, what makes individual agents behave as they do? Here, we need accounts of the mechanisms of deliberation and action at the level of the individual. What are the main features of individual choice, motivation, reasoning, and preference? How do these differ across social groups? How do emotions, rational deliberation, practical commitments, and other forms of agency influence the individual's deliberations and actions? This area of research is purposively eclectic, including performative action, rational action, impulse, theories of the emotions, theories of the self, or theories of identity.

Second, how are individuals formed and constituted? ML gives great importance to understanding the processes through which individuals are formed and constituted—the concrete study of the social process of the development of the self. Here, we need better accounts of social development, the acquisition of worldview, preferences, and moral frameworks, among the many other determinants of individual agency and action. What are the social institutions and influences through which individuals acquire norms, preferences, and ways of thinking? How do individuals develop cognitively, affectively, and socially? So, ML points up the importance of discovering the microfoundations and local variations of identity formation and the construction of the historically situated self.

So far, we have emphasized the socially situated individual. But social action takes place within spaces that are themselves socially structured by the actions and purposes of others—by property, by prejudice, by law and custom, and by systems of knowledge. So, our account needs to identify the *local social environments* through which action is structured and projected:

the interpersonal networks, the systems of rules, and the social institutions. The social thus has to do with the behaviorally, cognitively, and materially embodied reality of social institutions. An institution is a complex of socially embodied powers, limitations, and opportunities within which individuals pursue their lives and goals. A property system, a legal system, and a professional baseball league all represent examples of institutions. Institutions have effects that are in varying degrees independent from the individual or "larger" than the individual. Each of these social entities is embodied in the social states of a number of actors—their beliefs, intentions, reasoning, dispositions, and histories. Actors perform their actions within the context of social frameworks represented as rules, institutions, and organizations, and their actions and dispositions embody the causal effectiveness of those frameworks. And, institutions influence individuals by offering incentives and constraints on their actions, by framing the knowledge and information on the basis of which they choose, and by conveying sets of normative commitments (ethical, religious, interpersonal) that influence individual action.

It is important to emphasize that ML affirms the existence of social constructs beyond the purview of the individual actor or group. Political institutions exist—and they are embodied in the actions and states of officials, citizens, criminals, and opportunistic others. These institutions have real effects on individual behavior and on social processes and outcomes—but always mediated through the structured circumstances of agency of the myriad participants in these institutions and the affected society. This perspective emphasizes the contingency of social processes, the mutability of social structures over space and time, and the variability of human social systems (norms, urban arrangements, social practices, etc.).

An institution, we might say, is an embodied set of rules, incentives, and opportunities that have the potential of influencing agents' choices and behavior. An institution is a complex of socially embodied powers, limitations, and opportunities within which individuals pursue their lives and goals. A property system, a legal system, and a professional baseball league all represent examples of institutions. Institutions have effects that are in varying degrees independent from the individual or "larger" than the individual. Each of these social entities is embodied in the social states of a number of actors—their beliefs, intentions, reasoning, dispositions, and histories. Actors perform their actions within the context of social frameworks represented as rules, institutions, and organizations, and their actions and dispositions embody the causal effectiveness of those frameworks. And, institutions influence individuals by offering incentives and constraints on their actions, by framing the knowledge and information on the basis of which they choose, and by conveying sets of normative commitments (ethical, religious, interpersonal) that influence individual action.

This approach highlights the important point that all social facts, social structures, and social-causal properties depend ultimately on facts about individuals within socially defined circumstances.

It is evident that ML lays open the possibility of a fairly limited social ontology. What exists is the socially constructed individual, within a congeries of concrete social relations and institutions. The socially constructed individual possesses beliefs, norms, opportunities, powers, and capacities. These features are socially constructed in a perfectly ordinary sense: the individual has acquired his or her beliefs, norms, powers, and desires through social contact with other individuals and institutions, and the powers and constraints that define the domain of choice for the individual are largely constituted by social institutions (property systems, legal systems, educational systems, organizations, and the like). However, this ontology is too limited for the research concerns of sociology and other social sciences. Social scientists need to be able to refer to higher-level social constructs such as institutions, organizations, structures, or normative systems. Inevitably, social organizations at any level are constituted by the individuals who participate in them and whose behavior and ideas are influenced by them; subsystems and organizations through which the actions of the organization are implemented; and the material traces through which the policies, memories, and acts of decision are imposed on the environment: buildings, archives, roads, etc. All features of the organization are embodied in the actors and institutional arrangements that carry the organization at a given time. That said, it is perfectly legitimate to identify higher-level social arrangements as entities and forces.

Ontological Individualism and Microfoundationalism

Ontological individualism is a simple and compelling theory of the social world. It holds that all social entities, forces, or processes are composed of the actions and interactions of individuals and nothing else. It rules out the idea that there might be a kind of social entity or force that is independent of the social actors who compose it.

The concept of microfoundations is a direct corollary of the thesis of ontological individualism. It insists on the compositional nature of the social. However, there is a recursive aspect of the theory that distinguishes it from reductionism. The individuals to whom microfoundations are traced are not a-social; rather, their psychology, beliefs and motives are constituted and shaped by the social forces they and others constitute. So, the microfoundational account of the workings of an organization may well refer to the locally embodied effects of that organization on the current psychology of the members of the organization; and their behavior in turn reproduces the organization in the next iteration. This is one compelling reason to prefer the idea of ML over that of methodological individualism. Providing microfoundations for a social fact does not mean the same as reducing the social fact to a collection of purely individual facts.

A microfoundation is

- a specification of the ways in which the properties and structure of a higher-level entity are produced by the activities and properties of lower-level entities.

In the case of the social sciences, this amounts to

- a specification of the ways that properties, structural features, and causal powers of a social entity are produced and reproduced by the actions and dispositions of socially situated individuals.

Or,

- an account of the mechanisms at the individual actor level (and perhaps at levels intermediate between actors and the current level—e.g. institutions) that work to create the structural and causal properties that we observe at the meso or macro level.

A fully specified microfoundational account of a meso-level social feature consists of an account that traces out (1) the features of the actors and (2) the characteristics of the action environment (including norms and institutions), which jointly lead to (3) the social pattern or causal power we are interested in. A microfoundation specifies the individual-level mechanisms that lead to the macro- or meso-level social fact. This is the kind of account that Thomas Schelling illustrates so well in *Micromotives and Macrobehavior* (Schelling 1978).

Providing an account of a social entity's microfoundations requires two things: knowledge about what it is about the local circumstances of the typical individual that leads him or her to act in such a way as to bring about this relationship and knowledge of the aggregative processes that lead from individual actions of that sort to an explanatory social relationship of this sort. So, if we are interested in knowing about the microfoundations of the causal properties of states and governments, we need to arrive at an analysis of the institutions and constrained patterns of individual behavior through which the state's characteristics are effected. We need to raise questions such as these: How do states exercise influence throughout society? What are the institutional embodiments at lower levels that secure the impact of law, taxation, conscription, contract enforcement, and other central elements of state behavior? If we are concerned about the workings of social identities, then we need to inquire into the concrete social mechanisms through which social identities are reproduced within a local population—and the ways in which these mechanisms and identities may vary over time and place. And, if we are interested in analyzing the causal role that systems of norms play in social behavior, we need to discover some of the specific institutional practices through which individuals come to embrace and conform to a given set of norms.

The microfoundations perspective requires that we consider the pathways by which socially constituted individuals are influenced by distant social circumstances, and how their actions in turn affect distant social outcomes. There is no action at a distance in social life; instead, individuals have the values that they have, the styles of reasoning, the funds of factual and causal beliefs, etc., as a result of the structured experiences of development that they have undergone as children and adults. On this perspective, large social facts and structures do indeed exist; but their causal properties are entirely defined by the current states of psychology, norm, and action of the individuals who currently exist. Systems of norms and bodies of knowledge exist—but only insofar as individuals (and material traces) embody and transmit them. So, when we assert that a given social structure causes a given outcome, we need to be able to specify the local pathways through which individual actors embody this causal process. That is, we need to be able to provide an account of the causal mechanisms that convey social effects.

If ontological individualism is true, then it is also true that all social entities, forces, and processes possess microfoundations. This does not mean that we always know how those microfoundations function, and it does not necessarily mean that we need to identify the microfoundations in order to study the higher-level social entity. The microfoundations approach suggests a coherent position about the nature of the social world and the nature of social explanation:

- There are discernible and real differences in level in various domains, including the domain of the social.
- Higher-level entities depend on the properties and powers of lower-level constituents and nothing else (ontological individualism).
- The microfoundations of a higher-level thing are the particular arrangements and actions of the lower-level constituents that bring about the properties of the higher-level thing.
- There are no "holistic" or non-reducible social entities.

Taken together, this position amounts to a fairly specific view of the social world.

One way of motivating the theory of microfoundations is to observe that it is a prescription against "magical thinking" in the social realm. There is no "social stuff" that has its own persistent causal and structural characteristics; rather, all social phenomena are constituted by patterns of behavior and thought of populations of individual human beings. And, likewise, social events and structures do not have inherent social-causal properties; rather, the causal properties of a social structure or event are constituted by the patterns of behavior and thought of the individuals who constitute them and nothing else.

There are a number of arguments that might be considered to cast doubt on the microfoundations thesis as formulated here. One argument is the possibility of downward and lateral causation from meso or macro level to meso level. Another is the possibility raised by John Searle and Brian Epstein that there may be social facts that cannot be disaggregated onto facts about individuals (the validity of a marriage, for example). (We will return to these considerations in chapter 4.) A third argument is the difficult question of whether there might be reasons for thinking that a lower level of organization below the conscious agent (e.g. the cognitive system or neurophysiology) is more compelling than a folk theory of individual behavior. Finally, the metaphor of levels and strata itself may be misleading or incoherent as a way of understanding the realm of the social; it may turn out to be impossible to draw clear distinctions between levels of the social. (This is the rationale for the idea of a "flat" social ontology to be discussed shortly.)

This concept is relevant to social ontology in this way. Social entities are understood to be compositional; they are assemblages constituted and maintained by the mentality and actions of individuals. So, providing an account of the microfoundations of a structure or causal connection—say a paramilitary organization or of the causal connection between high interest rates and the incidence of alcohol abuse—is a specification of the composition of the social-level fact. It is a description of the agent-level relationships and patterns of behavior that cohere in such a way as to bring about the higher-level structure or causal relationship. The concept of microfoundations is directly relevant to evaluating explanations. If we assert a causal or explanatory relation between one social entity or condition and another, we must be prepared to offer a credible sketch of the ways in which this influence is conveyed through the mentalities and actions of individuals.

The theory of microfoundations is also very consonant with the idea of social mechanisms. When we ask about the microfoundations of a social process, we are asking about the mechanisms that exist at a lower level that create and maintain the social process.

Much turns, however, on what precisely we mean to require of a satisfactory explanation: a full specification of the microfoundations in every case, or a sketch of the way that a given social-level process might readily be embodied in individual-level activities. If we accept the second version, we are licensing a fair amount of autonomy for the social-level explanation, whereas if we accept the first version, we are tending toward a requirement of reductionism from higher to lower levels in every case. I interpret the requirement in the second way; it is not necessary to disaggregate every claim, like "organizational deficiencies at the Bhopal chemical plant caused the devastating chemical spill," onto specific individual-level activities. We understand pretty well, in a generic way, what the microfoundations of organizations are, and it isn't necessary to provide a detailed account in order to have a satisfactory explanation.

This means that the microfoundations requirement can be understood in a weak and a strong version, and some theorists understand the idea as a requirement of reductionism. However, I defend the position in a weak form that does not imply a reductionist theory of social explanation. Here is an effort to simplify these issues into a series of assertions:

- All social forces, powers, structures, processes, and laws (social features) are ultimately constituted by mechanisms at the level of individual actors (*ontological principle*).
- When we assert the reality or causal powers of a social entity, we need to be confident that there are microfoundations that cause this social entity to have the properties we attribute to it (*microfoundations principle*).
- Social scientists will be better able to hypothesize microfoundations when they have richer theories of the actor (*heuristic principle*).

So, the ontological principle is simply that social entities are wholly fixed by the properties and dynamics of the actions of the actors that constitute them. In language to be further discussed in chapter 4, social entities supervene upon socially situated actors, and the activities and beliefs of socially situated actors serve to generate the properties of the meso-level social entity. The requirement of microfoundations simply reproduces the ontological principle, ruling out ontologically impossible social entities and causal powers. The requirement of microfoundations is not a requirement on what an explanation needs to look like; rather, it is a requirement about certain beliefs we need to be justified in accepting when we advance a claim about social entities. It is what Julie Zahle calls a "confirmation" requirement (or perhaps better, a justificatory requirement) (Zahle and Collin 2014). A better theory of the actor supports the discovery of microfoundations for social assertions. Further, it provides a richer "sociological imagination" for macro- and meso-level sociologists. So, the requirement of microfoundations and the recommendation that social scientists seek out better theories of the actor are also valuable as heuristics for social research: they provide intellectual resources that help social researchers decide where to look for explanatory links, and what kinds of mechanisms might turn out to be relevant.

RELATIONAL SOCIAL CONCEPTS

In thinking about ontology, we are often drawn to considering fixed, stable entities. However, posing the question this way leads us to think of persistent abstract things populating the social world—for example, structures, organizations, or institutions. But there are persistent phenomena in the social world that don't look much like *things* and look more like *activities* and *processes*. Grammatically, they have more in common with verbs than nouns. And, when many such social phenomena are described using nouns, we are often forced to interpret them in a non-referential way.

Take the social realities of friendship, solidarity, and inflation.

The first is a characteristic of social relationships; it is a relational concept. It does not make sense to think of "friendship" as a concatenation of monadic atoms of "friend units"; rather, the concept of friend evinces a set of relational characteristics between persons. So, "friendship" doesn't designate a continuing "thing" in the world; instead, it designates a complex relational and psychological feature of pairs of persons, widely separated across population and space. Our theory of friendship encapsulates our interpretation of the mental and behavioral states of persons who are in the relationship of friendship with each other.

Solidarity has this feature of relationality, and it adds a feature of social motivation and psychological orientation to a group. We can ask whether solidarity exists in the social world, and we can reasonably answer that it does. But when we affirm that "solidarity exists," we really mean that "there are numerous instances of groups and individuals in which members of the group willingly conform their behavior to the needs and purposes of the group." Our explanation of "solidarity" is likely to invoke abstract ideas about individuals within consciously constituted groups rather than something analogous to a social substance. So, solidarity is not a thing, but rather a dynamic feature of consciousness shared in varying ways by individuals who orient themselves to a group.

"Inflation" is a different sort of social noun. It refers to a complex social state of affairs reflecting a set of *processes* in which prices of goods are determined by market forces and prices are rising across a range of commodities. We cannot define the social reality of "inflation" without specifying a set of distributed social facts and identifying a number of social processes. So, inflation too does not look at all like a social thing.

Each of these social nouns corresponds to a social reality. But this reality does not look much like a set of fixed entities or composites of entities. The semantics of objects and things does not work well for this range of social vocabulary. And yet each of these terms identifies a domain that is perfectly well suited to empirical inquiry and discovery. The social reality of friendship practices differs across cultures; friendship practice has some degree of stability over time; and we can discover quite a bit about the culture, norms, and practices of friendship in a particular culture. The nouns "solidarity" and "inflation" are similar. Each is a legitimate object of empirical inquiry; and neither conforms to the ontology of "thing" with fixed location and properties.

What this discussion suggests is that our ontology of the social world needs to encompass not only a range and variety of *entities*—structures, institutions, organizations—but also ontological categories that reflect a more fluid set of social realities: processes, practices, rules, relations, and activities. This observation converges with the styles of thought of thinkers as various as Charles Tilly and Norbert Elias; Tilly refers to "relational realism" (McAdam, Tarrow, and Tilly 2001), and Elias is an advocate of "process sociology" (Elias and Schröter 1991).

Influence Concepts

There are other social concepts that similarly require background presuppositions about relationships. We may refer to these as "influence" concepts, including especially the concept of power. Power is an elusive social concept, because it is fundamentally relational and composite. The power that a person or group possesses can only be defined in relation to the domain of persons over whom this power can be wielded and the set of social resources that constitute the levers of this power. Power must be characterized in terms of domain and mechanisms. The question here is whether there are other social concepts that have a similar conceptual geography. If so, this may give us a better basis for explaining the concept of power.

Consider these possible sibling concepts: status, affluence, charisma, eloquence, humorous, . . . Each of these is what we might call an "influence" concept. It stipulates a capacity to bring about a particular kind of effect in other persons. It follows that these concepts are inherently relational; we cannot define "charisma" or "eloquence" without explicitly or implicitly specifying the group of people who respond to these qualities. Second, conveying influence requires a mechanism of influence; and in fact each of these examples depends upon some set of qualities or assets through which the individual with the property is able to exert this influence (admiration, laughter, persuasion, willingness to follow, willingness to obey).

Further, each of these characteristics is social in one way or another. "Status" depends on an audience that is prepared to "read" a person with certain attributes as possessing a certain status, and it depends on the individual being socially situated on such a way as to acquire those tags (the Mercedes, the $800 haircut, . . .). "Affluence" depends on having resources adequate to support consumption noticeably superior to that of most other people in this social setting—in fact, it is doubly social, in that it depends upon comparison with other consumers and on the affluent person's having access to socially defined resources, which implies a particular situation within a particular set of social relations (corporation, pirate gang, government bureau).

Power differs from these other influence terms in several ways. Most crucially, power is less dependent on the social psychology of others and more dependent upon material resources. Status and eloquence are pretty much in the eye of the beholder, whereas the power of a criminal boss depends largely on his ability to marshal force. Affluence is similar in this respect, while "funny" is more similar to status.

So, an important distinguishing feature within this conceptual space of social influence concepts is whether the attributes needed to wield influence are personal psychological traits or external, socially defined assets. John Stewart is humorous because he has a set of capabilities—quick verbal wit, droll timing, sarcastic imagination, extreme facial motility—that we are culturally prepared to find amusing. These traits are not inherently funny—presenting the same skit to a group of Navajo ranchers might elicit only puzzled looks. But in our comedy culture, the person who has Stewart's qualities, but at a less adept level, will not succeed in being funny. Al Capone was powerful because he had violent men available to do his bidding. This wasn't a feature primarily of his psychological characteristics but rather his particular social location and the material resources of violence he could call upon.

We might consider how charisma fits in this analysis, especially since this concept has almost as common appeal in political analysis as power. We might say that a charismatic person is one who has the ability to influence other people to want to act in the ways he or she asks of them. This influence is often described as subrational and subconscious: followers act out the exhortations of their charismatic leader out of emotional allegiance rather than rational judgment. So, the capacities required of the charismatic leader are features of personality and performance—the charismatic person needs the qualities that permit him or her to inspire followers. In this way, charisma is similar to being funny. But these capabilities also give the leader the ability to influence followers beyond their rational will—which makes charisma more similar to power.

ARE SOCIAL NETWORKS FUNDAMENTAL?

Chapter 2 offered an "actor-centered" perspective on the social world. This approach suggests that we think of social realities by considering the individual actors who constitute social phenomena and try to understand social patterns as the expression of common features of reasoning and motivation by stylized agents. This is roughly the strategy under way in rational choice theory, neoclassical economics, game theory, and methodological individualism. Or, we might begin with an account of group attributes—race, class, gender, ethnicity, and religion. This is roughly the way in which Durkheim, Giddens, and Du Bois begin—with a kind of macro-social set of categories in terms of which we attempt to understand social structure and behavior.

The concept of a social network does not fit neatly into either category. It is larger than a collection of individuals, in that we have to specify a set of *relationships* among individuals in order to define a social network. But it is much more concrete and agent-based than the super-categories of race, class, or gender turn out to be. So, my question here is a fundamental one: Is the concept of a social network one of a very small number of concepts that must be invoked in virtually every kind of social explanation? As such, is the concept of a social network, and the associated concepts of concrete social relationships it brings with it, a fundamental component of any satisfactory social ontology? And, does the concept of a social network define a crucial space between the micro and the macro? (A good recent effort to link social networks theory to an important area of social science research is Mario Diani and Doug McAdam, *Social Movements and Networks: Relational Approaches to Collective Action* (Diani and McAdam 2003).)

Several points are evident. One is that social networks do in fact constitute a key causal mechanism underlying many social processes. We can explain important features of social and political life by identifying the concrete social networks that exist within the population: the transmission of ideas, knowledge, and styles through a population; the selection of important leaders in government and industry; the effective reach of the state; the course of mobilization within a community around an important issue; and the effectiveness of a terrorist group, to name a few examples. A second point is that networks have specific features of topology and functioning that have causal consequences that are largely independent from the personal characteristics of the people who constitute it. For example, information may travel more quickly through a network of people containing many midsized nodes than one containing just a few mega-hubs. And, this structural fact may suffice to explain some social outcomes: for example, this rebellion succeeded (because of rapid transmission of information), whereas that one petered out (because of ineffective communications).

Consider two very different examples of group behavior: synchronized cheering in a stadium and the spread of boycotts in Alabama in the early 1960s. The first case involves no social network at all. Cheerleaders stationed around the field initiate the chant as the noise moves to their part of the stadium, and many fans respond when called. Fan behavior is explained by the fan's observation of the behavior of other fans and the motions of the cheerleader. The boycotts had a different dynamic. Organizations emerged which set about to mobilize support for the strategy of boycott. Some of this effort took the form of public calls to action. But a larger part of the mobilization occurred through the workings of extended networks of engaged people—ministers, union activists, student organizations, and civil rights groups. And, the effectiveness and pattern of dissemination of the call to action depended critically on the scope and structure of each of these networks of networks—networks among leaders of diverse organizations and subordinate networks clustered around each leader. (Doug McAdam describes these processes in detail in *Political Process and the Development of Black Insurgency, 1930–1970* (McAdam 1999).)

These examples seem to lead to a couple of observations. One is that social networks are not critical for *every* form of social action. But the exceptions are pretty simple cases of spontaneous coordination. And, second, the example of civil rights mobilization illustrates very clearly why we should expect that social networks are usually crucial. The reason is straightforward: almost all social outcomes require a degree of coordination, communication, and mobilization. A social network is not the only way of bringing these factors about—cheerleaders and television stations can do it too. But the causal importance of social networks is likely to be great in many cases. And, for this reason, it seems justified to conclude that social networks are in fact fundamental to social explanation. Likewise, it appears correct to say that they function as bridging mechanisms from micro to macro, in that they help to convey the actions of local agents onto larger social outcomes.

A FLAT SOCIAL ONTOLOGY?

It is common to think of the social world in terms of "levels" of social organization—micro, meso, and macro (Figure 3.1). We will return to this idea in chapter 4, with this diagram to represent the structure of the social world.

But is this perhaps a misleading ontology? Would we be better served by thinking of the social world as "flat"—involving processes and relations all at the same level? It sometimes appears that John Levi Martin has such an ontology in mind in *Social Structures* (Martin 2009), and Doug Porpora envisions such a possibility in "Four Concepts of Structure" (Porpora 1989). So, this is the idea I would like to explore here.

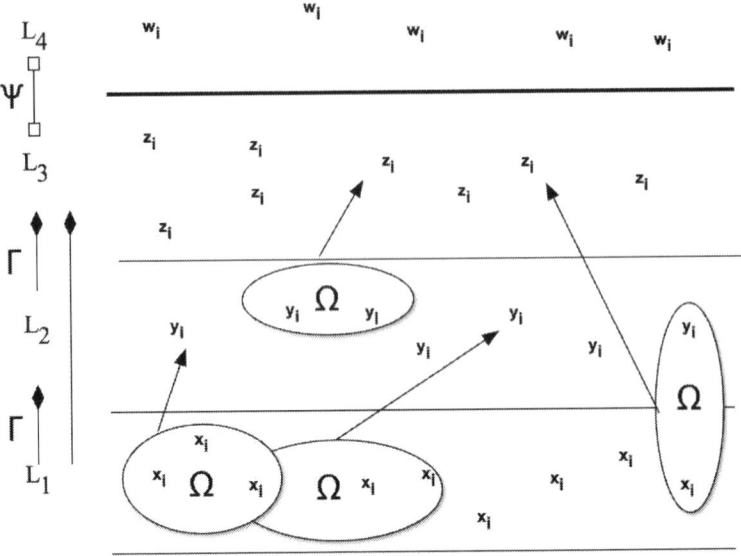

Levels of the social -- generation, microfoundation, emergence

Figure 3.1   Levels of the social.

What would that flat world look like? Here is one effort at formulating a flat social ontology (Figure 3.2).

- The social world exists as the embodiment of sets of individual persons with powers, capacities, and actions and interactions, and who stand in a vast range of concrete social relationships with each other.

Here is a passage from Porpora's article about structure mentioned above that seems to have this view in mind (Porpora 1989):

> In contrast with the previous conception of social structure, this one is not a version of sociological holism. It does not portray social structure as something that operates over the heads of human actors. Instead, social structure is a nexus of connections among them, causally affecting their actions and in turn causally affected by them. The causal affects of the structure on individuals are manifested in certain structured interests, resources, powers, constraints and predicaments that are built into each position by the web of relationships. These comprise the material circumstances in which people must act and which motivate them to act in certain ways. As they do so, they alter the relationships that bind them in both intended and unintended ways. (Porpora 1989: 200)

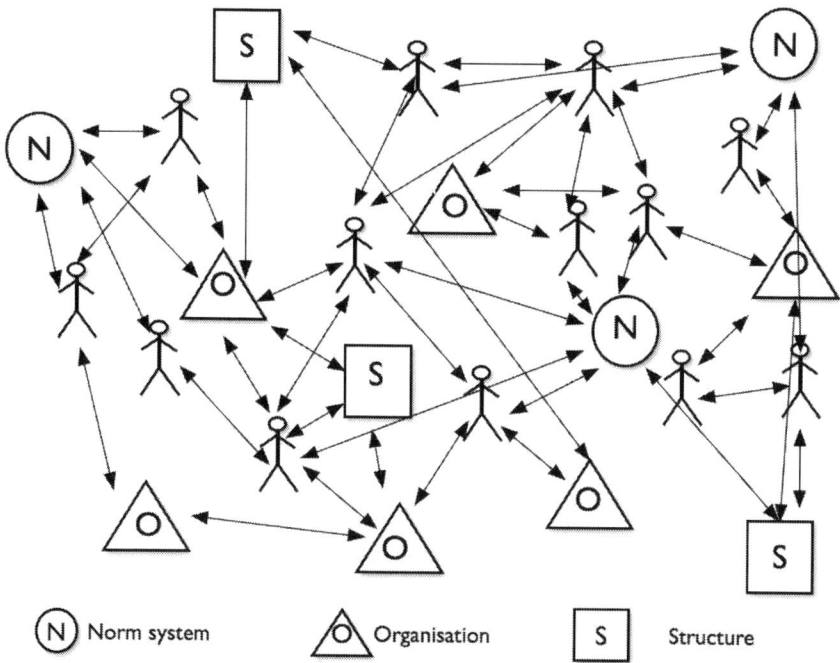

(N) Norm system   (△O) Organisation   [S] Structure

Figure 3.2   A flat social ontology.

What does this description leave out? For starters, it leaves out things we would have said were higher levels of the social reality: families, organizations, social movements, institutions, economies, clubs, and states. And, of course, these are legitimate social constructs. But are they inherently "higher level"? Or, are they compounds and extended aggregates of the lower-level stuff just mentioned—individuals with powers, actions, and relations?

Playing this idea out, we might consider that a social movement is a partially ordered group of individuals in association with each other. The organizations that call them forward are other groups of individuals, including their deliberative bodies and executives. The repressive organs of the state are yet other organized groups of individuals with powers and agency. And, in fact, the theory of strategic action fields seems to lean in this direction (Fligstein and McAdam 2012).

One important consideration that would count against the flat ontology is the idea that there are causal properties at a higher level that don't attach to entities at the base level. This view corresponds to the idea some sociologists have of emergence. It is sometimes maintained that social structures have properties at the structural level that cannot be reduced to the properties of the components of the structure. These are emergent properties. If this is so, then we will miss important explanations if we decline to recognize the reality of social structures. And, yet a social structure is plainly a higher-level social entity than a group of coordinated individuals. Its higher-level standing is a result of this fact: it is composed of objects at level 1; but it has properties that cannot be explained or derived from objects at level 1.

A related reason for rejecting the flat ontology is the idea that structures, institutions, or value systems—higher-level social things—may have legitimate causal properties that can be adequately discovered through study of these social things without more information about the base level (individuals in relations). This possibility doesn't necessarily imply that these are emergent properties, only that they are relatively autonomous from the base level. Here again, it seems reasonable to call these higher-level social entities—and therefore the flat ontology is not quite enough.

Another important consideration is the evident fact that social compounds have compositional structure. A fish is more than a collection of living cells; it has a stable structure and an internal organization that serves the needs of the fish organism. So, it is entirely appropriate to refer to fish as well as living cells. And, it seems correct to observe that something like this is true of some social entities as well—government agencies, worship organizations, and corporations.

Finally, it is hard to dispute that social things like kinship systems, business firms, and armies have stable and knowable characteristics that can be studied empirically. We shouldn't adopt an ontology that excludes legitimate topics for empirical research.

So, it seems that the parsimonious social theory associated with a flat ontology does not work. It forces us to overlook explanatory factors that are important for explaining social outcomes. And, it unreasonably asks us to ignore important features of the social world of which we have reasonably good understanding. In fact, the flat ontology is not far removed from the ontology associated with some versions of methodological individualism.

So, how might a bounded conception of higher-level social entities look? A formulation of a minimal multilayer alternative to the flat ontology might go along these lines:

- The social world consists of individuals and relations at the base level plus stable compounds of items at this level that have quasi-permanent properties and non-reducible causal powers that have effects on items at the base level.

Here, the criterion of higher-level standing in use is as follows:

- Possession of causal properties not reducible to (or needing reduction to) properties at the base level

By analogous reasoning, we might consider whether there are more complex configurations of base and level 1 entities, which themselves have properties that are emergent from or autonomous from base and level 1, and so forth, iteratively.

Are there level 2 entities by this criterion? For example, might the state be a level-2 entity, in that it encompasses organizations and individuals and it possesses new causal properties not present at level 1? In principle this seems possible. The state is a complex network of organizations and individuals. And, it is logically possible that new causal powers emerge that depend on both base and level 1, but that do not require reduction to those lower-level properties.

So, the language of levels of the social appears to be legitimate after all. It gives us a conceptual vocabulary that captures composition and complexity, and it allows us to identify important social-causal powers that would not be accessible to us on the flat ontology. We return to this set of issues in chapter 4.

STRUCTURES

Social structures and other social "things" are ontologically peculiar in some ways. Most especially, they are abstract, distributed, and nonmaterial. We cannot put a culturally dominant food aversion or a group prejudice in a box and weigh it. And yet, many of us want to say that social structures are "real," and not merely theoretical constructs. One important aspect of something's being real is that it has causal powers: the specific properties of the thing bring about differences in the world on the behavior of other things. This is a version of the interventionist theory of causation associated with Jim Woodward (Woodward 2003): change something about C and you bring about a change in E.

My position is a delicate one. On the one hand I advocate an actor-centered approach to sociology and the social sciences. I defend the idea that social claims need microfoundations in a specific (weak) sense. And, on the other hand, I believe that structures (institutions, value systems, organizations, practices) have a degree of stability that permits us to couch causal claims in terms of those structures directly, rather than needing to supplement those claims with disaggregated foundations at the level of the individual. So, I will argue in chapter 4 for the idea that we can sometimes regard causal powers of social entities as "relatively autonomous" from individual-level facts.

By meso-level structures I mean to refer to those like the following:

- National Science Foundation
- Nuclear Regulatory Commission

- IBM corporation
- AFL-CIO
- German paramilitary organizations, 1930
- German ideology of cultural despair, 1910
- Islamic norms of *Zakat*
- . . .

In each case, there are numerous actors assigned to roles, governed by rules defining their activities, and leading to a certain kind of functioning in the broader social environment. Generically, I would define a meso-level structure as follows:

- A composite of individuals and roles that incorporates a set of rules and norms for internal and external actors, and that possesses procedures of inculcation and enforcement through which internal and external actors are brought to comply with the rules and norms (to some degree).

I would define a normative system as

- a set of rules, norms, and expectations embodied in a population of actors and meeting a threshold level of success in coordinating and constraining behavior.

We have a number of sociological concepts that capture social items at this level: organization, bureaucracy, institution, normative community, social network, communications system, legal system, civil war, military coup, and advocacy group. It is evident that social entities often incorporate elements of several of these kinds of things. Organizations and structures often incorporate or depend upon normative systems, and normative systems often generate organizations and institutions that convey their impact to the young and adult actors.

What about other mid-level social things—ethnic group, electorate, financial crisis, . . . ? These strike me as being compounds of a miscellaneous set of social things—there are bits of organizations, normative systems, affinity groups, and social networks in each of them. The concept of assemblage seems to fit these nouns well.

The "meso" qualifier is a bit more difficult to specify. It is intended to focus our attention on mid-level social arrangements, between actors and global institutions like the US state, global Islam, and the world trading system. The intuitive idea is straightforward. These are the smaller-scale, lower-level social arrangements or units of which macro structures are composed.

The question of the ontological status of social structures is addressed by sociological theorist James Coleman (1990) from the point of view of methodological individualism. Basically, the idea propounded by Coleman and more recently by the analytical sociologists is that all social properties, including causal powers, work through the activities of individuals, and we need ideally to replace claims that appear to attribute causal powers to structures with theories that disaggregate these powers onto the patterned activities of individuals. This is a reductionist theory.

Other theorists, notably Dave Elder-Vass, want to assert that social structures have "emergent" properties and powers. An emergent property, according to Elder-Vass, is one that is possessed by the aggregate but not by the composing units. On this account, there are causal properties of structures that cannot be represented as the aggregate effect of individual actors.

My own approach depends on a line of reasoning long familiar in the special sciences. It is antireductionist, in that it denies that we need to derive higher-level properties from lower-level properties. It accepts the compositional ontology: social structures are composed of individual actors. But it asserts explanatory autonomy for theoretical statements about mid-level mechanisms.

One particularly direct way of supporting the idea that structures have meso effects is to establish correlations at that level for a few examples. But this is not the only way we establish causation in other areas of the sciences. We do experiments ("remove X and observe whether Y persists"), we analyze the outcomes of "natural" experiments, we do comparative studies, and we engage in process tracing of particular cases. We even engage in theoretical analysis to try to determine what causal powers a certain entity ought to be expected to have given its constitution.

So, there is ample room for sociologists to assert and investigate the causal properties of social structures. And, given appropriate attention to the principle of microfoundations, we have a social ontology that supports the legitimacy of such claims as well.

Do Social Structures Exist?

Are there such things as "social structures"? In what do they consist? What sorts of social powers do they exercise? Anthony Giddens is one of the theorists whose ideas are most often discussed in connection with the idea of social structures. His book *Central Problems in Social Theory: Action, Structure, and Contradiction in Social Analysis* is a classic statement of some of his views (Giddens 1979). Here is how he frames his core concern in a key essay, "Agency, Structure":

The principal issue with which I shall be concerned in this paper is that of connecting a notion of human action with structural explanation in social analysis. The making of such a connection, I shall argue, demands the following: a theory of the human agent, or of the subject; an account of the conditions and consequences of action; and an interpretation of "structure" as somehow embroiled in both those conditions and consequences. (49)

He defines a structure as a set of "rules and resources, organized as properties of social systems" (66).

A recent treatment of the reality of social structures is presented in Dave Elder-Vass's *The Causal Power of Social Structures* (Elder-Vass 2010). Elder-Vass accepts along with Giddens the point that agency and structure are inseparable; neither functions as a solely sufficient cause of social outcomes. But he argues strongly for the idea that social structures have causal powers that are not reducible to facts about individuals. He places his analysis generally within the tradition of critical realism (Bhaskar 1975). And, he relies heavily on the theory of supervenience to solve the riddle of how structures can be composed of individual-level activity and yet possess autonomous causal powers (Kim 1993, 2005).

Here is the core of Elder-Vass's ontology of structures: structures are composed of individuals in relation to each other; structures have "emergent" causal powers that are not simply the sum of the causal powers of the component individuals; these emergent powers derive from the relations between the components; and for any particular causal power of the structure it must be possible to provide an explanation of the power in terms of mechanisms involving the individuals and their relations.

The bulk of the book takes the form of an effort to work out this view in detail with respect to two important types of social structures: organizations and normative circles. A bank is an organization (which in turn fits into a web of other organizations). A normative circle is a set of overlapping sets of individuals who both embody and conform to a normative rule or ideal. (Elder-Vass traces the idea here back to Durkheim and Simmel.)

The idea of norm circles plays a related role in Elder-Vass's social ontology. If we were to distill the idea down to its simplest form, it seems to go along these lines: individuals have the capacity to form ideas, rules, and representations of various kinds. They reinforce their ideas and beliefs through interactions with other individuals who (approximately) share those mental representations. This is what makes a given norm system or conceptual framework a social feature rather than simply an individual feature. The representations are constantly tuned through interactions with other members of this representation-sharing group. These representations include ideas, conceptual frameworks, beliefs, and norms. The groups of people who share these and interact on the basis of them constitute a norm circle.

Consider a few candidates for social structures: the global trading system, the Federal government, the Chinese peasantry of the 1930s, the English class system, the Indian marriage system, race in the United States, the city of Chicago. Are these items examples of "social structures"?

What are the central assumptions we make in designating something as a social structure? (Note that the term "social structure" can be used in at least two important senses: first, as a causally operative institutional complex (the state or the market as causal social structures), and second, as a description of facets of the organization of society (demographic structure, urban-rural structure, structure of race and ethnicity, income structure). Here, I will focus on the first sense of the term.)

Several ideas appear to be core features in our ordinary understanding of this concept. A social structure consists of rules, institutions, and practices. A social structure is socially embodied in the actions, thoughts, beliefs, and durable dispositions of individual human beings. A social structure is effective in organizing behavior of large numbers of actors. A structure is coercive of individual and group behavior. A social structure assigns roles and powers to individual actors. A social structure often has distributive consequences for individuals and groups. A social structure is geographically dispersed. Social structures can cause social outcomes involving both persistence and change.

We might try to reduce these intuitions to a definition: a social structure is a system of geographically dispersed rules and practices that influence the actions and outcomes of large numbers of social actors.

Now back to our original question: Do such things exist? Before proceeding to an answer, a few points are evident. Any social entity must possess microfoundations in human mentalities and actions. There is no such thing as a social entity that lacks human embodiment—any more than there are works of art that lacks material embodiment. Social entities "supervene" upon human individuals.

This point also applies to any statements we might make about the putative causal powers of a social entity. So, claims about the causal properties of social structures must be compatible with there being microfoundations for those powers. How does an extended social structure exert influence over the actions of located individuals?

And, there is a final parallel point about claims about the geographical scope and coherence of a social entity. If we want to maintain that an entity exercises influence as a coherent and extended entity, we need to be able to specify the mechanisms through which this takes place. How does the Federal state exert its control and influence over the vast scope of the United States and its population?

So, with these qualifications about the unavoidable need for microfoundations—are there social structures?

Several of the instances offered above fit the terms of our provisional definition. They are large complexes of rules and practices that influence behavior and outcomes. And, it is straightforward to begin to sketch a description of the microfoundations upon which they exist: the social components through which these structures are embodied and through which they exercise influence on individuals and groups. The US Federal Government functions as a system of branches of government, each with its own departments governed by formal and informal rules. And, the "reach" of the state down to the local and individual level is secured by the socially implemented forms of power that are locally expressed (bank inspectors, law enforcement agencies, tax auditors, . . .).

This is an example of a large social structure that operates through a high degree of formal institutionalization. But some of the examples mentioned above depend primarily on informal mechanisms—the workings of widespread beliefs and attitudes, along with a diffused willingness of individuals to "enforce" the requirements of the structure. Structures relying primarily on informal mechanisms include the Indian marriage system or the English class system.

Is "race" a structure in American society? Plainly, it possesses some of the key elements identified above. The reality of race leads to an uneven distribution of opportunities and outcomes, so "race" is a social fact with distributive consequences. It has the element of coercion: racial prejudice and patterns of discrimination are imposed on individuals without an "opt-out" possibility. And, we can identify many of the social mechanisms through which race and racial discrimination work; so the category possesses microfoundations. Today, many of those mechanisms are "informal" rather than "formal"; but, of course, the legal institutionalization of racial discrimination is a recent fact in American history. So, "race" is a structural feature of American society.

Several of the examples mentioned above appear to fall outside the category of social structure, however, for example "Chinese peasantry." These examples appear to be large factors that play a role in large social structures, but are more akin to elements than systems. So, the structure that defines "Chinese peasantry" is the system of property, agriculture, and kinship that defines the peasant's role and opportunities in society; the category of "peasant" identifies one node within that system or structure.

What about "the city of Chicago"? Is this a structure or some other category of social entity? I am inclined to say that the city of Chicago is a complex social entity, not a structure. It falls *within* a variety of structures in America and the world—the global trading system, the electoral process, and the politics of national funding for large cities; and it embodies within it a variety of smaller structures—the public school system, lending practices, nepotism.

But the city itself does not function as a regulative system coordinating the activities of large numbers of individuals. Rather, it is a complex social entity composed of a mix of social practices, behaviors, systems, and relationships.

ORGANIZATIONS AS STRATEGIC ACTION FIELDS

Sometimes a rethinking of ontology and social categories results in an important step forward in social theory. This appears to be the case in some recent reflections on the relationships that exist between the sociology of organizations and social movements theory. The presumption of existing writings on these fields is that they refer to separate but related phenomena. One is more about social actors and the other is more about stable social structures. What happens when we consider the possibility that they actually refer to the same kinds of social phenomena?

This is the perspective taken by Neil Fligstein and Doug McAdam (2012). They describe their approach succinctly in their article "Toward a General Theory of Strategic Action Fields" (Fligstein and McAdam 2011) in these terms:

> We assert that scholars of organizations and social movements—and for that matter, students of any institutional actor in modern society—are interested in the same underlying phenomenon: collective strategic action. (2011: 2)

Fligstein and McAdam formulate their innovative approach in terms of the idea of "strategic action fields." They put it forward that "strategic action fields . . . are the fundamental units of collective action in society" (2011: 3). Power and advantage play key roles in their construction: "We too see SAFs as socially constructed arenas within which actors with varying resource endowments vie for advantage. Membership in these fields is based far more on subjective 'standing' than objective criteria" (2011: 3).

Here is how they formulate the theory in *A Theory of Fields* (2012). The basic idea is that the fundamental structure of social life is "agents behaving strategically within a field of resources and other agents." Here is what they mean by strategic action fields.

> A strategic action field is a constructed mesolevel social order in which actors (who can be individual or collective) are attuned to and interact with one another on the basis of shared (which is not to say consensual) understandings about the purposes of the field, relationships to others in the field (including who has power and why), and the rules governing legitimate action in the field. A stable field is one in which the main actors are able to reproduce themselves and the field over a fairly long period of time. (2012: 1)

Fligstein and McAdam do not give fundamental ontological status to structures or organizations, and they do not presuppose a dichotomy between
agents and structures. Instead, organizations and institutions are ensembles
of agents-in-fields, at a range of levels. Here is what they have to say about
firms, which can be extended to organizations more generally:

> Firms are nested strategic action fields in which there are hierarchical dependent
> relationships between the component fields. Each plant and office is a strategic
> action field in its own right. Typically firms are organized into larger divisions in
> which management controls resource allocation and hiring. (2012: 60)

This theory possesses microfoundations at the level of situated actors; this is
the thrust of the second chapter in the book. Their account is largely organized around the idea of social skill at the level of the actor. What is especially
relevant here, though, is the "macro-sociology" of the theory. In particular,
how do our concepts of meso-level social structures like institutions and organizations get reframed when we use the language of strategic action fields?
And, substantively, how can we account for the relative level of stability
that organizations and institutions possess, if they are simply composites of
strategically motivated actors? The strategic-field description suggests a high
degree of fluidity, as strategies and coalitions shift. But instead, we observe a
reasonable level of stability in organizations much of the time, persisting over
multiple generations of actors.

Part of the answer to the question of stability depends on the idea that Fligstein and McAdam introduce of "internal governance units."

> In addition to incumbents and challengers, many strategic action fields have
> internal governance units that are charged with overseeing compliance with field
> rules and, in general, facilitating the overall smooth functioning and reproduc-
> tion of the system. (2012: 13)

Organizations are configured around incumbents who are assigned roles and
powers that give them both an interest and an ability to maintain the workings
of the organization. So, stability is not a primitive quality of an organization; instead, it is a consequence of the specific interlocking assignments of
interests and powers within the various networks of agents that make up the
organization. Stability is a dynamic feature of the organization, reproduced by
the actions of incumbents. And, change in the organization occurs when there
is significant alteration in those interests and powers.

> Field stability is generally achieved in one of two ways: the imposition of hierar-
> chical power by a single dominant group or the creation of some kind of political
> coalition based on the cooperation of a number of groups. (2012: 14)

On this approach, then, stability is a consequence of the configuration of a given system of strategic fields, rather than an axiomatic property of the organization.

Here are types of social items they include in this theory:

> strategic action fields; incumbents, challengers, and governance units; social skill and the existential functions of the social; the broader field environment; exogenous shocks, mobilization, and the onset of contention; episodes of contention; settlement. (2012: 8)

Their approach is couched at the level of social ontology. The development of the theory of strategic action fields as a prime component of organizations and institutions is a move against the idea of the fixity of social "structures," institutions, and organizations. For example, they write against the ontology of new institutionalism: "The general image for most new institutionalists is one of routine social order and reproduction"—or, in other words, a static set of rules and constraints within which action takes place. Their ontology, on the other hand, emphasizes the fluidity of the constraints and circumstances of action from the actors' points of view; so the field shifts as actors undertake one set of strategies or another. "This leaves substantial latitude for routine jockeying and piecemeal change in the positions that actors occupy" (2012: 12).

So, both stability and change are incorporated into a single framework of analysis: actors react strategically to the field of constraints and positions within which they act, with results that sometimes reinforce current positions and other times disrupt those positions.

Fligstein and McAdam attempt to account for what looks like institutional rigidity by calling out the power of some actors to maintain their positions in the social order: "Most incumbents are generally well positioned and fortified to withstand these change pressures. For starters they typically enjoy significant resource advantages over field challengers" (2012: 20). But institutions should not be expected to maintain their structures indefinitely: "The expectation is that when even a single member of the field begins to act in innovative ways in violation of field rules, others will respond in kind, precipitating an episode of contention" (2011: 9).

Their language suggests a parallel with assemblage theory discussed in chapter 1, in the sense that social constructs fit upward and downward into strategic action fields at a range of levels. "We conceive of all fields as embedded in complex webs of other fields" (8). But at the other end of the spectrum of theory differentiation, their account also seems to make contact with rational choice theory, where both actions and rules are subject to deliberation and change by prudential actors.

There are several features of this approach that seem especially valuable for social theory. One is the fact that it directly challenges the tendency toward reification that sometimes blocks sociological thinking—the idea that social "things" like states persist largely independently from the individuals who make them up. This new approach leads to a way of thinking about the social world that emphasizes contingency and plasticity rather than rigid and homogeneous social structures. It is consistent with the thinking that leads to the idea of "methodological localism"—the idea that social phenomena rest upon "molecules" of socially constructed, socially situated individuals. Further, their analysis is explicitly couched at the meso level—neither macro nor micro.

Though this theory provides a new way of thinking about organizations, it has a good deal of consonance with the ideas about organizations and actors put forward by Crozier and Friedberg some forty years ago in *Actors and Systems: The Politics of Collective Action* (Crozier and Friedberg 1980). Crozier and Friedberg too looked at organizations as arenas of strategic and opportunistic action by agents. They too emphasized the role of cooperation and alliances within organizations. And, they too looked at organizations as solutions to problems of collective action. Crozier and Friedberg's premise is that actors within organizations have substantially more agency and freedom than they are generally afforded by orthodox organization theory, and we can best understand the workings and evolution of the organization as (partially) the result of the strategic actions of the participants (instead of understanding the conduct of the participants as a function of the rules of the organization).

Crozier and Friedberg look at organizations as solutions to collective action problems—tasks or performances that allow attainment of a goal that is of interest to a broad public, but for which there are no antecedent private incentives for cooperation. Organized solutions to collective problems—of which organizations are key examples—do not emerge spontaneously; instead, "they consist of nothing other than solutions, always specific, that relatively autonomous actors have created, invented, established, with their particular resources and capacities, to solve these challenges for collective action" (15). And, they emphasize the inherent contingency of these particular solutions; there are always alternative solutions, neither better nor worse.

This is an appealing point of view for several reasons. First, it is consistent with the view argued in chapter 1 concerning the plasticity of institutions. Second, it seems to fit very well with the ideas associated with methodological localism: Crozier and Freidberg lend support to the view that we can best understand a range of extended social phenomena as the result of the actions and thoughts of the socially situated and socially constituted actors who make up its various locales.

The authors address the constraining power of institutions and organizations by using the idea of "narrowing the field of play" (*champs d'interaction aménagés*) to describe the workings of an organization. Essentially this suggests that an organization commonly succeeds in ruling out certain strategies for the participants while leaving open others. And, perhaps this helps to explain part of the stability of many organizations over time: organizations succeed in limiting the freedom of choice of participants, though not down to a single option. For example, a junior faculty person may choose a strategy of flattering the department chair to increase the likelihood of receiving tenure; but he or she cannot threaten the chair with bodily harm unless support is provided. Crozier and Freidberg do not reject the facts of power and constraint within an organization. Rather, they reject the idea that these social systems of power leave actors with no alternative choices. Agents are capable of forming their own perceptions of the social relations in which they find themselves; and they are capable of acting strategically in trying to gain advantage within those relations.

So, the theories of organizations that are developed by Fligstein and McAdam as well as Crozier and Freidberg seem to provide support for several insights into the nature of the social that have emerged from arguments here. These theories of organization as fields of strategic action give us a basis for understanding organizations and institutions as reasonably stable social entities that depend nonetheless on the actions and strategies of the individual actors who make them up.

COLEMAN'S HOUSE-OF-CARDS INTERPRETATION

James Coleman offers a helpful position on the question of the reality of social structures in his landmark book, *Foundations of Social Theory* (1990). Coleman advocates for a view of research and theory in sociology that emphasizes the actions of situated purposive individuals, and he deliberately avoids the idea of persistent social structures within which actors make choices. His focus is on the relations among actors and the higher-level patterns that arise from these relations.

> The social environment can be viewed as consisting of two parts. One is the "natural" social environment, growing autonomously as simple social relations develop and expand the structure. A second portion is what may be described as the built, or constructed, social environment, organizations composed of complex social relations. The constructed social environment does not grow naturally through the interests of actors who are parties to relations. Each relation must be constructed by an outsider, and each relation is viable only through its connections to other relations that are part of the same organization. . . . The structure is like a house of cards, with extensive interdependence among the different relations of which it is composed. (43–44)

This is a fascinating formulation. Essentially Coleman is offering a sketch of how we might conceive of a social ontology that suffices without reference to structures as independent entities. We are advised to think of social structures and norms as no more than coordinated and mutually reinforcing patterns of individual behavior. The emphasis is on individual behavior within the context of the actions of others. As he puts the point later in the book, "The elementary actor is the wellspring of action, no matter how complex are the structures through which action takes place" (503). Essentially, there is no place for structures in Coleman's boat.

Coleman takes a similar approach to the topic of social norms, one of the engines through which social structures are generally thought to wield influence on action:

> Much sociological theory takes social norms as given and proceeds to examine individual behavior or the behavior of social systems when norms exist. Yet to do this without raising at some point the question of why and how norms come into existence is to forsake the more important sociological problem in order to address the less important. (241)

Coleman offers an example of the house-of-cards interdependence in question here in his discussion of problems arising within bureaucracies as a result of the cost of oversight and policing:

> Many kinds of behavior in bureaucracies derive from this fundamental defect: stealing from an employer, loafing on the job, featherbedding (in which two persons do the work of one), padding of expense accounts, use of organizational resources for personal ends, and waste. (79)

These kinds of behavior will swamp the organization, unless there are other actors within the organization who will undertake the costly activity of observing and punishing bad behavior. This might come about because of a formal incentive—people are paid to be auditors. Or, it might come about from internalized but informal motives acting in other persons—envy, a sense of fairness, or loyalty to the organization.

A good illustration in this context is the category of conventional practices of behavior. (David Lewis shows how conventions emerge from intentional behavior at the individual level; *Convention: A Philosophical Study* (Lewis 1969).) Let's say that a study finds that Americans overtip in small local restaurants. Here is a possible explanation. There is no rule or enforcement mechanism that punishes poor tippers. But because the restaurant is local, the client knows he or she will be returning; and because it is small, he or she knows that today's behavior will be noted and remembered. Further, the server recognizes the dynamic and reinforces it by providing small non-obligatory extras to the client—a free dessert on a birthday, a good table for a special occasion, and a larger pour from the wine bottle. This is an example of social behavior that fits Coleman's description of a "house of cards" pattern of interdependency between client and server. If the server stops playing his or her role, the client is less inclined to overtip the next time; and if the supererogatory tip is not forthcoming, the server is less likely to be generous with service at the next visit. The pattern is stable, and it can be explained fully in Coleman-like terms. Each party has an interest in continuing the practice, and the pattern is reinforced.

Anyone who accepts that social entities and forces rest upon microfoundations must agree that something like Coleman's recursive story of self-reinforcing patterns of behavior must be correct. But this does not imply that higher-level social structures do not possess stable causal properties nonetheless. The "house-of-cards" pattern of interdependency between auditor and worker, or between server and client, helps to explain how the stable patterns of the organization are maintained; but it does not render superfluous the idea that the structure itself has causal properties or powers. The microfoundations thesis does not entail reductionism.

COLLECTIVE ACTORS

A related question is whether our social ontology should include collective actors. Do we want to include supra-individual entities among the social objects that are capable of agency and action? Does a crowd, a business firm, or a state agency act as a unified actor?

What is involved in acting as a group? What is the difference between a crowd of pedestrians crossing Massachusetts Avenue in Cambridge when the light changes and a group of students marching into Harvard Hall in an attempt to initiate a protest? How about the difference between a group of history graduate students pursuing research simultaneously but separately on early New England diseases in Widener Library and a research group of scientists collaborating to discover the mechanism of HIV transmission at the cellular level?

The intuitive answer to these questions is pretty clear. A group activity requires some level of collective intentions and purposes on the parts of the participants toward each other and toward the group itself. A group is more than an ensemble of individuals performing a similar set of actions (pedestrians, independent researchers). Rather, we want to see some indication that the individuals regard themselves as members of the group, that they embrace some conception of the action that members of the group propose to perform, and that they individually choose their plans of action out of consideration of this group or collective purpose. In a group's actions, the individuals who make up the group are oriented toward the group and its goals and purposes. In other words, groups are constituted by some form of group-oriented intentionality on the part of individual members, and group actions are performed by individuals who have adopted a set of beliefs and attitudes toward other members of the group and its collective purposes.

There are quite a few complications that arise here, however. Here is one: many collective activities involve participants with a wide range of affiliation with the collective purpose. There are core members who explicitly and emphatically declare adherence to the collective goal and plan. There are some who are willing followers without a clear idea of the purpose or plan. There are opportunistic joiners who have their own private reasons for joining the group project. And, there may even be a degree of disagreement within the group about goals, strategies, and tactics—with the result that many committed members nonetheless differ from each other with respect to their collective intentions. And, these aren't sharp distinctions in most cases—so, a given collectivity may consist of a deeply mixed group of individuals with respect to their understandings, purposes, and affinities for the collective action.

Several philosophers have focused on this set of problems surrounding group intentionality. Margaret Gilbert thinks there is a sharp distinction between group intentions and individual intentions (Gilbert 1989). More recently, Raimo Tuomela refers to "we" intentions and "I" intentions in order to explain the defining characteristics of group behavior in *The Philosophy of Social Practices: A Collective Acceptance View* (Tuomela 2002). Both Gilbert and Tuomela seem to think that groups have intentions that are autonomous from the purposes and intentions of members of the group—a sort of Durkheimian view of the autonomous reality of the mentality of groups. What these approaches have in common is a desire to postulate a strong distinction in levels between group intentions and individual intentions.

Gilbert's primary contention is that the notion of a collectivity—individuals constituting a group—is the central feature of social ontology. And, she maintains that this concept can best be analyzed by the idea of a "plural subject"— the referent of the first-person plural pronoun, "we." The core of Gilbert's theory of social groups involves the idea of the *mutual recognition by a set of persons* that they are engaged in some joint actions or beliefs. "A set of people constitute a social group if and only if they constitute a plural subject"; and a plural subject is "a set of people each of whom shares with oneself in some action, belief, attitude, or similar attribute" (204). Gilbert argues that the pronouns "us" and "we" are the linguistic elements through which we refer to plural subjects in English. And, she believes that plural subjects exist; they are not fictions or constructions, but agents who have beliefs, perform actions, and succeed or fail in carrying out their intentions. According to Gilbert, "Social groups are plural subjects, collective beliefs are the beliefs of plural subjects, and social conventions are the 'fiats' of plural subjects" (408). Gilbert argues against the individualism of Max Weber, by arguing that collectivities are the central subject of the social sciences, and that collectivities cannot be subsumed under individualist concepts. Thus, Gilbert suggests that her theory offers support for holism over individualism (3).

I do not find this collectivist approach to "individuals behaving as groups" at all convincing, for several reasons. One is the point mentioned above about the heterogeneity of individual motivations and purposes within a group activity. This seems to imply that there couldn't be a coherent, univalent group intention that stands separate from the individuals who constitute the group. Instead, there are only the somewhat polyglot collective intentions within agents, with some degree of within-group communication and shaping about their shared collective purposes.

Second, there is the general skeptical point about "spooky" social entities—entities that are thought to have an existence independent from the states of agency and mind of the individuals who make up the social world. How could one possibly imagine that there is a collective intention associated with the Burmese monks in 2007, standing separate and independent from the beliefs, assumptions, loyalties, and adherences of many individual monks and networks of monks?

And, here is a third puzzle. We need to have some idea of the concrete social processes through which group-oriented intentions are created at the individual level in particular social circumstances. We need to know something about the microfoundations of group formation. It doesn't help to simply postulate "collective intentions"; we need to have a concrete sociology of the ways in which individuals come to have group-oriented beliefs, values, and motives.

Finally, the "autonomous collectivity" view does not work very well when we try to use it to interpret the practice of gifted social scientists who attempt to explain collective action. E. P. Thompson, James Scott, Chuck Tilly, Doug McAdam, and William Sewell all devote a lot of their effort to explaining how specific social collectivities came to define themselves as "groups" and came to act in a collective way. But their approaches are invariably based on understanding the many threads of mobilization, structure, and meaning at the disaggregated level that eventually build up to a movement. Thompson's metal workers, Scott's Southeast Asian peasant rebels (Scott 1976), Tilly's Vendeans (Tilly 1970), McAdam's civil rights activists and followers (McAdam 1999), and Sewell's Marseillaise craftsmen (Sewell 1980) all reflect the variation and concrete historical construction of individual consciousness within concrete political movements that confirms the variability and agentic nature of social movements and group identity.

That said, there is still a crucial role for group-oriented thoughts and purposes at the level of at least some of the participants in a group. Without these group intentions at the individual level, we couldn't say that there is a group at all—only a collection of individually oriented individual actors. Something like the following must be true for at least some of the members of a group action:

- X regards a set of other individuals as constituting a group G to which he or she belongs.
- X believes that G has a common interest or need N.
- X is motivated to join in concert with others in G in such a way as to bring about N.
- X believes that some significant number of other members of the group share these collective thoughts, purposes, and motives.
- X believes that some significant number of G will act accordingly.
- X has a consequent motivation to engage in the collective action.

One additional condition seems to be pragmatically required in order for these conditions to arise: there must be some tangible process of *communication and mobilization* through which the group-oriented intentional states mentioned here are created in the various individuals.

So, there are mandatory group-oriented states of mind that are part of the constitution of a group. But notice this key fact: these features of beliefs, intentions, and motives that I have mentioned are all located at the level of the individual actors. There is no higher-level collectivity that possesses an independent "group intention." So, a group is constituted by the states of intentionality and belief of its members and by the concrete processes of communication and mobilization through which a degree of group-orientedness and coherence emerges within the states of mind of the participants. Weber was right after all in this important respect (Weber 1930). Fundamentally, there are only three social-intentional states postulated here: *affiliation*, *mutual recognition*, and *solidarity*. And, there is a postulate about the microsocial processes through which these are cultivated: *mobilization*, *communication*, and *embodied social networks*.

It is worth noting that this analysis in turn is entirely compatible with the perspective of ML discussed earlier.

REALITY OF NORMATIVE SYSTEMS

The role of norms in social behavior is a key question for sociology. Is a norm, or a system of norms, a sociological reality? We discussed the role of social norms within the sphere of the actor in chapter 2; now let us consider the social embodiment of a system of norms.

We can offer mundane examples of social norms deriving from a wide range of social situations: norms of politeness, norms of fairness, norms of appropriate dress, norms of behavior in business meetings, norms of gendered behavior, and norms of body language and tone of voice in police work. In each case, we suppose that (a) there is a publicly recognized norm governing the specified conduct within a specific social group, (b) the norm influences individual behavior in some way, and (c) sanctions and internal motivations come into the explanation of conformant behavior. Norm breakers may come in for rough treatment by the people around them—which may induce them to honor the norm in the future. And, norm conformers may do so because they have internalized a set of inhibitions about the proscribed behavior.

The role of norms in social behavior is also a key question for sociology. Is a norm a sociological reality? And, do individuals behave in conformance to norms?

The questions about the social embodiment of a norm are the most difficult. Does the embodiment of a given norm consist simply in the fact that a certain percentage of people in fact behave in accordance with the rule—for whatever reason? Does the norm exist in virtue of the fact that people consciously champion the norm and impose sanctions on violators? Might we imagine that human beings are normative animals and absorb normative systems in the way that we absorb grammatical systems—by observing and inferring about the behavior of others?

As for the third cluster of questions about genesis and persistence, there is a range of possibilities here as well. The system may have been designed by one or more deliberate actors. It may have emerged through a fairly random process that is guided by positive social feedback of some sort. It may be the resultant of multiple groups advocating for one set of norms or another to govern a given situation of conflict and/or cooperation. And, conceivably, it may be the result of something analogous to natural selection across small groups: the groups with a more efficient set of norms may outperform competing groups.

For example, how should we explain the emergence and persistence of a particular set of norms of marriage and reproduction in a given society? Is it causally relevant to observe that "this set of norms results in a rate of fertility that matches the rate of growth of output"? How would this functionally desirable fact play a causal role in the emergence and persistence of this set of norms? Is there any sort of feedback process that we can hypothesize between "norms at time t," "material results of behavior governed by these norms at $t + 1$," and "persistence/change of norms at time $t + 2$"? The business practices of a company are consciously adjusted over time to bring about better overall performance; but what about spontaneously occurring sets of social norms? How do these change over time? Do individuals or groups have the ability to deliberately modify the norms that govern their everyday activities?

It seems inescapable that norms of behavior exist in a society and that individuals adjust their behavior out of regard for relevant norms. The micro-foundations of how this works are obscure, however, in that we do not really have good answers to the parallel questions: How do individuals internalize norms? And, how do informal practices of norm enforcement work? And, what social-causal factors play a role in the emergence, persistence, and change of a system of norms at a given time?

Code of the Street

Consider a detailed sociological example of an embodied set of norms. Elijah Anderson provides a striking exploration of the norms that guide behavior in inner-city Philadelphia in *Code of the Street: Decency, Violence, and the Moral Life of the Inner City* (Anderson 1999). Anderson wants to understand the content of the "code of the street"—the values around which young inner-city men and women orient their actions and aspirations. And, in the urban world of the late 1990s in America, a lot of that code circles around violence and aggression. Anderson wants to know how inner-city youth think about violence, and he wants to understand why impoverished urban neighborhoods have become so much more violent than their counterparts were when W. E. B. Dubois studied them early in the twentieth century.

> Here I take up more directly the theme of interpersonal violence, particularly between and among inner-city youths. While youth violence has become a problem of national scope, involving young people of various classes and races, in this book I am concerned with why it is that so many inner-city young people are inclined to commit aggression and violence toward one another. (preface)

Here is a strong description of the underculture of violence that Anderson identifies on Germantown Avenue:

> The inclination to violence springs from the circumstances of life among the ghetto poor—the lack of jobs that pay a living wage, limited basic public services (police response in emergencies, building maintenance, trash pickup, lighting, and other services that middle-class neighborhoods take for granted), the stigma of race, the fallout from rampant drug use and drug trafficking, and the resulting alienation and absence of hope for the future. (Anderson 1999: 32)

Consistent with the basis ethnographic insight mentioned above, Anderson wants to understand two things: What is the "code of the street"; what are those norms of behavior and masculinity that come together in inner-city Philadelphia (or Detroit, Miami, or Chicago)? And, second, what were the historical and social circumstances that shaped the emergence of this set of norms?

Here is Anderson's preliminary answer to the first question:

> At the heart of this code is a set of prescriptions and proscriptions, or informal rules, of behavior organized around a desperate search for respect that governs public social relations, especially violence, among so many residents, particularly young men and women. Possession of respect—and the credible threat of vengeance—is highly valued for shielding the ordinary person from the interpersonal violence of the street. (11)

The answer to the second question is more complex. Anderson's answer has to do with widespread alienation among urban young people from the legitimacy of basic social institutions, including the criminal justice system. But the more general historical cause that he explores is the history of racial discrimination and impoverishment that American cities have almost always witnessed. Racism and almost insurmountable segregation have created a thoroughly disaffected underclass in American cities.

A particularly powerful part of the book is Anderson's extensive use of individual stories—decent people, crack addicts, young mothers, working poor, and others. The long story of John Turner, the final chapter in the book, is particularly powerful. These stories serve to document Anderson's key lines of interpretation—the meaning of the street code, the way the violence of the street is experienced and accommodated, and the ways that these men and women think about the world they inhabit. This use of detailed personal stories from field notes means that the reader has at least a degree of independence from Anderson's narrative, since there is always the possibility of interpreting these vignettes differently from Anderson.

DO CULTURAL FACTS REQUIRE MICROFOUNDATIONS?

What can we say about the possible microfoundations of normative systems, cultural facts and social practices? Candidates for such factors include the social prevalence of symbols, meanings, practices, rituals, traditions, grammars, and the like. These items too require microfoundations. Cultural items are sometimes thought to be supra-individual and independent from the concrete individuals who live within their scope. And, it is true that culture exercises a specific kind of independence. But no less than any other social characteristic can cultural features evade their embodiment in individual actors and institutions.

Consider the norms of *zakat* (charity) as a profound part of Muslim identity. If we want to maintain that this norm is a real part of Muslim identity and that it explains certain social outcomes, then we need to know how these elements of identity are conveyed to children and practitioners at the local level. What are the concrete social mechanisms of inculcation and communication through which a Bangladeshi child comes to internalize a full Muslim identity, including adherence to the norms of *zakat*? To what extent are there important differences within Bangladeshi society in the forms of identity present in Muslims—urban–rural, male–female, and rich–poor? And, equally interestingly—in what ways do those processes give rise to a Muslim identity in Bangladesh that is somewhat different from that in Indonesia, Morocco, or Saudi Arabia?

Identities, cultures, and systems of meaning are no less embodied in the states of mind of actors than are the calculating features of rationality that underlie a market society. So, the fault of methodological individualists in this sphere is not that they fail to recognize the inherent autonomy of systems of cultural meaning; it is rather that they adhere to a theory of the actor that does not give sufficient attention to the variations and contingencies that characterize actors in various social and historical contexts. Ideas about the independence of cultural items from the level of individuals are suggestive and interesting, and I think they need to be fully confronted by an actor-centered sociology. But I do not believe they are incompatible with an actor-centered sociology.

Take the independence of a code of behavior from the specific individuals who are subject to the code. It is true that a single individual can only rarely influence the code, which is embodied in the thoughts and actions of countless others. But the reality of the code at any given time is in fact entirely dependent on those thoughts and actions (and artifacts created by previous actors). Moreover, the individual's embodiment of the code of behavior is in turn caused by a series of interactions through childhood and adulthood within a social setting.

It is certainly true that facts about culture make a difference in meso- and macro-level outcomes. A collective farm that was populated by actors who embodied Chairman Mao's ideal of "socialist man" would have functioning characteristics very different from those observed—no "easy riders," lots of earnest Stakhanovites. So, standard organizational analysis of the tendencies toward low productivity in collective agriculture is dependent on something like a purposive agent theory of the actor. Different kinds of actors give rise to different kinds of organizations.

This does not mean, however, that we could not have reasonably good understandings of "organizations" under differently realized structures of agency. This seems to be part of the work that Andreas Glaeser is doing in

Political Epistemics: The Secret Police, the Opposition, and the End of East German Socialism (Glaeser 2011). Glaeser tries to understand how organizations like the Stasi functioned in a setting in which participants' understandings and motivations were changing rapidly.

So, we can answer the question posed above. Cultural entities and practices do require microfoundations, and it is in fact a fruitful avenue of sociological and ethnographic investigation to discover the concrete social mechanisms and pathways through which these entities come to be embodied in various populations in the ways that they are.

POLITICAL CULTURE AND TECHNOLOGICAL CHANGE

Let us close this discussion with an example that treats several large-scale social things as suitable objects of study by a historical social scientist. Frank Dobbin provides a careful analysis of the political cultures and institutions of three countries in order to explain substantial and consequential differences in outcomes in the structure of the transportation systems that each country built over the better part of a century.

Here is the problem Dobbin takes on. A powerful new technology—the railroad—was developed in the first part of the nineteenth century. The nature and characteristics of the technology were essentially homogeneous across the national settings in which it appeared in Europe and North America. However, it was introduced and built out in three countries—the United States, Britain, and France—in markedly different ways. The ways in which the railroads and their technologies were regulated and encouraged were very different in the three countries, and the eventual rail networks had very different properties in the three countries. The question for explanation is this: Can we explain the differences in these three national experiences on the basis of some small set of structural or cultural differences that existed among the three countries and that causally explain the resulting differences in build out, structure, and technical frameworks? Or, possibly, are the three historical experiences different simply because of the occurrence of a large but cumulative number of unimportant and nonsystemic events?

These are the questions that historical sociologist Dobbin poses in his book, *Forging Industrial Policy: The United States, Britain, and France in the Railway Age* (Dobbin 1994). He argues that there were significantly different cultures of political and industrial policy in the three countries that led to substantial differences in the ways in which government and business interacted in the development of the railroads. "Each Western nation-state developed a distinct strategy for governing industry" (1). The *laissez-faire* culture of the United States permitted a few large railroad magnates and corporations to make the crucial decisions about technology, standards, and routes that would govern the development of the rail system. The regulated market culture of Great Britain favored smaller companies and strove to prevent the emergence of a small number of oligopolistic rail companies. And, the technocratic civil service culture of France gave a great deal of power to the engineers and civil servants who were charged to make decisions about technology choice, routes, and standards.

These differences led to systemic differences in the historical implementation of the railroads, the rail networks that were developed, and the regulatory regimes that surrounded them. The US rail network developed as the result of competition among a small number of rail magnates for the most profitable routes. This turned out to favor a few east-west trunk lines connecting urban centers, including New York, Boston, Chicago, and San Francisco. The British rail network gave more influence to municipalities who demanded service; as a result, the network that developed was a more distributed one across a larger number of cities. And, the French rail network was rationally designed to conform to the economic and military needs of the French state, with a system of rail routes that largely centered on Paris.

This example illustrates the insights that can be distilled from comparative historical sociology. Dobbin takes a single technology and documents a range of outcomes in the way in which the technology is built out into a national system. And, he attempts to isolate the differences in structures and cultures in the three settings that would account for the differences in outcomes. He offers a causal analysis of the development of the technology in the three settings, demonstrating how the mechanism of policy culture imposes effects on the development of the technology. The inherent possibilities represented by the technology intersect with the economic circumstances and the policy cultures of the three national settings, and the result is a set of differentiated organizations and outcomes in the three countries. The analysis is rich in its documentation of the social mechanisms through which policy culture influenced technology development; the logic of his analysis is more akin to process tracing than to the methods of difference and similarity in Mill's methods.

The research establishes several important things. First, it refutes any sort of technological determinism, according to which the technical characteristics of the technology determine the way it will be implemented. To the contrary, Dobbin's work demonstrates the very great degree of contingency that existed in the social implementation of the railroad. Second, it makes a strong case for the idea that an element of culture—the framework of assumptions, precedents, and institutions defining the "policy culture" of a country—can have a very strong effect on the development of large social institutions. Dobbin emphasizes the role that things like traditions, customs, and legacies play in the unfolding of important historical developments. And, finally, the work makes it clear that these highly contingent pathways of development nonetheless admit of explanation. We can identify the mechanisms and local circumstances that led, in one instance, to a large number of firms and hubs and in the other, a small number of firms and trunk lines.

Chapter 4

Reduction and Emergence

Earlier chapters have focused attention on the nature of social entities and their relation to social actors. In this chapter, we will pursue some of the conceptual and theoretical problems that emerge from these concerns. We will consider the idea of reductionism—the notion that social phenomena can be reduced to the actions and interactions of individuals. Here, we will also consider the notions of generativity and supervenience—the notion that social phenomena are "generated" by the actions and interactions of individuals, and nothing else.

The second largest theme in this chapter is the topic of emergence and relative explanatory autonomy. Do social phenomena have properties that cannot or need not be derived from the behavior of individuals after all? Are social outcomes "emergent" in some strong sense? Do facts about complexity imply that we cannot derive or predict social outcomes, no matter how much we know about the circumstances and actions of individuals? Is it possible to be a generativist without being forced to assume that social outcomes are predictable in principle?

AN ONTOLOGICAL DIAGRAM

Figure 4.1 provides an illustration of how the entities and processes of the social world might be arranged.

Figure 4.1 represents the social world as a set of layers of entities, processes, powers, and laws. Entities at L_2 are composed of or caused by some set of entities and forces at L_1. Likewise, L_3 and L_4. Arrows labeled with W indicate *microfoundations* for L_2 facts based on L_1 facts. Diamond-tipped arrows indicate the relation of *generative dependence* from one level to

115

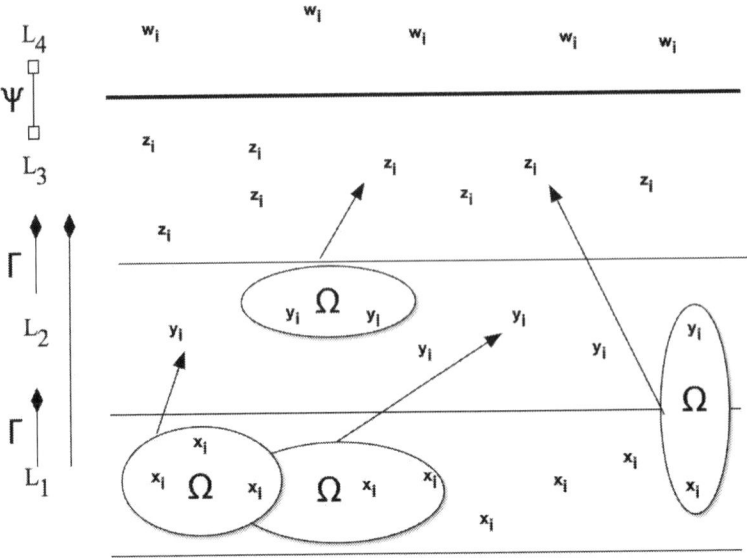

Levels of the social -- generation, microfoundation, emergence

Figure 4.1   Levels of the social.

another. Square-tipped lines indicate the presence of *strongly emergent* facts at the higher level relative to the lower level. The solid line (L_4) represents the possibility of a level of social fact that is not generatively dependent upon lower levels. The vertical ellipse at the right indicates the possibility of microfoundations narratives involving elements at different levels of the social world (individual and organizational, for example).

We might think of these levels as "individuals," "organization, value communities, social networks," "large aggregate institutions like states," etc.

This is only one way of trying to represent the structure of the social world. The notion of a "flat" ontology was considered in chapter 3. Another structure that is excluded by this diagram is one in which there is multidirectional causation across levels, both upward and downward. For example, the diagram excludes the possibility that L_3 entities have causal powers that are original and independent from the powers of L_2 or L_1 entities. The laminated view described here is the assumption built into debates about microfoundations, supervenience, and emergence. It reflects the language of micro-, meso-, and macro levels of social action and organization.

Here are definitions for several of the primary concepts.

- *Microfoundations* of facts in L_{n+1} based on facts in L_n: accounts of the causal pathways through which entities, processes, powers, and laws of L_n

bring about specific outcomes in L_{n+1}. Microfoundations are small causal theories linking lower-level entities to higher-level outcomes.

- *Generative dependence* of L_{n+1} upon L_n: the entities, processes, powers, and laws of L_{n+1} are generated by the properties of level L_n and nothing else. Alternatively, the entities, processes, powers, and laws of L_n suffice to generate all the properties of L_{n+1}. A full theory of L_n suffices to derive the entities, processes, powers, and laws of L_{n+1}.
- *Reducibility* of L_{n+1} to L_n: it is possible to provide a theoretical or formal derivation of the properties of L_{n+1} based solely on facts about L_n.
- *Strong emergence* of properties in L_{n+1} with respect to the properties of L_n: L_{n+1} possesses some properties that do not depend wholly upon the properties of L_n.
- *Weak emergence* of properties in L_{n+1} with respect to the properties of L_n: L_{n+1} possesses some properties for which we cannot (now or in the future) provide derivations based wholly upon the properties of L_n.
- *Supervenience* of L_{n+1} with respect to properties of L_n: all the properties of L_{n+1} depend strictly upon the properties of L_n and nothing else.

These characteristics serve to capture important features of ontology. There are implications for methodology that derive from some of these ideas as well. In particular, the idea of generative dependence suggests that it should be possible to construct models that derive upper-level properties from assumptions about lower-level entities and structures. This is the idea that the tools of computer-based simulation of the aggregate consequences of individual behavior can be a very powerful tool for sociological research and explanation. So, the tools of agent-based modeling and other simulations of complex systems have a very natural place within the generativist approach.

What are the logical relations among these concepts? Consider these statements about putative facts at levels L_n and L_{n+1}:

1. UM: all facts at L_{n+1} possess microfoundations at L_n and lower.
2. XM: some facts at L_{n+1} possess only inferred but unknown microfoundations at L_n and lower.
3. SM: some facts at L_{n+1} do not possess any microfoundations at L_n.
4. SE: L_{n+1} is strongly emergent from L_n and lower.
5. WE: L_{n+1} is weakly emergent from L_n and lower.
6. GD: L_{n+1} is generatively dependent upon L_n and lower.
7. R: L_{n+1} is reducible to L_n.
8. D: L_{n+1} is determined by L_n and lower.
9. SS: L_{n+1} supervenes upon L_n and lower.

Here are some of the logical relations that appear to exist among these statements.

1. UM entails GD
2. UM entails ~SE
3. XM entails WE
4. SE entails ~UM
5. SE entails ~GD
6. GD entails R
7. GD entails D
8. SM entails SE
9. UM entails SS
10. GD entails SS

On this analysis, the question of the availability of microfoundations for social facts can be seen to be central to all the other issues: reducibility, emergence, generativity, and supervenience can all be defined in terms of the presence or absence of microfoundations.

There are several positions that we can take with respect to the availability of microfoundations for higher-level social facts. If we have convincing reason to believe that all social facts possess microfoundations at a lower level (known or unknown), then we know that the social world supervenes upon the micro level; strong emergence is ruled out; weak emergence is true only so long as some microfoundations remain unknown; and higher-level social facts are generatively dependent upon the micro level.

If we take a pragmatic view of the social sciences and conclude that any given stage of knowledge provides information about only a subset of possible microfoundations for higher-level facts, then we are at liberty to take the view that each level of social ontology is at least weakly emergent from lower levels— basically, the point of view advocated under the banner of "relative explanatory autonomy." This also appears to be roughly the position taken by Herbert Simon.

If we believe that it is impossible in principle to fully specify the microfoundations of all social facts, then weak emergence is true, supervenience is false, and generativity is false. (For example, we might believe this to be true because of the difficulty of modeling and calculating a sufficiently large and complex domain of units.) This is the situation that Fodor believes to be the case for many of the special sciences.

If we have reason to believe that some higher-level facts simply do not possess microfoundations at a lower level at all, then strong emergence is true; the social world is not generatively dependent upon the micro-world; and the social world does not supervene upon the micro-world. This is the view taken by strong emergentists.

In other words, it appears that each of the concepts of supervenience, reduction, emergence, and generative dependence can be defined in terms of the availability of microfoundations for some or all of the facts at a higher level based on facts at the lower level. Strong emergence and generative dependence turn out to be logical contraries (witness the final two definitions above).

The second diagram, Figure 4.2, is mentioned frequently in this book and elsewhere in the literature on the philosophy of social science. It is referred to as "Coleman's Boat," and it derives from an effort by James Coleman (1990) to specify the relationships that exist between macro- and micro levels of the social world—social entities and individuals. The diagram specifies four possible directions of influence. Macro-level facts can influence individuals in their propensities for action (values, incentives, penalties). This is represented by arrow 1, the descending strut. Individuals through their actions can interact with other individuals and form new social propensities, represented by arrow 2. Individuals with various kinds of social propensities—social alliances, new motivations for action, social movements—can aggregate to new macro-level facts. This process is represented by arrow 3. Finally, we might imagine that macro-entities can directly influence other macro-entities (arrow 4). But Coleman rules out this form of social causation. In his treatment of the social world, any influence from a macro-social condition can only proceed through its effects on individuals at the micro level; and consequently their actions can aggregate to a change at the macro-level. So, macro-level events and structures can have macro-level effects, but only through the mediation of individuals. (The diagram is adapted from Hedström and Ylikoski (2010), and the labels for the struts are their contribution.)

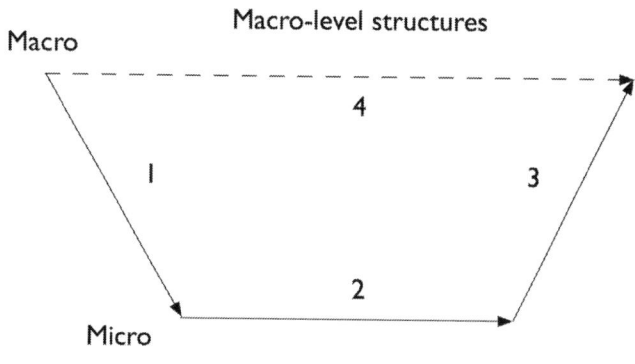

Figure 4.2 Coleman's boat (drawn after Hedström and Ylikoski 2010: 59).

REDUCTION

Let us begin with the view that the properties of social entities should be reducible in principle to facts about the properties of the things that compose them—individuals. There is nothing peculiar about the idea that some entities are complex assemblages of other, simpler entities. This fact by itself does not establish that reductionism is true. Virtually every entity in which we have an interest is a compound of simpler entities—genes, enzymes, or a protein molecule. A table has characteristics that depend on the physical features and arrangement of the materials that make it up, but those "table" characteristics are very different from the features of the composing elements—hardness, stability, load-bearing capacity, etc. And, there is no reason whatsoever to insist that "tables do not exist—only bits of wood exist." Tables are identifiable composite objects, and they have causal properties that we can invoke in explanations. So, the fact that there are characteristics of the composite that are dissimilar from the characteristics of the elements is not peculiar. This is equally true of social entities as well. The efficiency or corruptibility of a tax-collecting bureau is not a characteristic of the individuals who compose it; it is rather a system-level characteristic that derives from the incentives, oversight mechanisms, and physical infrastructure of the organization.

So, composite entities are not suspect in general. However, there are a couple of challenging questions that we need to confront about composite entities. First, can we explain the properties of the composite by knowing everything about the properties of the elements and the nature of their arrangement and interactions? Can we *derive* the properties of the whole from the properties of the components? Take metallurgy: Can we derive the properties of the alloy from the physical characteristics of the tin and copper that make it up? Or, are there "emergent" properties that somehow do not depend solely on the properties of the components?

Second, can we attribute causal powers to composite entities directly, or do we need to disaggregate causal claims about the aggregate onto some set of claims about the causal powers of the elements? Do we need to disaggregate the load-bearing capacity of the table onto a set of facts about the properties of the elements (legs, table top) and their configuration? It is certainly true that we can derive the load-bearing capacity of the table from this set of facts; this is what civil engineers do in modeling bridges, for example. The philosophical question is whether we ought to regard this causal property as simply a way of summarizing the underlying physics of the table or as a stable causal property in its own right.

Let's begin with the strongest thesis available: the idea that the facts of the social world are generated by the facts about individuals. This is the idea that the components of social entities—actors doing things with various beliefs and expectations about the world—serve to produce all the properties and powers of the social world. The components of the ingot of steel—iron, carbon, other trace elements—*generate* all the properties of the alloy metal; there are no other factors besides the components and their process of composition that affect the alloy's physical properties. This relationship between components and whole also implies the relationship of supervenience between the two levels; there can be no difference at the higher level without some difference at the lower level.

Related but distinct from generativity is the idea that the social world is *reducible* to facts about the actions and intentions of individuals. The idea of reductionism comes down to derivability of the facts or regularities of one level of phenomena from our knowledge of the things of which this level is composed. Suppose we observe that large groups commonly encounter problems of under-provision of public goods. We can perhaps reduce this group-level fact to a set of facts about individuals if we can demonstrate that individuals have a rational incentive to "free ride" when confronted with an indivisible public good. The group-level fact is logically derivable from facts about individuals. This was the thrust of Mancur Olson's analysis of collective action problems (Olson 1965).

In the social sciences, the reductionist impulse amounts to something along these lines: the properties and dynamics of social entities need to be explained by the properties and interactions of the individuals who constitute them. Social facts need to be reducible to a set of individual-level facts and laws. Similar positions arise in psychology ("psychological properties and dynamics need to reduce to facts about the activities and properties of the central nervous system") and biology ("complex biological systems like genes and cells need to reduce to the biochemistry of the interacting systems of molecules that make them up").

The idea of generativity was mentioned above: the idea that the properties of a higher-level thing are generated by the properties of the lower-level things of which it is composed. This idea is sometimes thought to be equivalent to reductionism, but it is not. Let's grant for the moment that the facts about B jointly serve to generate the facts about A. Then A supervenes upon B, by definition. Do these facts imply that A is reducible to B, or that facts of A can be or should be reduced to B? Emphatically not. Reducibility is a feature of the relationship between bodies of knowledge or theories—our knowledge of A and our knowledge of B. To reduce A to B means deriving what we know about B from what we know about A. For example, the laws of planetary motion are derivable from the law of universal gravitation: by working through the mathematics of gravity, it is possible to derive the orbits of the planets around the sun. So, the laws of planetary motion are reducible to the law of universal gravitation.

Generativity is not a feature of theories; instead, it is an ontological feature of the world. Physicalism is such a conception. Physicalism maintains that facts about the physical body, including the nervous system, jointly generate all mental phenomena. Generativity involves the idea that, taking the full reality of the properties and powers of B, the properties of A result. The properties of the entities at level B suffice to generate all the properties of the entities at level A. But there is no assurance that our current knowledge about B permits a mathematical derivation of A. Further, there is no assurance that a "full and complete theory" of B would permit such a derivation—because there is no assurance that such a theory exists at all. And, then, there is the issue of computability: it may be radically in feasible to perform the calculations necessary to derive A from B. And, so, it is clear that reducibility does not follow from generativeness.

Social reductionism is referred to as methodological individualism (MI). MI is a doctrine in the philosophy of the social sciences about the relationship between society and individuals. The idea of MI is one that has appealed to some philosophers and social thinkers for almost as long as there has been systematic thinking about social science. Modern philosophy of social science began in the nineteenth century, and John Stuart Mill's theories of social knowledge contained the assumption of MI (Mill 1988). Max Weber also put forward the doctrine in *The Methodology of the Social Sciences* (Weber 1949). A classic statement was presented by J. W. N. Watkins (Watkins 1968), "Methodological Individualism and Social Tendencies." (Lars Udehn's *Methodological Individualism: Background, History and Meaning* is a very good study of the long history of the debate over this issue (Udehn 2001).)

Reductionism has a bad flavor within much of philosophy, but it is worth dwelling on the concept a bit more fully. Why would the strategy of reduction be appealing within a scientific research tradition at all? Here is one reason: there is obvious explanatory gain that results from showing how the complex properties and functionings of a higher-level entity are the result of the properties and interactions of its lower-level constituents. This kind of demonstration serves to explain the upper-level system's properties in terms of the entities that make it up. This is the rationale for Peter Hedström's metaphor of "dissecting the social" (Hedström 2005). The explanatory strategy illustrated by Thomas Schelling in *Micromotives and Macrobehavior* (Schelling 1978) proceeds in exactly this fashion. Schelling wants to show how a complex social phenomenon (say, residential segregation) can emerge as the result of a set of preferences and beliefs of the independent individuals who make up the relevant population. And, this is also the approach that is taken by researchers who develop agent-based models.

However, the insistence upon reduction is often frustrating to other scientists and philosophers. It often seems to be a way of changing the subject away from our original scientific interest. Consider the field of cognitive psychology. We start out, let's say, with an interest in motion perception, looking at the perceiver as an information-processing system, and the reductionist keeps insisting that we turn our attention to the organization of a set of nerve cells. But we weren't interested in nerve cells; we were interested in the computational systems associated with motion perception. So, reductionism seems to be a demand to change the question driving our research.

Another reason to be frustrated with "methodological reductionism" is the conviction that mid-level entities have stable properties of their own. So, it is not necessary to reduce those properties to their underlying constituents; rather, we can investigate those properties in their own terms, and then make use of this knowledge to explain other things at that level.

Finally, it is often the case that it is simply impossible to reconstruct with any useful precision the micro-level processes that give rise to a given higher-level structure. The mathematical properties of complex systems are crucial on this point: even relatively simple physical systems, governed by deterministic mechanical laws, exhibit behavior that cannot be calculated on the basis of information about the starting conditions of the system. A solar system with a massive star at the center and a handful of relatively low-mass planets produces a regular set of elliptical orbits whose future positions and velocities can be calculated precisely. But a three-body gravitational system creates computational challenges that make it impossible to predict the future state of the system; even small errors of measurement or intruding forces can significantly shift the evolution of the system.

William Wimsatt is a philosopher of biology whose writings about reduction have illuminated the topic significantly (Wimsatt 2006). Wimsatt distinguishes among three varieties of reductionism in the philosophy of science: inter-level reductive explanations, same-level reductive theory succession, and eliminative reduction (2006: 448). He finds that eliminative reduction is a nonstarter; virtually no scientists see value in attempting to eliminate references to the higher-level domain in favor of a lower-level domain. Inter-level reduction is essentially what was described above. And, theory-succession reduction is a mapping from one theory to the next of the ontologies that they depend upon.

What is most useful about Wimsatt's approach is the fact that he succeeds in de-dramatizing this issue. He puts aside the comprehensive and general claims that have sometimes been made on behalf of "methodological reductionism" in the past, and considers specific instances in biology where scientists have found it very useful to investigate the vertical relations that exist between higher-level and lower-level structures. This takes reductionism out of the domain of a general philosophical principle and into that of a particular research heuristic.

Are there good reasons to believe that we ought to restrict social explanations to theories that specify reductive links between social facts and individual-level facts? My judgment is that it is not scientifically useful to do so, for several reasons. First is the point about computational limits: even if the outcome of a riot is "fixed" by the full psychological states of participants *ex ante* and their strategic interactions during the event, it is obviously impossible to gather that knowledge and aggregate it into a full and detailed model of the event. So, deriving a description of the outcome from a huge set of facts about the participants is impossible. Second, it is telling that we need to refer to the strategic interactions of participants in order to model the social event; this means that the social event has a dynamic internal structure that is sensitive to sub-events that occur along the way. (Jones negotiates with Smith more effectively than Brown negotiates with Black. The successful and failed negotiations make a difference in the outcome but are unpredictable and contingent.) Third, the facts at the social level rarely aggregate to simple laws or regularities that might have been derived from lower-level laws and regularities; instead, social outcomes are contingent and varied.

This set of considerations suggests that reductionism is not a valid requirement on social research and explanation. Some social phenomena are amenable to this "vertical" scheme of explanation. But others are not, and there is no compelling reason to exclude non-reductionist theories and explanations of social phenomena.

Supervenience

Let us now turn to another appealing answer that has been offered to the question of the relationship between levels of entities, the theory of supervenience (Kim 2005). The theory of supervenience is appealing in part because it accepts the ontology of levels and dependency across levels, but does not require reductionism. It requires that the real properties of the lower level serve to determine the real properties of the higher level. But it does not presuppose that it is possible or necessary to discover the links between levels, or to derive the higher level from what we know about the lower level.

According to the theory of supervenience, facts at one level of description are fixed or determined by facts at a lower level of description. To say that X supervenes upon Y is to say that there is no difference between states of affairs concerning X for which there is not also a difference in states of affairs concerning Y. This is a less restrictive doctrine than reductionism because it does not require that we provide derivations of the facts of X from facts of Y.

This theory derives largely from the work of philosopher Jaegwon Kim over the past thirty years. (See *Physicalism, or Something Near Enough*

(Kim 2005) for a recent formulation of the theory.) A level of description is said to supervene upon another level just in case there can be no differences of state at the first level without there being a difference of state in the second level. The theory was first applied to mental states and states of neurophysiology: "No differences in mental states without some difference in neurophysiology states." Supervenience theory implies an answer to the question of whether one set of facts "fixes in principle" the second set of facts.

Here is how Julie Zahle puts the point in her contribution to Turner and Risjord's *Philosophy of Anthropology and Sociology* (Turner and Risjord 2006):

> Social entities, their properties, actions, etc. may be said to supervene upon individuals, their actions, and so on, insofar as: (1) there can be no difference at the level of social wholes, their properties, actions, etc., unless there is also a difference at the level of individuals, their properties, actions, and so on; (2) individuals, their actions, etc. fix or determine what kinds of social wholes, properties, etc. are instantiated. (327)

Supervenience does not imply "reducibility in principle," let alone "reducibility in practice" between levels. In order to have reducibility, it is necessary to have a system of statements describing features of the lower level that are sufficient to permit deductive derivation of all of the true statements contained in the higher-level domain. If it is a social fact that "collective action tends to fail when groups are large," then there would need to be set of statements at the level of individual actors that logically entail this statement. Two additional logical features would appear to be required for reduction: a satisfactory set of bridge statements (linking the social term to some construction of individual-level terms; "collective action" to some set of features of individual agents, so there is a mapping of concepts and ontologies between the two domains) and, at least, some statements at the lower level that have the form of general laws or lawlike probabilistic statements. These are very strenuous assumptions.

Does the idea of supervenience help answer the question of the ontological status of social entities? May we say things like "the causal powers of a labor union supervene upon the organized behaviors of the individuals who make it up"? Is it helpful to judge that social entities supervene upon facts about individuals and nothing else? And, does this leave room for the idea of social causation and relative explanatory autonomy? Are we able to acknowledge the dependence of the social world on facts about individuals without abandoning the idea that there is social causation and social science?

Perhaps surprisingly, Kim thinks that the theory will *not* assist us in the last two ways, at least when it comes to psychology:

This view [supervenience] provides the burgeoning science of psychology and cognition with a philosophical rationale as an autonomous science in its own right: it investigates these irreducible psychological properties, functions, and capacities, discovering laws and regularities governing them and generating law-based explanations and predictions. It is a science with its own proper domain untouched by other sciences, especially those at the lower levels, like biology, chemistry, and physics. This seductive picture, however, turns out to be a piece of wishful thinking, when we consider the problem of mental causation—how it is possible, on such a picture, for mentality to have causal powers, powers to influence the course of natural events. (15)

Ned Block addresses this issue in his article "Do Causal Powers Drain Away" (Block 2003). He introduces the idea of "causally efficacious properties" and argues that Kim's arguments against persistent causal properties at the upper level do not in fact succeed.

In my view, the only claims about MI that seem unequivocally plausible today are the ontological requirements—the various formulations of the notion that social things are composed of the actions and thoughts of individuals and nothing else. This position is sometimes referred to as "ontological individualism." In my view, ontological individualism is true of the social world. This implies as well that the supervenience claim and the microfoundations claim are true as well.

But to concede that xs are composed of ys does not entail the need for any kind of reductionism from x to y. And, this extends to the idea of explanatory reduction as well. So, MI does not create valid limits on the structure of social explanations, and meso-level explanations are not excluded.

Further, there is a wholly implausible part of the theory that needs to be jettisoned: the idea that we can carve out the individual as separate from and prior to the social. In classical physics, the analogous claim is supportable. Sodium atoms are homogeneous and interchangeable. But it is not plausible in the human world. Social facts intertwine with the mind and actions of individuals all the way down. So, from the start, it would seem that the program of MI should be formulated in terms of reduction from the big social to the small social, not the nonsocial.

So, it seems as though we can now draw several conclusions about the field of social reductionism and methodological individualism. The ontological thesis is true, but it is compatible with a range of different ideas about within- and cross-level explanation. So, reductionism does not follow. Second, the assumed micro level cannot be a hypothetical pre-social or non-social individual. Finally, there is no reason to associate the plausible core of ontological individualism with one specific theory of action, the rational-intentional theory. We cannot presuppose that microeconomics and rational choice theory are the best theories upon which to base derivations of macro from micro. As pragmatist sociologists now argue emphatically, there are compelling theories of the actor that do not privilege the model of conscious deliberative choice. (These arguments were reviewed in chapter 2.) Ontological individualism does not entail that individuals are egoists or purely self-regarding. It does not entail that individuals are not social. It does not entail that social facts do not have causal consequences—for other social facts and for individual behavior. It is indeed possible to reframe almost all substantive sociological theory in terms that are consistent with the reasonable conditions implied by ontological individualism. Even Durkheim's central theories can be formulated in a way that is compatible with ontological individualism. And, from the other direction, even a theorist with as clear a commitment to MI as Max Weber, is still able to make "macro" or "holistic" claims about the causal importance of factors such as religion or morality.

HOLISM AND EMERGENT SOCIAL PROPERTIES

So far, we have considered a group of approaches to the social sciences that proceed on the basis of ontological individualism. What considerations can be offered in support of some version of ontological holism? Here are a couple of arguments that avoid the accusation of "spooky holism."

First is a very reasonable point deriving from pragmatic objections to reductionism mentioned above. If we know on ontological grounds that the behavior of the whole depends upon the features and behavior of the constituent parts and nothing else—the heart of the theory of supervenience—but also know that it is entirely hopeless to attempt to calculate the one based on facts about the other—then it is justified to consider the whole as if it embodied causal processes at the macro level. So, there is a pragmatic argument available that recommends the autonomy of social facts based on the infeasibility of derivability.

Second is the plausibility of the idea that there are large historical or social forces that are for all intents and purposes beyond the control of any of the individuals whom they influence. The fact that a given population exists as a language community of German speakers or Yoruba speakers has an effect on every child born into that population. The child's neurocognitive system is shaped by this social reality, quite independently from facts about the child's agency or individuality. The grammar of the local language is an autonomous social fact in this context—even though it is also a fact that depends upon its being embodied in the particular brains and behaviors of the countless individuals who constitute this community. This is equally true when we turn to systems of attitudes, norms, or cognitive systems of thinking.

It is obvious but trivial to observe that the ways in which individuals come to learn a language flow through other individuals who already possess the grammar, norms, or folk beliefs—this is the ontological reality captured by the microfoundations thesis. But a point in favor of a modest holism is this: the fact of the commonality of Yoruba grammar can be viewed as if it were an autonomous fact—even though we know it depends on the existence of Yoruba speakers. The key point of the holism thesis here remains: that the social facts of the current grammar are coercive with respect to current Nigerian children in specific communities. And, it is likewise with respect to other aspects of social cognition and norms. This takes us some distance toward Durkheim's central view—the autonomy of social facts.

Now what about social structures? Can some instances of social structures be treated as if they were autonomous with respect to the individuals whom they affect? Consider the lending system that operates in a particular setting. We can specify a collection of rules and practices *X, Y, Z* that regulate the transactions that occur within this system. The individual who wants to borrow from a bank or other financial institution is unavoidably subject to these rules and practices. He or she does not have the option of rewriting the rules in a more rational or fair or socially progressive way; at a given point in time, the rules and practices are fixed independently from the wishes or intentions of the people involved in the institution. Once again, it is trivially true that these rules are embodied in the knowledge, beliefs, and actions of other individuals; but these rules function as if they were autonomous. And, this is true for institutions at the full range of scope, from the local to the global.

The advocate for a modest social holism might maintain two plausible positions: first, that all social facts are embodied in the states of mind and behavior of individuals (consistent with ontological individualism); but second, that some social facts (institutions, social practices, systems of rules) have explanatory autonomy independent from any knowledge we might be able to provide about the particular ways in which these facts are embodied in individuals. The first is an ontological point and the second is a point about explanation.

These points in favor of a modest holism are compatible with other important points about social entities—the points about heterogeneity, plasticity, and opportunistic transformation that have been made in chapters 1 and 3. In other words, we aren't forced to choose between "agent" and "structure"; rather, agents influence structures and structures influence agents.

These arguments suggest two things. First, holism and individualism are not so sharply opposed as perhaps they appear. But second, and more importantly, two styles of social explanation are validated and compatible: the compositional or aggregative model of explanation—explain the outcome as the aggregative consequence of the behavior of large numbers of individuals—and constraining or filtering explanations—the structuring of individual behavior that is created by the workings of social institutions. The first model of explanation corresponds well to the assumptions of methodological individualism, while the second corresponds to the idea that structures and large social factors cause patterns of individual behavior. And, neither has antecedent priority over the other. These two forms of explanation conform to the two struts of Coleman's boat.

Antireductionism: Brian Epstein's Critique

It was argued above that the theory of supervenience is all but trivially true in application to the social world in relation to the level of individual actors. This more or less follows from the key premise of ontological individualism, the idea that the social world is created and constituted solely by the actions and states of minds of large numbers of individuals. Brian Epstein argues against this apparent truism in several places, most notably in "Ontological Individualism Reconsidered" (Epstein 2007; see also Epstein 2015). The core of his argument is the idea that there are other factors influencing social facts besides facts about individuals. Social facts then fail to supervene in the strict sense: they depend on facts other than facts about individuals. There are indeed differences at the level of the social that do not correspond to a difference in the facts at the level of the individual. Here is how Epstein puts the core of his argument:

> My aim in this paper is to challenge this [the idea that individualism is simply the denial of spooky social autonomy]. But ontological individualism is a stronger thesis than this, and on any plausible interpretation, it is false. The reason is not that social properties are determined by something other than physical properties of the world. Instead it is that social properties are often determined by physical ones that cannot plausibly be taken to be individualistic properties of persons. Only if the thesis of ontological individualism is weakened to the point that it is equivalent to physicalism can it be true, but then it fails to be a thesis about the determination of social properties by individualistic ones. (3)

And, here is how Epstein formulates the claim of weakly local supervenience of social properties upon individual properties:

> Social properties weakly locally supervene on individualistic properties if and only if for any possible world w and any entities x and y in w, if x and y are individualistically indiscernible in w, then they are socially indiscernible in w. Two objects are individualistically or socially indiscernible if and only if they are exactly like with respect to every individualistic property or every social property, respectively. (9)

The causal story for supervenience of the social upon the individual perhaps looks like as shown in Figure 4.3a.

The causal story for non-supervenience that Epstein tells looks like as shown in Figure 4.3b.

In this case, supervenience fails because there can be differences in S without any difference in I (because of differences in O).

But maybe the situation is even worse, as emergentists want to hold (Figure 4.3c).

Here, supervenience fails because social facts may be partially "auto-causal"—social outcomes are partially influenced by differences in social facts that do not depend on differences in individual facts and other facts.

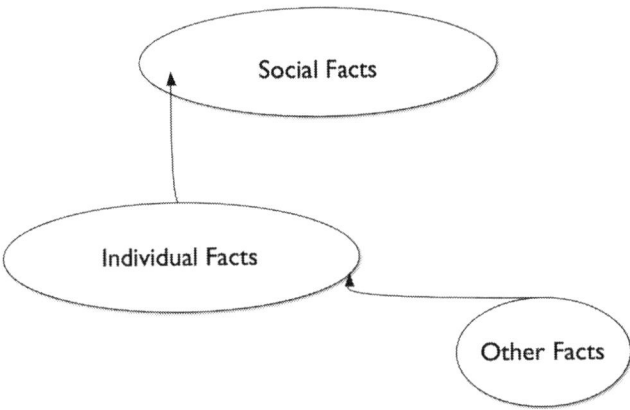

Figure 4.3a   Supervenience of social facts.

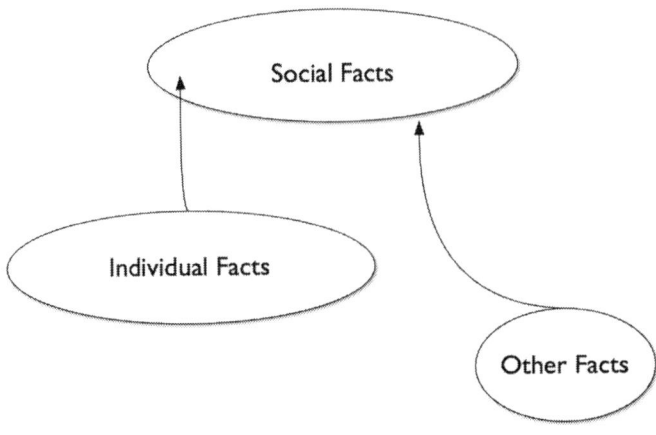

Figure 4.3b   Weak nonsupervenience of social facts.

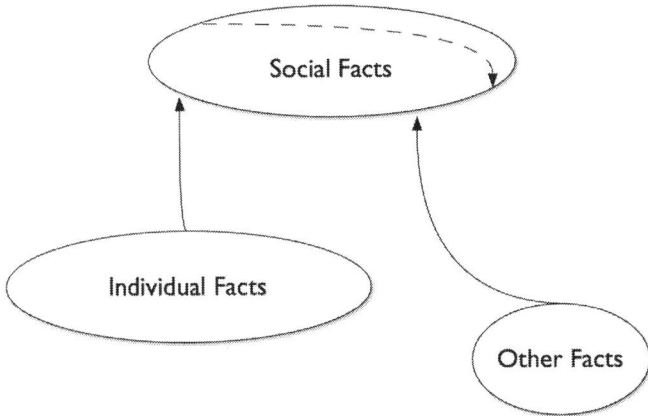

Figure 4.3c   Strong nonsupervenience of social facts.

As a first approximation, Epstein's line of thought is easy to grasp. The outcome of a game of baseball between the New York Yankees and the Boston Red Sox depends *largely* on the actions of the players on the field and in the dugout, but not *entirely and strictly*. There are background facts and circumstances that also influence the outcome but are not present in the motions and thoughts of the players. The rules of baseball are not embodied on the field or in the minds of the players; so, there may be possible worlds in which the same pitches, swings, impacts of bats on balls, catches, etc. occur; and yet, the outcome of the game is different. The Boston pitcher may be subsequently found to be ineligible to play that day, and the Red Sox are held to forfeit the game. The rule in our world holds that "tie goes to the runner," whereas, in alto-world, the tie may go to the defensive team; and this means that the two-run homer in the ninth does not result in two runs, but rather the final out. So, the game does not depend on the actions of the players alone, but on distant and abstract facts about the rules of the game.

So, what are some examples of "other facts" that might be causally relevant to social outcomes? The scenario offered here captures some of the key "extra-individual" facts that Epstein highlights, and that play a key role in the social ontology of John Searle: situating rules and interpretations that give semantic meaning to behaviors. Epstein highlights facts that determine "membership" in meaningful social contexts: being president and being the catcher on the Boston Red Sox. Both Epstein and Searle emphasize that there are a wide range of dispersed facts that must be true in order for Barack Obama to be president and Ryan Hanigan to be catcher. This is not a strictly "individual-level" fact about either man. Epstein quotes Gregorie Currie on this point: "My being Prime Minister . . . is not just a matter of what I think and do; it depends on what others think and do as well. So my social characteristics are clearly not determined by my individual characteristics alone" (Epstein 2007: 11).

So, according to Epstein, local supervenience of the social upon the individual fails. What about global supervenience? He believes that this relation fails as well. And, this is because, for Epstein, "social properties are determined by physical properties that are not plausibly the properties of individuals" (Epstein 2007: 20). These are the "other facts" in the diagrams above. His simplest illustration is this: without cellos there can be no cellists (24). And, without hanging chads, George W. Bush would not have been president. And, later, one can be an environmental criminal because of a set of facts that were both distant and unknown to the individual at the time of a certain action (33).

Epstein's analysis is careful and convincing in its own terms. Given the modal specification of the meaning of supervenience (as offered by Jaegwon Kim and successors), Epstein makes a strong case for believing that the social does not supervene upon the individual in a technical and specifiable sense. However, I am not convinced that very much follows from this finding. For researchers within the general school of thought of "actor-centered sociology," their research strategy is likely to remain one that seeks to sort out the mechanisms through which social outcomes of interest are created as a result of the actions and interactions of individuals. If Epstein's arguments are accepted, it implies that we should not couch that research strategy in terms of the idea of supervenience. But this does not invalidate the strategy, or the broad intuition about the relation between the social and the actions of locally situated actors upon which it rests. These are the intuitions that I try to express through the idea of "methodological localism" above. And, since I also want to argue for the possibility of "relative explanatory autonomy" for facts at the level of the social (e.g., features of an organization), I am not too troubled by the failure of a view of the social and individual that denies strict determination of the former by the latter.

Searle on Status Function

John Searle is another philosopher who believes there are non-reducible social facts. Fundamentally, Searle's interest is in the nature of social ontology (Searle 2010):

> [The philosophy of society is] the study of the nature of human society itself: What is the mode of existence of social entities such as governments, families, cocktail parties, summer vacations, trade unions, baseball games, and passports? (Searle 2010: 5)

Searle's answer is categorical and dogmatic; there is precisely one human intentional activity that underlies all of social reality:

> Humans have the capacity to impose functions on objects and people where the objects and the people cannot perform the functions solely in virtue of their physical structure. [E.g. a five-dollar bill can't be physically transformed into a grande latte.] The performance of the function requires that there be a collectively recognized status that the person or object has, and it is only in virtue of that status that the person or object can perform the function in question. (7)

Status functions are fundamental, according to Searle, because they are the bearers of rights, obligations, and norms—what he refers to as "deontic powers." As a member of the American Philosophical Association, I have a right to attend the annual conference, and this right is embodied in the states of intentionality of other actors who recognize that status and the associated right. "So status functions are the glue that holds society together. They are created by collective intentionality and they function by carrying deontic powers" (9).

Searle thinks that rules, institutions, and collective intentions are the fundamental "atoms" of social phenomena; and—this is the dogmatic part—he thinks that these all depend on one mental action, which he refers to as a Status Function Declaration. He holds that we cannot understand the working of a rule, a socially embodied obligation, or a socially embodied right, without postulating a commonly recognized Status Function Declaration that establishes that practice. And, sure enough—a status function declaration is a form of a speech act.

> All institutional facts, and therefore all status functions, are created by speech acts of a type that in 1975 I baptized as "Declarations" . . . With the important exception of language itself, all of institutional reality, and therefore, in a sense, all of human civilization, is created by speech acts that have the same logical form as Declarations. . . . Institutional facts are without exception constituted by language, but the functioning of language is especially hard to see. (10, 11, 90)

So, speech acts, and the linguistic intentionality that they express, are the foundation of all social phenomena. "All of institutional reality is created by linguistic representation" (13). It all boils down to speech acts.

What this all seems to amount to is three points: (1) Social interactions always involve language, both internally in thought and externally in communication. (2) The idea of a norm is an inherently social idea that needs to be embodied in the beliefs and attitudes of the individuals in the group through linguistically framed mental representations. (3) Norms need to be shared and publicly articulated if they are to be socially real. Searle represents these three common ideas in a more technical vocabulary: individuals have individual and collective intentionality; individuals have deontic commitments; and deontic commitments result from status function declarations—speech acts of a specific kind.

Let's consider each of the points. Is intentionality inherently linguistic? Of course, adult human intentionality usually is—we can always paraphrase a state of consciousness as a linguistic declaration of some sort, and it is common to think of "thought" as internal speech. But is it possible to imagine purposiveness and intentionality in a nonlinguistic species? Can we find examples of nonhuman cooperation that appears to presuppose intentionality without language? The answers to these two questions appear to be affirmative. Examples of primate problem-solving, group hunting, and simple cooperation, in which the behavior of members of a group are oriented to the behavior of others, all appear in the animal behavior literature. (See Michael Tomasello and colleagues in *Why We Cooperate* (Tomasello 2009).)

Is it possible for a group of humans to embody a set of norms of behavior that are not explicitly formulated in language? Again, it seems that we have good empirical and theoretical reasons for thinking that "implicit norms," conventions, and practices exist. Searle himself gives some attention to what we would call "norms by convention," but only to argue that these examples are on their way to full-fledged status function declarations ("pre-institutional examples of the same logical form") (19). But David Lewis's extensive work on the topic in *Convention: A Philosophical Study* (Lewis 1969) (which Searle does not discuss) gives substantial support for the idea that conventions can emerge within a human group without formal linguistic articulation, and they can persist as a basis for organizing group behavior without requiring "codification" through a speech act. Here is a simple example:

> In my hometown of Oberlin, Ohio, until recently all local telephone calls were cut off without warning after three minutes. Soon after the practice had begun, a convention grew up among Oberlin residents that when a call was cut off the original caller would call back while the called party waited. Residents usually conformed to this regularity in the expectation of conformity by the other party to the call. In this way calls were easily restored, to the advantage of all concerned. New residents were told about the convention [deontic speech act!] or learned it through experience [no deontic speech act required!]. It persisted for a decade or so until the cutoff was abolished. (Lewis 1969: 43)

So, according to Lewis, coordination through tacit or implicit convention is a common feature of social life, and it does not require a deontic speech act for its effectiveness. (In fact, Lewis argues that the arrow points the other direction: language presupposes conventions rather than being a necessary condition to the possibility of a convention.) Lewis's analysis is responsive to condition (3) above as well. Lewis has demonstrated how a practice can become "common knowledge" and effective in regulating coordinative and cooperative behavior, without ever having been expressed through a deontic declaration.

So, it seems that Searle's insistence on the inescapable role of language and performative speech acts goes beyond what is justified by the facts. The social is not reducible to a set of logical characteristics of language. That said, it is of course true that human social life—coordination, planning, strategizing, conspiring, cooperating, and competing—is enormously dependent on our species' ability to use language to express our thoughts and intentions. But we don't gain very much by paraphrasing social action in the language of speech acts; the real challenge for the social scientist is to explain social outcomes, not to redefine them.

Most fundamentally, we would hope that the philosophy of society or the philosophy of social science will help to formulate better theories and better research questions in the social sciences. The hard part of the social sciences is not arriving at a logical analysis of how institutions and norms can be defined in terms of something else; it is rather the challenge of sorting out real human behavior within a set of institutions and explaining outcomes on that basis. But because of its single-minded focus on a single logical hypothesis, *Making the Social World* doesn't really do that. It is a formal treatment of the supposed relationship between institutions and speech acts that unfortunately does not provide substantive insight into the workings of real social institutions or human behavior.

Social Facts

One of the more convincing arguments for the existence of social facts that lie above the level of individual actors is the social reality of rules and ascriptive identities. Bob and Alice are married by Reverend Green at 7 pm, July 1, 2015. The social fact that Bob and Alice are now married is not simply a concatenation of facts about their previous motions, beliefs, and utterances. Rather, it depends also on several trans-individual circumstances: first, that their behaviors and performances conform to a set of legal rules governing marriage (e.g. that neither was married at the time of their marriage to each other, or that they had secured a valid marriage license from the county clerk); and, second, that various actors in the event possess a legal identity and qualification that transcend the psychological and observational properties they possess. (Reverend Green is in fact a legally qualified agent of a denomination that gives him the legal authority to perform the act of marriage between two qualified adults.) If Bob has permanently forgotten his earlier marriage in a moment of intoxication to Francine, or if Reverend Green is an imposter, then the correct performance of each of the actions of the ceremony nonetheless fails to secure the legal act of "marriage." Bob and Alice are not married if these prior conditions are not satisfied. So, the social fact that Bob and Alice are married does not depend exclusively on their performance of a specific set of actions and utterances.

Is this kind of example a compelling refutation of the thesis of ontological individualism (as Brian Epstein believes it is)? John Searle thinks that facts like these are fundamentally important in the social world; he refers to them as "status functions." And, Epstein's central examples of supra-individual social facts have to do with membership and ascriptive status. However, several considerations suggest to me that the logical status of rules and ascriptions does not have a lot of importance for our understanding of the ontology of the social world.

First, ascriptive properties are ontologically peculiar. They are dependent upon presuppositions and implicatures that cannot be fully validated in the present. Consider the contrast between these two statements about Song Taizu, founder of the Song Dynasty: "Song was a military and political mastermind" and "Song was legitimate emperor of China." The former statement is a factual statement about Song's embodied characteristics and talents. The latter is a complex historical statement with debatable presuppositions. The truth of the statement turns on our interpretation of the legal status of the seven-year-old "Emperor" whom he replaced. It is an historical fact that Song ruled long and effectively as chief executive; it is a legal abstraction to assert that he was "legitimate emperor."

Second, it is clear that systems of rules have microfoundations if they are causally influential. There are individuals and concrete institutions that convey and interpret the rules; there are prosecutors who take offenders to task; there are libraries of legal codes and supporting interpretations that constitute the ultimate standard of adjudication when rules and behavior come into conflict. And, individuals have (imperfect) grasp of the systems of rules within which they live and act—including the rule that specifies that ignorance is no excuse for breach of law. So, it is in fact feasible to sketch out the way that a system of law or a set of normative rules acquires social reality and becomes capable of affecting behavior.

Most fundamentally, I would like to argue that our interest is not in social facts *simpliciter*, but in facts that have causal and behavioral consequences. We want to know how social agglomerates behave, and in order to explain these kinds of facts, we need to know how the actors who make them up think, deliberate, and act. Whether Alice and Bob are *really* married is irrelevant to their behavior and that of the individuals who surround them. Instead, what matters is how they and others represent themselves. So, the behaviorally relevant question is this: do Alice, Bob, Reverend Green, and the others with whom they interact believe that they are married? So, the behaviorally relevant content of "*x* is married to *y*" is restricted to the beliefs and attitudes of the individuals involved—not the legalistic question of whether their marriage satisfied current marriage laws.

To be sure, if a reasonable doubt is raised about the legal validity of their marriage, then their beliefs (and those of others) will change. Assuming they understand marriage in the same way as we do—"two rationally competent individuals have undertaken legally specified commitments to each other, through a procedurally qualified enactment"—then doubts about the presuppositions will lead them to recalculate their current beliefs and status as well. They will now behave differently than they would have behaved absent the reasonable doubts. But what is causally active here is not the fact that they were not legally married after all; it is their knowledge that they were not legally married.

So, is the fact that Bob and Alice are *really* married a social fact? Or, is it sufficient to refer to the fact that they and their neighbors and family *believe* that they are married in order to explain their behavior? In other words, is it the logical fact or the epistemic fact that does the causal work? I think the latter is the case and that the purely ascriptive and procedural fact is not itself causally powerful. So, we might turn the tables on Epstein and Searle, and consider the idea that *only* those social properties that have appropriate foundations at the level of socially situated individuals should be counted as real social properties.

EMERGENCE

Now let's consider what appears to be a stronger version of holism, the theory of emergence. One view that has been taken about the causal properties of social structures is that they are *emergent*: they are properties that appear only at a certain level of complexity and do not pertain to the items of which the social structure is composed.

An important current source of thinking about emergence is the theory of critical realism. Roy Bhaskar holds that social entities are emergent from facts at the level of individuals. "Emergence is an irreducible feature of our world, that is, it has an irreducibly ontological character" (Bhaskar 1975: 103). However, this does not mean for Bhaskar that higher-level social things are not constituted by the properties of lower-level things (including individuals). Instead, he argues for the causal autonomy of the higher-level entities.

I have argued that complex objects are real (and that the complexity of objects is real); and that the concept of their agency is irreducible. Complex objects are real because they are causal agents capable of acting back on the materials out of which they are formed. Thus the behaviour of e.g. animate things is not determined by physical laws alone. (1975: 103)

This is a complicated view, but what it appears to amount to is what I will describe below as "relative explanatory autonomy" for the level of social entities. In other words, Bhaskar seems to want to embrace two ideas: social entities are "fixed" by lower-level facts and they exercise autonomous causal powers that can be independently investigated by social scientists.

This interpretation is not completely consistent with other statements that Bhaskar makes, however; for example, he writes:

From the normic and non-empirical nature of laws and their consistency with situations of dual control I conclude that the world is a world of agents incompletely described. Laws neither undifferentially describe nor uniquely govern the phenomena of our world. And this is accounted for by the fact that it is an incompletely described world of agents which are constituted at different levels of complexity and organization. (1975: 103)

He then goes on to distinguish three kinds of reducibility. In short, Bhaskar's view of emergence is not completely clear in *A Realist Theory of Science*.

Tuukka Kaidesoja takes an important step forward on this topic in *Naturalizing Critical Realist Social Ontology* (Kaidesoja 2013a) by arguing that Bhaskar intertwines three different kinds of emergence without clearly distinguishing them: compositional, transcendentally realist, and global level.

- *Compositional emergence*: A particular complex whole sometimes has properties that are not properties of any of its parts and not merely "aggregative" effects of the ensemble of parts (179–180).
- *Transcendentally realist emergence*: Abstract social structures, as distinct from social particulars, have properties that cannot be derived from the activities of individuals. "Transcendentally real emergent powers of social structures differ from the causal powers of concrete social systems composed of interacting persons" (182).
- *Global-level emergence*: Levels of reality (e.g. society, mind, matter) have emergent properties not derivable from the properties of lower levels of reality. "Each emergent level has its own synchronically emergent properties which are autonomous with respect to those of other levels" (186).

The three sets of ideas are successively more demanding, and Kaidesoja finds that they are inconsistent with each other. Moreover, there is a crucial complication: within the compositional version (but not within the other two versions) Bhaskar allows that the emergent factor is amenable to "micro-reductive explanation." This is essentially the position described above as "weak emergence," and it is advocated by several other theorists to be discussed shortly. It is a reasonable position. The other two versions, by contrast, are explicitly *not* compatible with micro-reductive explanation, and do not appear reasonable.

In fact, Kaidesoja finds that there are insolvable problems with the "transcendentally realist" and "global-level" versions of the theory of emergence, and he concludes that they are unsupportable. Kaidesoja therefore focuses his attention on the compositional version as the sole version of emergence that can be coherently asserted within critical realism.

R. Keith Sawyer, also a critical realist, supports this reading of Bhaskar. He believes that Bhaskar's serious commitment is to Kaidesoja's first version, the "compositional" version of emergence:

> Bhaskar implicitly accepted supervenience as an account of the relation between higher- and lower-level properties. He held that there is only one substance in the universe; synchronic emergent powers materialism "does not require the postulation of any substance other than Matter as the bearer of the emergent powers" (Bhaskar 1982: 282). He accepted the supervenience claim that societies "are unilaterally, existentially dependent on" the material world such that "any social change entails a natural change" (p. 281)—one of the implications of supervenience. (Sawyer 2005: 81)

David Elder-Vass treats the theory of emergence from a critical realist perspective in *The Causal Power of Social Structures: Emergence, Structure and Agency* (Elder-Vass 2010). He defines a property of a compound entity or structure as emergent when the property applies only to the structure itself and not to any of its components.

> A thing . . . can have properties or capabilities that are not possessed by its parts. Such properties are called emergent properties. (Elder-Vass 2010: 4)
>
> An emergent property is one that is not possessed by any of the parts individually and that would not be possessed by the full set of parts in the absence of a structuring set of relations between them. (17)

This definition of emergence is entirely compatible with the idea that the emergent property is derivable from knowledge about the component parts—or in other words, the weak emergence position. By Elder-Vass's criterion, most properties are emergent—for example, the sweetness of sugar, the flammability of woven cotton, and the hardness of bronze. It is obvious and unexceptional that there are "emergent" properties in this limited sense.

(Elder-Vass discusses this interpretation under the topic of "eliminative reductionism"; 2010: 24, 54.)

Now consider a view of emergence offered by Herbert Simon in his conception of a complex system in a 1962 article "The Architecture of Complexity" (Simon 1962). Here is how Simon defines the relevant notion of complexity:

> Roughly, by a complex system I mean one made up of a large number of parts that interact in a nonsimple way. In such systems, the whole is more than the sum of the parts, not in an ultimate, metaphysical sense, but in the important pragmatic sense that, given the properties of the parts and the laws of their interaction, it is not a trivial matter to infer the properties of the whole. In the face of complexity, an in-principle reductionist may be at the same time a pragmatic holist. (468)

Here, Simon favors a view that does not assert ontological independence of system characteristics from individual characteristics, but does assert pragmatic and explanatory independence. In fact, his position seems equivalent to the supervenience thesis: social facts supervene upon facts about individuals. But the implication for research is plain: it is useless to pursue a reductionist strategy for understanding system-level properties of complex systems. Simon undertakes to split the difference by referring to "reductionism in principle," or what I called above "weak emergence":

> reductionism in principle even though it is not easy (often not even computationally feasible) to infer rigorously the properties of the whole from knowledge of the properties of the parts. In this pragmatic way, we can build nearly independent theories for each successive level of complexity, but at the same time, build bridging theories that show how each higher level can be accounted for in terms of the elements and relations of the next level down. (Simon 1996 [1969]: 172)

This view emphasizes the computational and epistemic limits that sometimes preclude generating the phenomena in question—for example, the problems raised by nonlinear causal relations and causal interdependence. Many observers have noted that the behavior of tightly linked causal systems may be impossible to predict, even when we are confident that the system outcomes are the result of "nothing but" the interactions of the units and subsystems.

Non-reducible Emergence

The theory of weak emergence is a plausible one. Some holists have something stronger in mind, however: the idea that the properties of the whole cannot be derived from knowledge of the properties of the parts and their relations to each other. What gives the idea of emergence real bite—but also makes it fundamentally mysterious—is the additional idea that the property cannot be derived from facts about the components and their arrangements within the structure in question. By this criterion, none of the properties just mentioned are emergent, because their characteristics can in principle be derived from what we know about their components in interaction with each other.

This is the concept of emergence that is associated with holism and antireductionism, which we may refer to as strong emergence. Essentially it requires us to do our scientific work entirely at the level of the structure itself—discover system-level properties and powers and turn our backs on the impulse to explain through analysis.

Poe Wan highlights the important differences between these two schools of thought about emergence in his discussion of Niklas Luhmann and Mario Bunge (Wan 2011). Luhmann's conception (Luhmann, Baecker, and Gilgen 2013) is extravagantly holistic, endorsing strong emergence, whereas Bunge's conception is consistent with the idea that emergent characteristics are none-theless fixed by properties of the constituents. Wan argues that Luhmann has an "epistemological" understanding of emergence—the status of a property as emergent is a feature of its derivability or explicability on the basis of lower-level facts. Bunge's approach, on the other hand, is ontological: even if we can fully explain the higher-level phenomenon in terms of the proper-ties of the lower level, the property itself is still emergent. So, for Bunge, "emergence" is a fact about being, not about knowledge. Wan also notes that Luhmann wants to replace the "part-whole" distinction with the "environ-ment-system" distinction—which Wan believes is insupportable (180).

Here is Bunge's definition of emergence:

> To say that P is an emergent property of systems of kind K is short for "P is a global (or collective or non-distributive) property of a system of kind K, none of whose components or precursors possesses P." (Bunge 2003: 15)

Bunge's position here is exactly the same as the conception offered by Elder-Vass above. It defines emergence as novelty at the higher level—whether or not that novelty can be explained by facts about the constituents. Bunge's conception is consistent with methodological individualism, in my reading, whereas Luhmann's is not. Wan provides an excellent review of the history of thinking about this concept, and his assessment is persuasive. In particu-lar, his endorsement of Bunge's position of "rational emergentism" seems to get the balance exactly right: social properties are in some sense fixed by the properties of the constituents; they are nonetheless distinct from those underlying properties; and good scientific theories are justified in referring to these emergent properties without the need of reducing them or replacing them with properties at the lower level.

It is a fair question to ask whether the concept of emergence is less important than it initially appears to be. Part of the interest in emergence seems to derive from the impulse by sociologists and philosophers to try to show that there is a legitimate level of the world that is "social," and to reject the more extreme versions of reductionism.

Social scientists have a few concrete and important interests in the issue of emergence of social entities and properties. One is a concern for the autonomy of the social science disciplines. Is there a domain of the social that warrants scientific study? Or, can we make do with really good microeconomic theories, agent-based modeling techniques, and a dollop of social psychology and do without developed theories of the causal powers of social entities?

Another concern is apparently related, but on the ontology side of the story: are there social entities that can be studied for their empirical and causal characteristics independently from the individual activities that make them up? Do social entities really exist? Or, are there compelling reasons to conclude that social entities are too fluid and plastic to admit of possessing stable empirical properties? This concern is what drives Bhaskar's insistence on the emergent character of social entities and structures.

It seems that these concerns can be fully satisfied without appealing to a strong conception of emergence. We have perfectly good concepts that individuate entities at a social level, and we have fairly ordinary but compelling reasons for believing that these sorts of things are causally active in the world. But perhaps we can frame some simple ideas about the social world that will allow us to be more relaxed about whether these properties can be reduced to or explained by facts about actors (methodological individualism), or derived from facts about actors, or are instead strongly independent from the level of actors upon which they rest.

RELATIVE EXPLANATORY AUTONOMY

Consider the following background propositions about the social world. These are not trivial assumptions, but it would appear that a broad range of social thinkers would accept them, from enlightened analytical sociologists to many critical realists.

1. Social phenomena are constituted by the actions and thoughts of situated social actors. ("No pure social stuff, no ineffable special sauce.")
2. Actors are causally influenced by a variety of social structures and entities. ("Actors are socially constituted and socially situated.")

3. Ensembles have properties that derive from the interactions of the composing entities (actors). ("System properties derive from complex and dynamic relations and structures among constituents.")
4. There are social properties that are not the simple aggregation of the properties of the actors. ("System properties are not simply the sum of constituent properties.")
5. Ensembles sometimes have system-level properties that exert causal powers with regard to their own constituents. ("Systems exert downward causation on their constituents.")
6. The computational challenges involved in modeling large complex systems are often overwhelming. ("The properties and behavior of complex systems are sometimes incalculable based simply on information about constituents and their arrangements.")

These assumptions would serve to establish quite a bit of autonomy for social science investigation and explanation, without requiring us to debate whether social entities are nonetheless emergent. And, the ontologically cautious among us may be more comfortable with these limited and reasonably clear assumptions than they are with an open-ended concept of emergent phenomena and properties. Assumption 6 suggests that it is not feasible (and likely will never be) to deduce social patterns from individual-level facts. Assumptions 3 and 4 establish that social properties are "autonomous" from individual-level facts. Assumptions 1 and 2 establish the ontological foundation of social entities—the socially constituted individuals whose thoughts and actions constitute them. And, assumption 5 establishes that the causal powers of social entities are in fact important and autonomous from facts about individuals, in the very important respect that higher-level properties play a causal role in the constitution of lower-level entities (individuals). This assumption is reflected in assumption 2 as well.

So, perhaps, we might conclude that not much turns on whether social properties and powers are strongly emergent or not. Instead, we might be better advised to try to capture the issues in this area in different terms. The alternative that I favor is the idea of relative explanatory autonomy. This is the idea that mid-level system properties are often sufficiently stable that we can pursue causal explanations at that level, without providing derivations of those explanations from some more fundamental level. The six core assumptions mentioned above serve to capture the heart of this approach.

The explanatory challenge is very clear: if we want to explain meso-level outcomes on the basis of reference to emergent system characteristics, we can do so. But we need to have good replicable knowledge of the causal properties of the emergent features in order to develop explanations of other kinds of outcomes based on the workings of the system characteristics. I would also add that we need to have confidence that the hypothesized system-level characteristics do in fact possess microfoundations at the level of the individual and social actions that underlie them; or, in other words, we need to have reason for confidence that the emergent properties our explanations hypothesize do in fact conform to the supervenient relation.

I have expressed skepticism about the theory of strong emergence. But my view also incorporates the premise of antireductionism. These two views are compatible if we assume a meta-theory of *relative explanatory autonomy* for social explanations. The key insight here is that there are good epistemic and pragmatic reasons to countenance explanations at a meso level of organization, without needing to reduce these explanations to the level of individual actors. Here is a statement of the idea of relative explanatory autonomy, provided by a distinguished philosopher of science, Lawrence Sklar, with respect to areas of the physical sciences:

> Everybody agrees that there are a multitude of scientific theories that are conceptually and explanatorily autonomous with respect to the fundamental concepts and fundamental explanations of foundational physical theories. Conceptual autonomy means that there is no plausible way to define the concepts of the autonomous theories in terms of the concepts that we use in our foundational physics. This is so even if we allow a rather liberal notion of "definition" so that concepts defined as limit cases of the applicability of the concepts of foundational physics are still considered definable. Explanatory autonomy means that there is no way of deriving the explanatory general principles, the laws, of the autonomous theory from the laws of foundational physics. Once again this is agreed to be the case even if we use a liberal notion of "derivability" for the laws so that derivations that invoke limiting procedures are still counted as derivations. (Sklar 2006: 1)

The idea of relative explanatory autonomy has been invoked by cognitive scientists against the reductionist claims of neuroscientists. Of course, cognitive mechanisms must be grounded in neurophysiological processes. But this doesn't entail that cognitive theories need to be reduced to neurophysiological statements. Sacha Bem reviews these arguments in "The Explanatory Autonomy of Psychology: Why a Mind Is Not a Brain" (Bem 2011). Michael Strevens summarizes some of these issues in "Explanatory Autonomy and Explanatory Irreducibility" (Strevens 2011). And, Geoffrey Hellman addresses the issues of reductionism and emergence in the special sciences in "Reductionism, Determination, Explanation" (Hellman 2011).

These arguments are directly relevant to the social sciences, subject to several important caveats. First is the requirement of microfoundations: we need always to be able to plausibly connect the social constructs we hypothesize to the actions and states of minds of situated actors. And, second is the requirement of ontological and causal stability: if we want to explain a meso-level phenomenon on the basis of the causal properties of other meso-level structures, we need to have confidence that the latter properties are reasonably stable over different instantiations. For example, if we believe that a certain organizational structure for tax collection is prone to corruption of the ground-level tax agents and wants to use that feature as a cause of something else, we need to have empirical evidence supporting the assertion of the corruption tendencies of this organizational form.

Explanatory autonomy is consistent with our principle requiring micro-foundations at a lower ontological level. Here, we have the sanction of the theory of supervenience to allow us to say that composition and explanation can be separated. We can settle on a level of meso- or macro explanation without dropping down to the level of the actor. We need to be confident there are microfoundations, and the meso properties need to be causally robust. But if this is satisfied, we don't need to extend the explanation down to the actors.

Once we have reason to accept something like the idea of relative explanatory autonomy in the social sciences, we also have a strong basis for rejecting the exclusive validity of one particular approach to social explanation, the reductionist approach associated with MI and Coleman's boat. Rather, social scientists can legitimately aggregate explanations that call upon meso-level causal linkages without needing to reduce these to derivations from facts about individuals. And, this implies the legitimacy of a fairly broad conception of methodological pluralism in the social science, constrained always by the requirement of the in-principle availability of microfoundations.

What seems clear can be summarized in just a few points:

- Social entities and facts are determined and constituted by facts about individuals, their beliefs, their relations, and their actions. So, social entities and facts do in fact supervene upon facts about individuals.
- Social entities do have causal properties that can be discovered without needing to eliminate them in terms of properties of individuals.
- There is a legitimate and defensible level of explanation at which social scientists can hypothesize social properties and causal capacities; so, there is a place for a "relatively autonomous" social science. We are not forced to be reductionist.

My position, then, is that sociology is a special science in Fodor's sense and that sociologists both can and do treat their domain as relatively autonomous.

To be clear, I too believe that there is a burden of proof that must be met in asserting a causal power or disposition for a social entity—something like "the entity demonstrates an empirical regularity in behaving in such and such a way" or "we have good theoretical reasons for believing that X social arrangements will have *Y* effects." And, some macro concepts are likely cast at too high a level to admit of such regularities. That is why I favor "meso" social entities as the bearers of social powers. As new institutionalists demonstrate all the time, one property regime elicits very different collective behavior from its highly similar cousin. And, this gives the relevant causal stability criterion. Good examples include Robert Ellickson's new-institutionalist treatment of Shasta County and liability norms (1991) and Charles Perrow's treatment of the operating characteristics of technology organizations (1999). In each case, the microfoundations are easy to provide. What is more challenging is to show how these social causal properties interact in cases to create outcomes we want to explain.

CLOSING

The point here is a simple one for philosophers of social science: we should not let our debates about emergence, meso-level causation, and structural causal powers lead us to forget some of the fundamental and obvious facts about the social world. There is room for meso-level social causes within this story. But our thinking about meso-level causes and social structures needs always to be grounded in a concrete understanding of how social interaction happens at the local and individual levels. I have tried to formulate a description of this set of realities in terms of the idea of *methodological localism*. Margaret Archer's theory of morphogenesis points in a similar direction, as discussed in chapter 7. Of all the metaphors we sometimes use for describing the social world, E. P. Thompson's idea of the "making" of the English working class seems especially apt (Thompson 1966). MI is not a valid basis for the social science. But a related but less strident imperative is crucial: pay attention to the social actors who constitute the social world—they are all we have in the social world.

Chapter 5

Generativity and Complexity

Many of the topics considered in the earlier chapters have to do with the relation between macro and micro, and social and individual. These topics are potentially relevant to a very lively body of work emerging within the interdisciplinary fields of complex systems, computational mathematics, and simulation studies. This emerging synergy between advanced computational mathematics and the social sciences is possible because of the way that social phenomena emerge from the actions and thoughts of individual actors in relationship to each other. This is what allows us to join simulation models to methodology and explanation. Essentially, we can think of the upward strut of Coleman's boat (Figure 4.2)—the part of the story that has to do with the "aggregation dynamics" of a set of actors—and can try to create models that can serve to simulate the effects of these actions and interactions. A well-known example is Thomas Schelling's simulation of residential segregation (Schelling 1971). This chapter will consider some of the philosophical and methodological issues that arise from this intersection.

As we have seen at many points already, apparently simple assumptions about the social world give rise to very different ideas about ontology and methodology. This is true for the current chapter as well. One group of scientists examines the tools of agent-based simulation and conclude that it should be possible to generate all important social phenomena making use of these tools. These are the advocates of "generativity." Another group of scientists are struck by the unpredictability of complex systems and observe that complex systems have novel characteristics not found among the units. Complex systems possess features like "tight linkage," "nonlinearity," path dependence, and multiple systems of feedback that lead to dynamics that are difficult or impossible to predict, and leading complexity theorists argue that complex systems have "emergent" properties. These scientists are grouped under the umbrella of "complex adaptive systems," and they are agnostic about the ability of formal models to reproduce the workings of real social ensembles.

There are important differences as well as similarities across the field of simulation and complexity studies. For example, Joshua Epstein and Scott Page both make use of the methods of agent-based modeling (ABM), but they disagree about the idea of emergence. Page believes that complex adaptive systems give rise to properties that are emergent and qualitatively different from individual-level properties, whereas Epstein doesn't think the idea of emergence makes a lot of sense. Rather, Epstein's view depends on the idea that we can reproduce (generate) the macro phenomena based on a model involving the agents and their interactions. Macro phenomena are generated by the interactions of the units, whereas for Page and Miller, macro phenomena in some systems have properties that cannot be easily derived from the activities of the units.

We will note that there is a wide gap between "generativity in principle" and "reproduction of a complex social effect through computational simulation." We may call these two ideas "ontological generativity" and "computational generativity." The ontological fact that "states of units at level L_n suffice to generate the properties of entities at level L_{n+1}" does not imply that it is possible to design a simulation or model that derives the properties of the latter from the former—for the simple reason that simulations by their nature require abstraction from the full detail of the properties of the entities represented in the simulation.

GENERATIVITY

Chapter 4 considered several philosophical views of the relationships between individual-level and social-level dynamics. Overall, arguments there supported the thesis of "ontological individualism"—the view that the properties of individuals (including social characteristics and dispositions) fix the properties of higher-level social entities. This view can be described as the thesis of ontological generativity. This philosophical perspective on the social world gives encouragement to a simulation methodology that proceeds by attributing characteristics to base-level units and their action rules and derives population-level patterns of behavior. This approach is referred to as *agent-based modeling*. This approach attempts to model social outcomes using agent-based simulations. Here, the idea is that various features of the social world can be *generated* through formal simulation models. The simulation model is intended to show how the behavior of a set of agents aggregates to the social outcome in question. Joshua Epstein's three-volume work on agent-based models is a fundamental textbook for the field (Epstein 2006, 2013; Epstein and Axtell 1996). Here is how Epstein defines generativity in *Generative Social Science* (Epstein 2006):

> Agent-based models provide computational demonstrations that a given microspecification is in fact sufficient to generate a macrostructure of interest. . . . Rather, the generativist wants an account of the configuration's attainment by a decentralized system of heterogeneous autonomous agents. Thus, the motto of generative social science, if you will, is: If you didn't grow it, you didn't explain its emergence. (2006: 8)

Generativity is directly incompatible with the idea of strong emergence, and in fact Epstein takes pains to cast doubt on that idea.

> I have always been uncomfortable with the vagueness—and occasional mysticism—surrounding this word [emergence] and, accordingly, tried to define it quite narrowly. . . . There, we defined "emergent phenomena" to be simply "stable macroscopic patterns arising from local interaction of agents." (31)

It is very important to note here that these two ideas of "generativity" need to be clearly distinguished. The first is the idea introduced in chapter 4. This is an ontological theory of the ways in which more fundamental entities give rise to the properties of the more complex entities in which they are composed. It is a concept on the same level as the idea of supervenience. The second meaning is the computational science idea about models and simulations. A simulation of a complex system outcome O succeeds in generating the outcome if it embodies assumptions about the lower-level units and the rules of interaction they obey and demonstrates that a version of O is the result of a large number of iterations of the model. Ontological generativity does not entail computational generativity, and a volume of successes for computational generativity (empirically satisfactory simulations of important social effects) does not entail ontological generativity.

ABM Methodology

A particularly interesting avenue of approach to social analysis is agent-based simulation. Here, the basic idea is that we want to explain how a certain kind of social process unfolds. We can take our lead from the general insight that social processes depend on *microfoundations* at the level of socially situated individuals. Social outcomes are the aggregate result of intentional, strategic interactions among large numbers of agents. And, we can attempt to implement a computer simulation that represents the decision-making processes and the structural constraints that characterize a large number of interacting agents.

In brief, ABM is a collection of aggregative techniques aimed at working out the aggregate consequences of the hypothetical choices of a number of individuals interacting in a series of social environments. ABM models generally represent the actors' motivations and decision rules very abstractly— sometimes as economic actors, sometimes as local optimizers, sometimes as heuristically driven decision makers. An ABM model may postulate several groups of actors whose decision rules are different—predators and prey, landlords and tenants, and bandits and generals. The goal is to embody a set of behavioral assumptions at the actor level and then to aggregate the results of the actions and interactions of these actors at a macro-level. Joshua Epstein highlights four common characteristics of the ABM approach: heterogeneity of agents, autonomy of agents, spatial location of events, local interactions, and bounded rationality (Epstein 2006).

Thomas Schelling's *Micromotives and Macrobehavior* gives a clear exposition to the logic of this approach (Schelling 1978). Schelling demonstrates in a large number of convincing cases, how we can explain large and complex social outcomes as the aggregate consequence of behavior by purposive agents pursuing their goals within constraints. He offers a simple model of residential segregation, for example, by modeling the consequences of assuming that blue residents prefer neighborhoods that are at least 50% blue, and red residents prefer neighborhoods that are at least 25% red (Schelling 1971). The consequence is that a randomly distributed residential pattern becomes highly segregated in an extended series of iterations of individual moves based on their specified preferences about neighborhood composition.

It is possible to model various kinds of social situations by attributing a range of preferences and action rules across a hypothetical set of agents, and then run their interactions forward over a period of time. By running the simulation multiple times, it is possible to investigate whether there are patterned outcomes that recur across numerous timelines—or, sometimes, whether there are multiple equilibria that can result, depending on more or less random events early in the simulation.

Robert Axelrod's repeated prisoners' dilemma tournaments represent another influential example of agent-based simulations (Axelrod 1984). Axelrod demonstrates that reciprocity, or tit for tat, is the winning strategy for a population of agents who are engaged in a continuing series of prisoners' dilemma games with each other. The most ambitious examples of this kind of modeling (and predicting and explaining) are to be found in the Santa Fe Institute's research paradigm involving ABM and the modeling of complex systems.

This approach to social analysis is profoundly different from the "subsumption under theoretical principles" approach, the covering law model of explanation. It does not work on the assumption that there are laws or governing regularities pertaining to the social outcomes or complex systems at all. Instead, it attempts to generate descriptions of the outcomes as the aggregate result of the purposive and interactive actions of the many individuals who make up the social interaction over time. It is analogous to the simulation of swarms of insects, birds, or fish, in which we attribute very basic "navigational" rules to the individual organisms, and then run forward the behavior of the group as the compound of the interactive decisions made by the individuals.

How would this model of the explanation of group behavior be applied to real problems of social explanation? Agent-based models have been used extensively within the field of economic geography (Heppenstall et al. 2011). The contribution by Crooks and Heppenstall in this volume provides an especially good introduction to the approach ("Introduction to Agent-Based Modelling"). Crook and Heppenstall describe the distinguishing features of the approach in these terms:

> To understand geographical problems such as sprawl, congestion and segregation, researchers have begun to focus on bottom-up approaches to simulating human systems, specifically researching the reasoning on which individual decisions are made. One such approach is agent-based modelling (ABM) which allows one to simulate the individual actions of diverse agents, and to measure the resulting system behaviour and outcomes over time. The distinction between these new approaches and the more aggregate, static conceptions and representations that they seek to complement, if not replace, is that they facilitate the exploration of system processes at the level of their constituent elements. (Heppenstall et al. 2011: 86)

The goals of this description of a simulation of urban-suburban residential distribution over time have a lot in common with the nineteenth-century von Thunen's *Isolated State* analysis of a city's reach into the farm land surrounding it (Thunen 1826). What ABM adds to the analysis is the ability to use plentiful computational power to run models forward that include thousands of hypothetical agents; and to do this repeatedly so that it is possible to observe whether there are groups of patterns that result in different iterations. The results are then the aggregate consequence of the assumptions we make about large numbers of social agents—rather than being the expression of some set of general laws about "urbanization."

Federico Bianchi and Flaminio Squazzoni provide a very useful survey of the development and uses of agent-based models in the social sciences over the past twenty-five years (Bianchi and Squazzoni 2015). Here is their general definition of an ABM:

Agent-based models (ABMs) are computer simulations of social interaction between heterogeneous agents (e.g., individuals, firms, or states), embedded in social structures (e.g., social networks, spatial neighborhoods, or institutional scaffolds). These are built to observe and analyze the emergence of aggregate outcomes. By manipulating behavioral or interaction model parameters, whether guided by empirical evidence or theory, micro-generative mechanisms can be explored that can account for macro-scale system behavior, that is, an existing time series of aggregate data or certain stylized facts. (284)

This definition highlights several important features of the ABM approach:

- Unlike traditional rational choice theory and microeconomics, it considers *heterogeneous* agents.
- It explicitly attempts to represent concrete particulars of the social environment within which agents act.
- It is a micro- to macro strategy, deriving macro outcomes from micro activities.
- It permits a substantial degree of "experimentation" in the form of modification of base assumptions.
- It is possible to provide empirical evidence to validate or invalidate the ABM simulation of a given aggregate outcome.

Bianchi and Squazzoni note that the primary areas of application of agent-based models in social science research include a relatively limited range of topics. The first of these topics included uncoordinated cooperation, reciprocity, and altruism. Robert Axelrod's work on repeated prisoners' dilemmas represents a key example of modeling efforts in this area (Axelrod 1984).

Another extensive treatment of the methods of ABM techniques is Gianluca Manzo, *Analytical Sociology: Actions and Networks* (Manzo 2014). Manzo's volume proceeds from the perspective of analytical sociology and agent-based models. Manzo provides an account of explanation that highlights the importance of "generating" the phenomena to be explained. Here are several principles of methodology on this topic:

P4: in order to formulate the "generative model," provide a realistic description of the relevant micro-level entities (P4a) and activities (P4b) assumed to be at work, as well as of the structural interdependencies (P4c) in which these entities are embedded and their activities unfold;

P5: in order rigorously to assess the internal consistency of the "generative model" and to determine its high-level consequences, translate the "generative model" into an agent-based computational model;

P6: in order to assess the generative sufficiency of the mechanisms postulated, compare the agent-based computational model's high-level consequences with the empirical description of the facts to be explained (Manzo 2014: 9)

These observations serve to clarify the assumption of computational generativity that guides much thinking in the ABM literature.

What kinds of real social phenomena are amenable to treatment by the techniques of ABM? David O'Sullivan and his coauthors offer an assessment of this question in their contribution to Heppenstall et al., *Agent-Based Models of Geographical Systems* (Heppenstall et al. 2011). O'Sullivan and colleagues offer a basic taxonomy of different applications of ABM research.

> simple abstract models where the focus is on exploring the collective implications of individual-level decision making.
>
> more detailed [accounts that] locate virtual model agents in a representation of the real world setting of interest. Typically, such models operate at a regional or landscape scale
>
> some of the most ambitious models aim at detailed . . . representations of both the geographical setting and the processes unfolding in that setting (Heppenstall et al. 2011: 111–112)

This taxonomy depends on the degree of abstraction and realism that the model aspires to.

Here are a handful of research projects that are amenable to these techniques, most of which are illustrated in the Heppenstall volume.

- Land use patterns in peasant agriculture
- Residential patterns—urban and rural
- Patterns of burglaries
- Occurrence of interpersonal violence in civil war
- Traffic patterns—pedestrian and vehicular

These examples of potential ABM research applications have several things in common. They are situations where a number of independent individuals react to a social and natural environment with a set of goals; and they are usually situations where individuals make independent decisions but influence each other through their actions. These are situations of dynamic interactive choices. O'Sullivan and colleagues put these points this way:

> We consider the most fundamental characteristics of agents in spatial models to be goal-direction and autonomy. . . . However, more specific definitions of the concept may add any of flexibility, "intelligence," communication, learning, adaptation or a host of other features to these two. (Heppenstall et al. 2011: 115)

O'Sullivan et al. also pose an important question about what the circumstances are where the features of agents makes a difference in the social outcome:

This argument focuses attention on three model features: heterogeneity of the decision-making context of agents, the importance of interaction effects, and the overall size and organization of the system. If agents are the same throughout the system, then, other things being equal, an aggregate approach is likely to capture the same significant features of the system as an agent-based approach. (Heppenstall et al. 2011: 118)

Essentially, the point here is a simple one: if an aggregate outcome results from homogenous individuals making a decision about something on the same basis as everyone else, then we don't need an agent-based model. ABM techniques become valuable when heterogeneous agents interact with each other to bring about novel outcomes.

There are quite a few social situations that do not fit the terms of these models well. Some social processes are not simply the aggregate outcome of choices by a set of independent autonomous agents. For example, the flow of work through an architectural design studio is determined by the rules of the firm, not the independent choices of the employees, and the behavior of an army is largely determined by its general staff and command structure. O'Sullivan et al. put the point this way:

A more important question may be, "what should the agents in an ABM of this system represent?" If the interactions among individual actors in the real world are substantially channelled via institutions or other social or spatial structures, perhaps it is those institutions or social or spatial structures that should be represented as agents in an ABM rather than the individuals of which they are formed. (Heppenstall et al. 2011: 120)

So, a general question for ABM methodology is this: Where do structural social factors come into ABM models? Here, I am thinking of things like a system of regulation and law, a pattern of racialized behavior, the architecture of the transport system, a tax system, . . . We might treat these as parameters in the environment of choice for the agents. They are beyond the control of the agents and are regarded as constraints and opportunities.

It seems reasonable to judge that ABM techniques are very useful when we are concerned with phenomena that are aggregates of strategic behavior by individual actors, but they are not pertinent to many other questions that sociologists pose. In particular, they do not seem useful for sociological inquiries that are primarily concerned with the dynamics and effects of large social structures where the behavior of individuals is routine, homogeneous, or largely determined exogenously. These are the circumstances where the premises of the ABM approach—autonomy, heterogeneity, and activity—are not satisfied.

ABM Models of Civil Unrest

An important area of application of ABM models concerns the dynamics through which a stable community consisting of multiple groups may begin to polarize and fission into antagonisms and conflict. This is the topic of civil conflict. Suppose we have an urban population spread across space in a distribution that reflects a degree of differentiation of residence by income, religion, and race. Suppose religion is more segregated than either income or race across the region. And, suppose we have some background theoretical beliefs about social networks, civic associations, communication processes, and other factors influencing a disposition to mobilize. ABM methods have been constructed to allow us to probe different scenarios to see what effects these different settings produce for polarization and conflict.

Carlos Lemos et al. provide an overview of applications of ABM techniques in social conflict and civil violence in "ABM of social conflict, civil violence and revolution: state-of-the-art-review and further prospects." Here is an overview statement of their findings about one specific approach, the threshold-based approach:

> Social conflict, civil violence and revolution ABM are inspired on classical models that use simple threshold-based rules to represent collective behavior and contagion effects, such as Schelling's model of segregation [7] and Granovetter's model of collective behavior [15]. Granovetter's model is a theoretical description of social contagion or peer effects: each agent a has a threshold Ta and decides to turn "active"—e.g. join a protest or riot—when the number of other agents joining exceeds its threshold. Granovetter showed that certain initial distributions of the threshold can precipitate a chain reaction that leads to the activation of the entire population, whereas with other distributions only a few agents turn active. (section 3.1)

Armano Srbljinovic and colleagues attempt to model the emergence of ethnic conflict in "An Agent-Based Model of Ethnic Mobilisation" (Srbljinovic et al. 2003). Their goal is to better explain the emergence of polarized and antagonistic ethnic conflict in the former Yugoslavia; their method of approach is to develop an agent-based model that might capture some of the parameters that induce or inhibit ethnic mobilization. They refer to the embracing project as "Social Correlates of the Homeland War." They believe an ABM can potentially illuminate the messy and complex processes of ethnic mobilization observed on the ground:

> Our more moderate goals are based on a seemingly reasonable assumption that the results observed in a simplified, artificial society could give us some clues of what is going on, or perhaps show us where to centre our attention in

further and more detailed examination of a more complex real-world society. (paragraph 1.4)

They describe the 1980s and 1990s in this region in these terms:

> So, by the end of the eighties and the beginning of the nineties, the ethnic roles in the society of the former Yugoslavia, that were kept toward the middle of Banton's social roles-scale for more than forty years, now under the influence of political entrepreneurs, increased in importance. (paragraph 2.5)

And, they would like to explain some aspects of the dynamics of this transition. They single out a handful of important social characteristics of individuals in the region: (a) ethnic membership, (b) ethnic mobilization, (c) civic mobilization, (d) grievance degree, (e) social network, (f) environmental conditions, and (g) appeals to action. Each actor in the model is assigned a value for factors a–e; environmental conditions are specified; and various patterns of appeals are inserted into the system over a number of trials

The algorithm of the model calculates the degree of mobilization intensity for all the agents as a function of the frequency of appeals, the antecedent grievance level of the agent, and a few features of the agents' social networks. If we add a substantive hypothesis about the threshold of M after which group action arises, we then have a model of the occurrence of ethnic strife.

The model uses a "SWARM" methodology. It postulates 200 agents, half red and half blue; and, it calculates for each agent a level of mobilization intensity for a sequence of times, according to the following formula:

$$m^i(t + 1) = m^i(t) + (m^i_{app} + m^i_{socnet} + m^i_{cool})\Delta t$$

(Srbljinovic et al. (2003), paragraph 3.8)

This formula calculates the *i*th individual's new level of mobilization intensity *m* depending on the prior intensity, the delta created by the appeal, the delta created by the social network, and the "cooling" for the current period. (It is assumed that mobilization intensity decays over time unless restimulated by appeals and social network effects.)

This is a very interesting experiment in modeling of a complex interactive social process. But it also raises several important issues. Is the periodicity shown by Red and Blue mobilization intensities in the simulation a real effect, or is it an artifact of the design of the model? Second, it is important to notice the range of factors the simulation does not consider, which theorists like Tilly would think to be crucial: quality of leadership, quality and intensity of organization, content of appeals, differential pathways of appeals, and variety of political psychologies across agents. This simulation captures several important aspects of this particular kind of collective action. But it omits a great deal of substantial factors that theorists of collective action would take to be critical elements of the dynamics of the situation.

Epstein's Civil Violence Model

Let's look at one important ABM model in greater detail and see what its strengths and weaknesses are. Joshua Epstein makes use of ABM techniques to attempt to understand some of the dynamics of civil violence and ethnic cleansing (Epstein 2002, 2006). The goal of the model is to generate the dynamics of uncoordinated grievance-based rebellion by independent agents distributed over space. In a second version of the model, Epstein seeks to generate the dynamics of communal violence between two ethnic groups. The mechanics of the model are simple. Individuals are specified as "Agent" and "Cop." Agents are provided with a hardship level and a legitimacy level. They are given a specified level of risk aversiveness. Their action rule is governed by the relationship between their net grievance level and the perceived risk posed by a proximate cop. When grievance is high and risk is low, the agent chooses to become active (rebel). Cops are provided with a simpler specification: a location and a rule that specifies they arrest a random active agent within range. Now, run the simulation forward several hundred (or thousand) iterations and quantify the patterns that result.

Here is Epstein's description of the purpose of this simulation attempt in *Generative Social Science*:

> The aim of the modeling is to generate certain stylized facts and core dynamics of decentralized rebellions and spontaneous ethnic conflicts. It illustrates a number of themes of the Generative chapter. Autonomous agents interact locally on an explicit space. They exhibit bounded rationality in deciding whether or not to rebel, adapt to ever-changing information, and are heterogeneous by hardship, level of political grievance, propensity to take risks, and ethnic identity. Local conformity, global diversity, and punctuated equilibrium—hallmarks of complex systems—are clearly evident here, as is the potential for empirical reconstruction (e.g., of Rwanda or Bosnia) along the lines of the Anasazi work, and policy applications in the area of peacekeeping. (Epstein 2006: prelude, chapter 11)

Epstein's analysis of the results leads to several findings: the behavioral assumptions lead to individual deceptive behavior; the finding that free assembly catalyzes rebellious outbursts; the impact of periodic assaults on regime legitimacy; and the effects of reductions in presence of Cops. Among other "stylized facts" he describes this finding: "The model explains standard repressive tactics like restrictions on freedom of assembly and the imposition of curfews. Such policies function to prevent the random spatial clustering of highly aggrieved risk-takers, whose activation reduces the local cop-to-active ratio, permitting other less aggrieved and more timid agents to join in" (2002: 7248).

How good is this model as a way of understanding civil unrest? First, it is clear that it is based on extremely sparse behavioral assumptions. Scholars who study contentious politics like McAdam, Tarrow, and Tilly spend a great deal of effort examining rebels' motives and values; all of that is reduced to legitimacy, grievance, and risk aversion in this model. (Epstein is very clear himself about the sparseness of the behavioral assumptions; this is a strength, in his view.)

Another major shortcoming of this model of civil conflict is that it does not incorporate the workings of organizations into the dynamics of mobilization. And yet, scholars like Tilly (McAdam, Tarrow, and Tilly 2001) and Bianco (Bianco 2001) make it clear that organizations are critical to the development and scope of mobilization of a populace. So, a model of civil conflict needs to be able to incorporate the effects of organizations in the mobilization and activation of large groups of individual agents. Here, I will explore what we might want from an ABM that incorporates organizations.

These limitations make it clear that this model is not a basis for explanation of any specific empirical case. The behavioral assumptions included in the model are vastly too simplified to do justice to real examples of social unrest, and the absence of organizations is a serious shortcoming as well.

Can Organization Be Introduced into the Epstein Model?

Ideally, we would like to see a model that incorporates the workings of one or more political organizations as part of the dynamics of rebellion. How might organizations be introduced into an agent-based model of social contention along the lines of Epstein's? I can imagine two quite different approaches. First, we might look at organizations as higher-level agents within the process. As each organization works its way through the population, it gains or loses members; and this affects individual behavior and the geographical distribution of activated agents. This would be an attempt to directly model the mechanism of mobilization through organizational mobilization by representing organizations as an additional type of agent. This approach is entirely compatible with the ABM approach, in that ABM theorists specifically encourage heterogeneity of agents. This simulation would simply increase the range of agents by including organizations as well as individuals. A simpler approach is to represent organizations as environmental factors, analogous to disease vectors, which percolate through the population of agents and alter their behavior. The first option is a substantial complication, but the second option can be explored easily within NetLogo. (NetLogo is particularly welcoming to the nonexpert in this regard, since it is easy to go back and forth between the code and the graphical representation of the model (Wilensky 1999).)

In the next few pages, I will illustrate two efforts of my own to modify the Rebellion model (Wilensky 2011b) to introduce the factor of organization. This is possible because the model is provided in the NetLogo library, and users are able to modify the code. The idea I would like to shed light on is the notion that organizations are themselves adaptive agents; organizations recruit followers; and followers are changed in their behavioral characteristics as a result of membership.

Here, I will implement the idea of using an epidemiological model to capture the effects of political mobilization through organization. I will consider mobilization to a political party as being akin to infection by a contagious disease. This could be implemented in a competitive fashion, with two or more organizations competing for members. Here, however, I will examine the simple case where there is only one organization and it has a specified probability of infection from cadre to agent by proximity. One of the sample models provided by the NetLogo library is EpiDEM Basic (Wilensky 2011a). This model simulates an infectious disease moving through a population through person-to-person contact.

We can adapt this model to a political context by understanding "infection" as "recruitment to the organization." I have modified the model to allow for reinfection after an agent has been cured (disaffiliated from the organization). This corresponds to exit and reentrance into a political organization. This leads the model to reach various levels of equilibrium within the population depending on the settings chosen for infectiousness, cure rates, and cure time frames. The screenshot below illustrates the model. The graph represents the percentage of the population that have been recruited to the organization at each tick. The infection rate (mobilization success) surges to nearly 100% in the early ticks of the model, but then settles down to a rough equilibrium for the duration of the run. Orange figures are organization members, while blue are not members (either because they have never affiliated or they have disaffiliated).

This model (Figure 5.1) does not immediately contribute to a more realistic version of the Rebellion model, but it serves to illustrate how the infection model might be adapted to represent mobilization.

An important shortcoming in this implementation is that it is forced to represent every agent as a "cadre" for the organization as soon as he or she is recruited, whereas on the ground it is generally a much smaller set of professional cadres who serve as the vectors of proselytization for the party. This accounts for the early surge in membership to almost 100%,

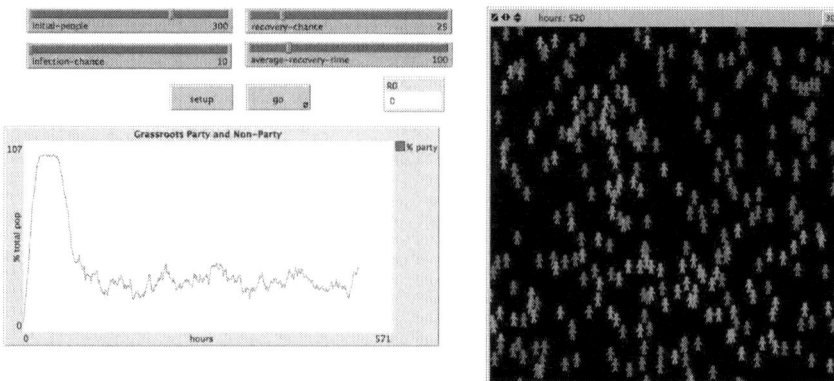

Figure 5.1   EpiDEM model of organizational recruitment.

which then moderates to the 30% level. The initial surge derives from the exponential spread of infection prior to the period in which cures begin to occur. On the current settings of recruitment and defection, the population stabilizes at about 30% membership in the party. Ideally, the model could be further modified to incorporate "infection" by only a specified set of cadres rather than all members.

Two fundamental questions arise about this hypothetical simulation. First, is the simulation assumption that "organizational mobilization is like an infectious disease" a reasonable one? Or, does organizational mobilization have different structural and population dynamics than the spread of a disease? For example, diseases percolate through direct contact; perhaps, organizational mobilization has more global properties of diffusion. And, second, does the resulting simulation give rise to patterns that have realistic application to real processes of social contention? Do we learn something new about social contention and mobilization by incorporating the additional factor of "organization" in this way that the Epstein model by itself does not reveal?

It would be possible to merge this party mobilization model with the Epstein model of rebellion (also provided in the NetLogo library), allowing us taking party membership into account as a factor in activation. In other words, we could attempt to model two processes simultaneously: the "infection" of new party members through a contagion model and the differential activation of agents according to whether they are exposed to a party member or not. This is complicated, though, and there is a simpler way of proceeding: simply represent the workings of an organization with an exogenously given number of party cadres. This can be implemented very simply into the Epstein Rebellion model.

For the second modification of the Epstein model I, will represent the effect of the presence or absence of an organization "on the ground" as a factor leading to differential activation by agents. How does an organization influence agents? There are multiple possible avenues, but one important vector is the presence in neighborhoods of representatives of the organization. Accordingly, I introduce a new kind of agent, "Cadre," and I modify the agent's behavior rule to be conditional, depending on whether a cadre is visible or not. If a cadre is present, the agent's activation threshold is lowered significantly. The causal assumption is this: the presence of a cadre in a neighborhood increases the threshold for action. The logic of this modification is this: for a given agent, if there is a cadre in the neighborhood, then the threshold for action is low, whereas if there is no cadre in the neighborhood, the threshold for action is high.

Table 5.1 presents the snippet of code that incorporates these changes.

Now run the model with two sets of assumptions: no cadres and 1% cadres.

The two panels represent these two scenarios (0% cadres (Figure 5.2) and 1% cadres (Figure 5.3)). As these panels illustrate, the behavior of the population of agents is substantially different in the two cases. In both scenarios, there are sudden peaks of activism (measured on the "Rebellion Index" panel). But those peaks are both higher and more frequent in the presence of a small number of activists. So, we might say the model succeeds in illustrating the difference that organization makes in the occurrence of mobilization. A few party activists substantially increase the likelihood of rebellion.

Or, does it? Perhaps not. The modifications introduced here are very simple, and they succeed in addressing a primary concern raised earlier about the

Table 5.1 Modifications to REBELLION code

```
;;AGENT BEHAVIOR
to determine-behavior
     if any? (agents-on neighborhood) with [party?] [;; increase activation if party
     cadre nearby
     set active? (grievance-risk-aversion * estimated-arrest-probability >
     partythreshold)]
     if not any? (agents-on neighborhood) with [party?] [;; increase activation if party
     cadre nearby
     set active? (grievance-risk-aversion * estimated-arrest-probability > threshold)]
     ;; ifelse party? [set active? (grievance-risk-aversion * estimated-arrest-probability >
     partythreshold)]
[set active? (grievance- risk-aversion * estimated-arrest-probability > threshold)];;
MODIFIED
     ;; set active? (grievance-risk-aversion * estimated-arrest-probability >
     partythreshold);; MODIFIED
     ;; set active? (grievance-risk-aversion * estimated-arrest-probability > threshold)
     end
```

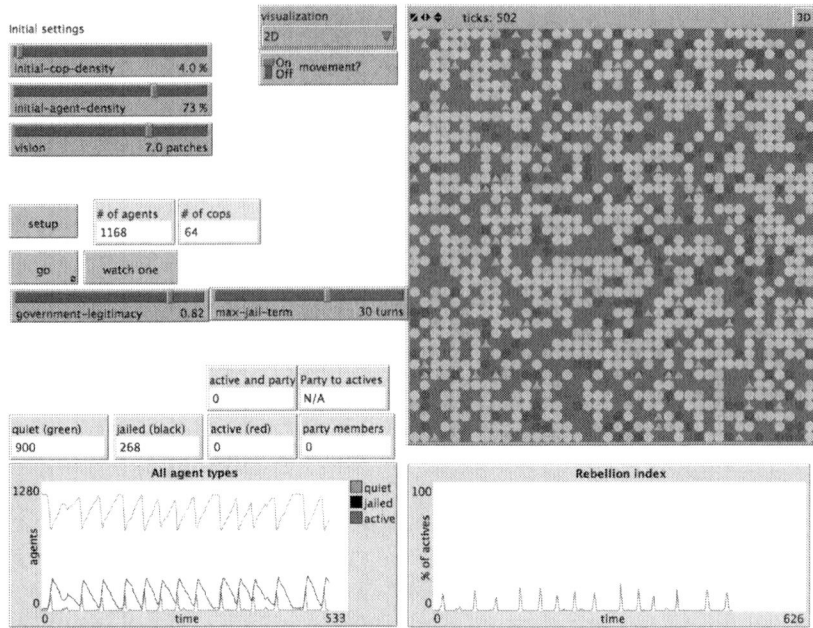

Figure 5.2   Scenario 1: occurrence of mobilization with no party members.

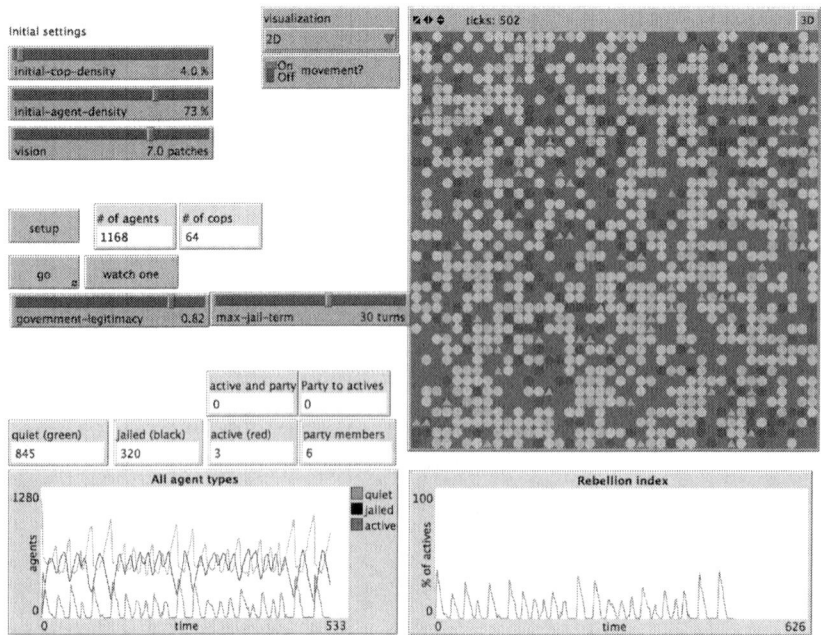

Figure 5.3   Scenario 2: occurrence of mobilization with 1% party members.

original version of Epstein's model: the fact that it does not take the presence of organization into account as a causal factor in civil unrest. But the realism of the model is still low. For example, the Rebellion model is specifically intended to capture the relationship between cops and agents. But it is not interactive in the other way in which rebellious behavior spreads: the process in which rising density of activation in a neighborhood increases the probability of activation for each individual. In other words, neither the original implementation nor this simple extension allows introduction of the spatial dimensions of mobilization and civil unrest (aside from the original random location of party activists).

But most fundamentally, the extension I have presented here is still an enormously abstract representation of the workings of organizations in the context of civil unrest and mobilization. I've boiled the workings of a political organization down to a single effect: if a neighborhood is exposed to a party cadre, the individuals in that neighborhood are substantially more likely to become active. And, the model behaves accordingly; there is more activism when there are more cadres. But we can't really interpret this as the derivation of a social effect from an independent set of assumptions; rather, the implementation of the idea of organization simply assumes the fact that cadres amplify activation by others in the neighborhood. In other words, the model is built to embody the effect I was expecting to see.

This exercise makes a couple of points. First, agent-based models have the virtue of being very explicit about the logic of action that is represented. So, it is possible for anyone to review the code and to modify the assumptions, or to introduce factors that perhaps should be considered.

But second, no one should imagine that agent-based models reproduce reality. Any ABM is implemented by (1) codifying one or more assumptions about the factors that influence a given collective phenomenon and (2) codifying the rules of action for the kinds of agents that are to be represented. Both kinds of assumption require extreme abstraction from the reality of a social setting, and therefore models can almost invariably be challenged for a lack of realism. It is hard for me to see how an agent-based model might be thought to be explanatory of a complex social reality such as the Cairo uprising.

ABM models of unrest and rebellion warrant study. They attempt to codify the behavior of individuals within geographic and social space and to work out the dynamics of interaction that result. But it is very important to recognize the limitations of these models as predictors of outcomes in specific periods and locations of unrest. These simulation models probably don't shed much light on particular episodes of contention in Egypt or Tunisia during the Arab Spring. The "qualitative" theories of contention that have been developed probably shed more light on the dynamics of contention than the simulations do at this point in their development.

Limitations of ABM Simulations

Here are some important concerns this discussion suggests about the validity of various ABM approaches to social conflict:

• Simulations often produce results that appear to be artifacts rather than genuine social tendencies.
• Simulations leave out important features of the social world that are prima facie important to outcomes: for example, quality of leadership, quality and intensity of organization, content of appeals, differential pathways of appeals, and variety of political psychologies across agents.
• The factor of the influence of organizations is particularly important and nonlocal.
• Simulations need to incorporate actors at a range of levels, from individual to club to organization.

Epstein makes it clear that he is interested in the capacity of this model to shed light on the logic of civil unrest, given very sparse behavioral assumptions. But it is very important to recognize the limitations of these models as predictors of outcomes in specific periods and locations of unrest. These simulation models probably don't shed much light on particular episodes of contention in Egypt or Tunisia during the Arab Spring. The "qualitative" theories of contention that have been developed probably shed more light on the dynamics of contention than the simulations do at this point in their development.

In chapter 2, we considered the idea of an "actor-centered" approach to the social sciences. How does this approach relate to the ABM approach? The most important difference between the two approaches is the issue of granularity and abstraction concerning the nature of the actors. Actor-centered researchers are critical of the methodological move toward abstraction in the description of the actor. They believe that the socially embedded and rather specific features of deliberation and action that they investigate in various historical and cultural settings are crucial, and these features are lost when we move to a more abstract desire-belief-opportunity (DBO) approach. ABM theorists argue that abstraction about the agent is necessary if a social situation is supposed to be tractable—to model the behavior of a population of agents we need to be able to represent their decision rules in a reasonably compact and mathematically representable way. So, if we take the view that each individual is a unique bundle of mental frameworks and action practices, we will have to give up the enterprise of modeling their collective behavior.

However, this appears to be a difference of nuance rather than a fundamental inconsistency of approaches. As we have seen, heterogeneity is a core tenet of ABM methodology. Unlike microeconomics, ABM models are fully consistent with postulating a range of actors with different preferences and decision rules. And, it is plausible to hope that ABM models might be strengthened by incorporating more of the specificity of social actors that is provided by the actor-centered approach. So, ABM researchers themselves appear to be open to incorporating more realistic assumptions about actors' motivations and reasoning frameworks.

This suggests that there is perhaps more fertile ground between the actor-centered sociology (ACS) and ABM frameworks than has yet been worked out. ACS focuses its attention on the question of refining our understanding of how actors are constituted, and ABM provides a rich set of techniques for transporting from assumptions about individual actors to the simulated result of aggregating these actors' behaviors onto a collective pattern.

The hybrid approach still requires abstraction about actors. But perhaps it is worth considering adjusting the focus, from "farmers in an environment" to "Kenyan farmers with *X, Y, Z* features of goals and reasoning schemes." Perhaps, the disaggregation of types of actors needs to go even further. And, perhaps the question of "what kinds of actors are involved in land use in Kenyan agriculture?" needs to be driven by empirical investigation rather than methodological fiat or computational convenience.

One important step in this direction is that Joshua Epstein's attempt broadens the behavioral assumptions used in ABM by introducing the idea of "agent-zero" (Epstein 2013). He seeks to introduce emotional and social motivations to complement the more standard rational-intentional assumptions invoked in most simulations. "As defined here, the agent's total disposition to act will be an explicit mathematical function of these" (Epstein 2013: 3).

> Specifically, my central objective here is to develop a simple explicit model of individual behavior in groups that includes some representation of "the passions," of (imperfect) reason, and of social influence. In other words, I will offer an exploratory synthesis of three (partially understood and obviously intertwined) processes:
>
> • The emotional
> • The cognitive
> • The social
>
> To this end, I introduce a new theoretical entity, Agent_Zero, endowed with emotional/affective, cognitive/deliberative, and social modules whose—often nonconscious—interactions determine his or her observed behavior. (Epstein 2013: 1–2)

This is an important step because it makes a meaningful effort to incorporate a richer conception of the actor into ABM models.

COMPLEXITY AND CHAOS

Now, let us turn to another perspective within the field of computational social science: the study of complex systems. This group shares some assumptions and methods with the generativist paradigm just discussed, but is distinguished by the fact that it emphasizes the substantial qualitative differences that emerge in complex systems and that deserve study in their own right. This observation underlies the development of chaos theory in the social sciences (Kiel and Elliott 1996; Resnicow and Page 2008). Kiel and Elliott describe this development in the introduction to this volume:

> The mathematical foundation of chaos theory and the unique vernacular of this new science can deter some researchers from exploring the dynamics of nonlinear systems. Terms such as periodicity, sensitive dependence on initial conditions, and attractors are not the usual vernacular of the social sciences. (19)

Resnicow and Page identify some of the elements leading to chaotic behavior at the population level with respect to health in these terms:

> Health behavior change may mirror other complex systems found in nature that involve multiple component parts that interact in a nonlinear fashion. Factors such as knowledge, attitude, belief, and efficacy no doubt exert influence on health behavior change. They may be thought of as the particle components of the motivational quantum. However, the interaction of these factors resembles a complex system. For example, which particular bits of knowledge, attitude, belief, and environmental constraints and the amount of each required to tip the system for a particular individual or a particular behavior is virtually impossible to predict. (Resnicow and Page 2008: 1383)

These ideas about nonlinear causal processes and unpredictable changes at the system level are highly relevant to understanding the social world. So, let us consider some of the main ideas of complexity theory as an approach to the social sciences.

Herbert Simon is one of the seminal thinkers in the study of complexity. His 1962 article "The Architecture of Complexity" (Simon 1962) put forward several ideas that have become core to the conceptual frameworks of the field. So, it is worthwhile highlighting a few of the key ideas that were put forward in that article. Here is Simon's definition of complexity:

Roughly, by a complex system I mean one made up of a large number of parts that interact in a nonsimple way. In such systems, the whole is more than the sum of the parts, not in an ultimate, metaphysical sense, but in the important pragmatic sense that, given the properties of the parts and the laws of their inter-action, it is not a trivial matter to infer the properties of the whole. In the face of complexity, an in-principle reductionist may be at the same time a pragmatic holist. (Simon 1962: 468)

Notice several key ideas contained here, as well as several things that are not said. First, the complexity of a system derives from the "nonsimple" nature of the interaction of its parts (subsystems). A watch is a simple system, because it has many parts but the behavior of the whole is the simple sum of the direct mechanical interactions of the parts. The watch spring provides an (approxi-mately) constant impulse to the gearwheel, producing a temporally regular motion in the gears. This motion pushes forward the time registers (second, minute, hour) in a fully predictable way. If the spring's tension influenced not only the gearwheel but also the size of the step taken by the minute hand, or if the impulse provided by the spring varied significantly according to the alignment of the hour and second hands and the orientation of the spring, then the behavior of the watch would be "complex." It would be difficult or impossible to predict the state of the time registers by counting the ticks in the watch gearwheel. So, this is a first statement of the idea of complexity: the fact of multiple causal interactions among the many parts (subsystems) that make up the whole system.

A second main idea here is that the behavior of the system is difficult to predict as a result of the nonsimple interactions among the parts. In a complex system, we cannot provide a simple aggregation model of the system that adds up the independent behaviors of the parts; rather, the parts are influenced in their behaviors by the behaviors of other components. The state of the sys-tem is fixed by interdependent subsystems, which implies that the system's behavior can oscillate wildly with apparently similar initial conditions. (This is one explanation of the Chernobyl nuclear meltdown: engineers attempted to "steer" the system to a safe shutdown by manipulating several control sys-tems at once; but these control systems had complex effects on each other, with the result that the engineers catastrophically lost control of the system.) This suggests that complex systems have emergent properties. Here is the version of emergence that Simon favors in *The Sciences of the Artificial* (Simon 1996 [1969]):

By adopting this weak interpretation of emergence, we can adhere (and I will adhere) to reductionism in principle even though it is not easy (often not even computationally feasible) to infer rigorously the properties of the whole from knowledge of the properties of the parts. In this pragmatic way, we can build nearly independent theories for each successive level of complexity, but at the same time, build bridging theories that show how each higher level can be accounted for in terms of the elements and relations of the next level down. (Simon 1996: 172)

A third important point here is Simon's distinction between "metaphysical reducibility" and "pragmatic holism." He accepts what we would today call the principle of supervenience: the state of the system supervenes upon the states of the parts. But he rejects the feasibility of performing a reduction of the behavior of the system to an account of the properties of the parts. He does not discuss the concept of emergence in detail here, but this would be another way of putting his point: a metaphysically emergent property of a system is one that cannot in principle be derived from the characteristics of the parts. A pragmatically emergent property is one that supervenes upon the properties of the parts, but where it is computationally difficult or impossible to map the function from the state of the parts to the state of the system. This point is relevant to the idea of "relative explanatory autonomy" provided in chapter 4. The latter idea postulates that we can sometimes discover system properties (causal powers) of a complex system that are in principle fixed by the underlying parts, but where it is either impossible or unnecessary to discover the specific causal sequences through which the system's properties come to be as they are.

Another key idea in this article is Simon's idea of a hierarchic system.

> By a hierarchic system, or hierarchy, I mean a system that is composed of inter-related subsystems, each of the latter being, in turn, hierarchic in structure until we reach some lowest level of elementary subsystem. (Simon 1996: 468)
>
> I have already given an example of one kind of hierarchy that is frequently encountered in the social sciences: a formal organization. Business firms, governments, universities all have a clearly visible parts-within-parts structure. (Simon 1996: 469)

Here, the idea is also an important one. It is a formal specification of a particular kind of ensemble in which structures at one level of aggregation are found to be composed separately of structures or subsystems at a lower level of aggregation. Simon offers the example of a biological cell that can be analyzed into a set of exhaustive and mutually independent subsystems nested within each other. It is essential that there is a relation of enclosure as we descend the hierarchy of structures: the substructures of level S are entirely contained within it and do not serve as substructures of some other system S. It is difficult to think of biological examples that violate the conditions of hierarchy—though we might ask whether an organism and its symbiote might be best understood as a nonhierarchical system. But examples are readily available in the social world. Labor unions and corporate PACs play significant causal roles in modern democracies. But they are not subsystems of the political process in a hierarchical sense: they are not contained within the state, and they play roles in nonstate systems as well. (A business lobby group may influence both the policies chosen by a unit of government and the business strategy of a health care system.)

Simon appears to believe that hierarchies reduce the complexity of systems; and they support the feature of what we would now call "modularity," where we can treat the workings of a subsystem as a self-enclosed unit that works roughly the same no matter what changes occur in other subsystems. Simon puts this point in his own language of "decomposability." A system is decomposable if we can disaggregate its behavior onto the sum of the independent behaviors of its parts. A system is "nearly decomposable" if the parts of the system have some effects on each other, but these effects are small relative to the overall workings of the system.

At least, some kinds of hierarchic systems can be approximated successfully as nearly decomposable systems. The main theoretical findings from the approach can be summed up in two propositions:

> (a) In a nearly decomposable system, the short-run behavior of each of the component subsystems is approximately independent of the short-run behavior of the other components; (b) in the long run, the behavior of any one of the components depends in only an aggregate way on the behavior of the other components. (Simon 1996: 474)

One idea that is not contained in Simon's 1962 version of complexity is that of causal nonlinearity. Nonlinearity is a problem for the "near decomposability" view that Simon wanted to take of complexity in the 1962 version, because it casts doubt on the ability to disentangle causal influences deriving from interconnected subsystems. Small differences in initial conditions can lead to large differences in outcome. This is a key aspect of chaos theory and the varieties of turbulent phenomena that provide the best examples of chaotic systems. And, this casts some doubt on one of the central conclusions of the 1962 paper:

> The fact, then, that many complex systems have a nearly decomposable, hierarchic structure is a major facilitating factor enabling us to understand, to describe, and event to "see" such systems and their parts. Or perhaps the proposition should be put the other way round. If there are important systems in the world that are complex without being hierarchic, they may to a considerable extent escape our observation and our understanding. (477)

This is a decidedly pre-chaos understanding of the nature of complex systems. Many contemporary complexity theorists would reject the idea that social processes are commonly the result of "nearly decomposable, hierarchic structures." So, it is a genuine change for the mathematics of chaos theory to be included in the 1996 version. Complexity research has moved forward since 1962, and Simon recognizes this in the 1996 chapter. What we don't find here is any discussion of whether actual social processes and systems display chaotic behavior in this well-defined sense. And, we don't see Simon shifting his position on "nearly decomposable" systems.

So, why does Simon expect that systems will generally be hierarchical, and hierarchies will generally be near decomposable? It turns out that this is an expectation that derives from the notion that systems were created by designers (who would certainly favor these features because they make the system predictable and understandable) or evolved through some process of natural selection from simpler to more complex agglomerations. So, we might expect that hydroelectric plants and motion detector circuits in frogs' visual systems are hierarchical and near decomposable.

But here is an important point about social complexity. Neither of these expectations is likely to be satisfied in the case of social systems. Take the causal processes (subsystems) that make up a city. And, consider some aggregate properties we may be interested in—emigration, resettlement, crime rates, school truancy, real estate values. Some of the processes that influence these properties are designed (zoning boards, school management systems), but many are not. Instead, they are the result of separate and non-teleological processes leading to the present. And, there is often a high degree of causal interaction among these separate processes. As a result, it might be more reasonable to expect, contrary to Simon's line of thought here, that social systems are likely to embody greater complexity and less decomposability than the systems he uses as examples.

There seem to be several key factors that create indeterminacy or emergence within complex social systems. One is the fact of causal interdependency, where the state of one mechanism influences the state of another mechanism that is itself a precursor to the first mechanism. This is the issue of feedback loops or "coupled" causal processes. Second is nonlinearity: small differences in input conditions sometimes bring about large differences in outputs. Whenever an outcome is subject to a threshold effect, we will observe this feature; small changes short of the threshold make no change in the output, whereas small changes at the threshold bring about large changes. And, third is the adaptability of the agent itself. If the agent changes behavioral characteristics in response to earlier experience (through intention, evolution, or some other mechanism), then we can expect outcomes that surprise us, relative to similar earlier sequences. And, in fact, mechanisms display features of each of these characteristics. They are generally probabilistic, they are often nonlinear, they are sensitive to initial conditions, and at least sometimes they "evolve" over time.

Are there examples of social processes and phenomena that display chaotic characteristics over time? Take the occurrence of massive street demonstrations as an example; are there aspects of chaos in the technical sense involved in the outbreak of street mobilization? Do small, apparently random events have large effects on the eventual outcome?

It would appear that this is the case when we look at the cases of uprising and passivity in different cities during the Arab Spring of 2011. Some social scientists have tried to understand the likelihood of uprising as an increasing function of economic crisis, regime weakness, and regime brutality. This implies a linear assumption about the causal role of these three forces. But it seems plausible to speculate that random events like a broken phone chain, an Internet outage, or the defection of a key leader could push the process of mobilization into a different direction. Moreover, it seems that contemporary research on social complexity pays a lot of attention to nonlinearity, path dependency, and sequential processes of social mobilization—leaving a lot of room for the kinds of turbulent effects that are observed in traffic flow, storm generation, and water dripping from a leaking tap. This is the kind of work that becomes more important in more recent treatments of complex systems.

So, oddly enough, it seems that one could fairly say that Simon's views of social complexity—as expressed in the 1996 third edition of *The Sciences of the Artificial* as well as in his groundbreaking "Architecture of Complexity" in 1962—are significantly incomplete, given the way that complexity theorists are now thinking about social processes. Simon did not incorporate the guiding assumptions of "complex adaptive systems theory" into his own thinking and remained convinced of the adequacy of the ideas of hierarchical systems and nearly decomposable systems as late as 1996.

Let us turn now to another major figure in the development of complexity science, John Holland. Holland argues that emergence is a key discovery within the study of complex adaptive systems. Here are the high-level features that Holland attributes to complex systems:

- self-organization into patterns, as occurs with flocks of birds or schools of fish
- chaotic behaviour where small changes in initial conditions ("the flapping of a butterfly's wings in Argentina") produce large later changes ("a hurricane in the Caribbean")
- "fat-tailed" behaviour, where rare events (e.g. mass extinctions and market crashes) occur much more often than would be predicted by a normal (bell-curve) distribution

- adaptive interaction, where interacting agents (as in markets or the Prisoner's Dilemma) modify their strategies in diverse ways as experience accumulates. (Holland 2014: 5)

In 1997, Holland argued that complex adaptive systems produce emergent properties at the level of the complex system:

> Emergence is a common feature of complex adaptive systems (cas)—ant colonies, networks of neurons, the immune system, the Internet, and the global economy, to name a few—where the behavior of the whole is much more complex than the behavior of its parts. (Holland 1997: 12)

He describes emergence in similar terms almost twenty years later:

> Each of these complex systems exhibits a distinctive property called emergence, roughly described by the common phrase "the action of the whole is more than the sum of the actions of the parts." (Holland 2014: 1)

However, Holland notes the ambiguity described in chapter 4 about two different ways of understanding emergence (strong and weak):

> Emergence itself is a property without a sharp demarcation. There are conflicting definitions, some claiming that emergence should be a holistic property, incapable of being reduced to the interaction of parts. That is not the interpretation used here. Instead this book concentrates on interactions where the aggregate exhibits properties not attained by summation. (2014: 3)

And, he makes it clear that his intended meaning is weak emergence, not strong emergence. So, his view is that complex systems create new properties—properties not attached to the units that compose them—but he is committed to the idea that these properties can be derived from the workings of the units to the extent that we can represent the complex interactions that exist among them.

Let us turn now to a very contemporary contribution to complexity science, John Miller and Scott Page's *Complex Adaptive Systems: An Introduction to Computational Models of Social Life* (Miller and Page 2007). Miller and Page look at certain kinds of social phenomena as constituting what they call "complex adaptive systems," and they try to demonstrate how some of the computational tools developed in the sciences of complex systems can be deployed to analyze and explain complex social outcomes.

A key premise of their understanding of complexity theory is that a population of units has "emergent" properties that result from the interactions of units with dynamic characteristics. Call these units "agents." The "agent" part of the description refers to the fact that the elements (persons) are self-directed units. Social ensembles are referred to as "complex adaptive systems"—systems in which outcomes are the result of complex interactions among the units and in which the units themselves modify their behavior as a result of prior history. Here is their summary description of adaptive social systems:

> Adaptive social systems are composed of interacting, thoughtful (but perhaps not brilliant) agents. It would be difficult to date the exact moment that such systems first arose on our planet—perhaps it was when early single-celled organisms began to compete with one another for resources. . . . What it takes to move from an adaptive system to a complex adaptive system is an open question and one that can engender endless debate. At the most basic level, the field of complex systems challenges the notion that by perfectly understanding the behavior of each component part of a system we will then understand the system as a whole. (Miller and Page 2007: 5)

Page and Miller believe that social phenomena often display emergence in a way that we can make sense of. Here is the umbrella notion they begin with:

> The usual notion put forth underlying **emergence** is that individual, localized behavior aggregates into global behavior that is, in some sense, disconnected from its origins. Such a disconnection implies that, within limits, the details of the local behavior do not matter to the aggregate outcome. (2007: 44)

And, they believe that the notion of emergence is applicable at several levels of social description, including "disorganized complexity" (the central limit theorem, the law of large numbers) and "organized complexity" (the behavior of a system of interacting agents).

> Under organized complexity, the relationships among the agents are such that through various feedbacks and structural contingencies, agent variations no longer cancel one another out but, rather, become reinforcing. In such a world, we leave the realm of the Law of Large Numbers and instead embark down paths unknown. While we have ample evidence, both empirical and experimental, that under organized complexity, systems can exhibit aggregate properties that are not directly tied to agent details, a sound theoretical foothold from which to leverage this observation is only now being constructed. (53)

The key to complexity of a system (as contrasted to complicatedness) is the fact of deep interdependency among the components of a system. What happens to one component has broad consequences for the other components. So, a complicated system is essentially just an aggregation of parallel components, whereas a complex system is one in which the functioning of each component is affected by the functioning of the others. Another important feature of complex systems is the fact of heterogeneity of the units. In contrast to typical economic models, where every individual has the same decision rules, in a complex system the theorist is able to represent a range of different kinds of agents.

Organized complexity, in their view, is a substantive and important kind of emergence in social systems, and this concept plays a key role in their view of complex adaptive systems. But what kind of emergence is this—weak or strong? A careful reading indicates that most contributors to this field of research have weak emergence in mind when they refer to the concept.

Finally, let us turn to a sustained attempt to understand social change within the basic assumptions of complexity theory. How should we attempt to analyze dynamic social processes in contexts in which the object of choice involves the actions of other agents whose choices jointly determine the outcome and where the outcome is unpredictable? Robert Axelrod and Michael Cohen address these issues in *Harnessing Complexity: Organizational Implications of a Scientific Frontier* (Axelrod and Cohen 1999). They define a complex adaptive system in the same terms as Miller and Page: a body of causal processes and agents whose interactions lead to outcomes that are unpredictable. The interactions among agents often have unpredictable consequences; and, the agents themselves adapt their behavior based on past experiences: "They interact in intricate ways that continually reshape their collective future."

The terms "complexity" and "chaos" are often used interchangeably; but Axelrod and Cohen distinguish sharply between them in these terms:

> Chaos deals with situations such as turbulence that rapidly become highly disordered and unmanageable. On the other hand, complexity deals with systems composed of many interacting agents. While complex systems may be hard to predict, they may also have a good deal of structure and permit improvement by thoughtful intervention. (xv)

Axelrod and Cohen make use of three high-level concepts to describe the development of complex adaptive systems: variation, interaction, and selection. Variation is critical here, as it is in evolutionary biology, because it provides a source of potentially successful innovation—in strategies, in organizations, in rules of action. The idea of adaptation is central to their analysis—in this case, adaptation and modification of strategies by agents in light of current and past success. Interaction occurs when agents and organizations intersect in the application of their strategies—often producing unforeseen consequences. (The strategy of open-source software development is one example that they look at, and the interactions that occurred as open-source innovations encountered closed-source innovations.) An organization or a population is best served, they argue, when there is a regular source of innovations (variations); when these innovations are implemented in the form of variant strategies; and when it is possible to cultivate more successful variations and to damp out less successful (selection). Here is how they summarize their view:

> Agents, of a variety of types, use their strategies, in patterned interaction, with each other and with artifacts. Performance measures on the resulting events drive the selection of agents and/or strategies through processes of error-prone copying and recombination, thus changing the frequencies of the types within the system. (Axelrod and Cohen 2000)

Consider a simple example—a fictional assembly of 1,000 Egyptian citizens in January 2011, interested in figuring out what to do in light of their long-standing grievances and the example of Tunisia. Will the group erupt into defiant demonstration or dissolve into private strategies of self-preservation? The dynamics of the situation are fundamentally undetermined. The outcome depends on things like who speaks first, how later speakers are influenced by earlier speakers, whether the PA system is working adequately, which positions happen to have a critical mass of supporters, the degree to which the government can make credible threats of retaliation, the presence of experienced organizers, and a dozen other factors. So, we cannot predict whether this group will move toward resistance or accommodation, even when we assume that all present have serious grievances against the Egyptian state.

The fact of path dependence comes into this scenario, in that the order of actions by the agents can influence the outcome. So, we could run the Egypt scenario forward multiple times and arrive at different outcomes repeatedly. We might imagine a tool along the lines of a Monte Carlo simulation that models the range of possible outcomes; but, in the sorts of systems Axelrod and Cohen are interested in, the range of outcomes is very wide with no "modal" and most probable outcomes at the core.

Axelrod and Cohen want to go beyond understanding complexity; they want to design some strategies for harnessing complexity. That is, they want to arrive at some interventions that designers and planners can undertake that will improve predictability and the ability of planners to bring about desirable outcomes.

The difficulty of prediction in the future development of a complex system derives in part from the adaptiveness of the agents who make it up; but it also derives from the fact of nonlinearity of causation in complex systems. Small influences can have large effects; there is often a discontinuity between the magnitude and direction of a cause and its effect.

What makes prediction especially difficult in these settings is that the forces shaping the future do not add up in a simple, systemwide manner. Instead, their effects include nonlinear interactions among the components of the system. The conjunction of a few small events can produce a big effect if their impacts multiply rather than add. (14)

Decision theorists distinguish between situations of parametric rationality and strategic rationality. In the former, the decision maker is playing against nature, with a fixed set of probabilities and causal properties; in the latter, the decision maker is playing against and with other rational agents, and the outcome for each depends upon the choices made by all. Game theory offers a mathematical framework for analyzing strategic rationality, while expected utility theory is advanced as a framework for analyzing the problem of choice under risk and uncertainty. The fundamental finding of game theory is that there are equilibria for multiperson games, both zero sum and nonzero sum, for any game that can be formulated in the canonical game matrix of agents' strategies and joint outcomes. Whether those equilibria are discoverable for ordinary strategic reasoners is a separate question, so the behavioral relevance of the availability of an equilibrium set of strategies is limited. And, here is the key point: neither parametric rationality nor equilibrium-based strategic rationality helps much in the problem of decision-making within a complex adaptive system.

The situation that Axelrod and Cohen describe here is an instance of strategic rationality, but it doesn't yield to the framework of mathematical game theory. This is because we can't attach payoffs to combinations of strategies for the separate agents; this follows from the unpredictability assumption built into the idea of complexity. And, second, complex adaptive systems are usually in a dynamic process of change, so that the system never attains an equilibrium state.

Axelrod and Cohen are hoping to provide counsel for how decision makers can "harness" complexity—that is, how they can design policies and strategies that perhaps push a complex situation in a favorable direction, or that insulate an organization from the worst outcomes that the complex system may produce.

Harnessing complexity . . . means deliberately changing the structure of a system in order to increase some measure of performance, and to do so by exploiting an understanding that the system itself is complex. (9)

Agents of a variety of types use their strategies, in patterned interaction, with each other and with artifacts. Performance measures on the resulting events drive the selection of agents and/or strategies through processes of error-prone copying and recombination, thus changing the frequencies of the types within the system.

And, they arrive at eight rules of thumb for "harnessing complexity" when it comes to organizations and social policies:

• Arrange organizational routines to generate a good balance between exploration and exploitation.
• Link processes that generate extreme variation to processes that select with few mistakes in the attribution of credit.
• Build networks of reciprocal interaction that foster trust and cooperation.
• Assess strategies in light of how their consequences can spread.
• Promote effective neighborhoods.
• Do not sow large failures when reaping small efficiencies.
• Use social activity to support the growth and spread of valued criteria.
• Look for shorter-term, finer-grained measures of success that can usefully stand in for longer-run, broader aims (156–158).

So, how should we understand these heuristics as a conclusion to this analysis? These heuristics function as an "operating manual" for leaders and policy makers attempting to bring about good effects within a population of agents demonstrating adaptive complexity. They do this, apparently, by reducing the degree of unpredictability of individual agents' choices—through trust, positive neighborhoods, avoiding discouragement, and reinforcing positive behavior. Perhaps these are plausible meta-strategies for intervening within a complex adaptive social system.

What is worrisome, though, is the implicit functionalism that seems to underlie the argument: the idea that agents of goodwill and having the long-term best interests of the population in mind are making the rules. But what happened to the predators—the organized crime figures, the drug lords, the conspirators, the predatorial businesses, and the anti-democrats? Won't they too be looking to exploit (harness) the workings of complexity? Axelrod's earlier work on repeated prisoners' dilemmas explicitly took into account the availability of strategies designed to exploit the cooperators; and, his work on cooperation emphatically makes the point that cooperation is often deployed for antisocial and predatory purposes (cartels, extortion rackets, . . .) (Axelrod 1984). Shouldn't this counter-social agency be incorporated into this analysis of complex adaptive systems as well? As Charles Tilly points out, crime and piracy also depend upon "trust networks" and innovative forms of predation (Tilly 2005).

During the 1980s, the Reagan administration wanted to create a "Star Wars" antimissile shield, and some of their policy makers argued that we could solve the technical challenges because the United States had succeeded in putting a man on the moon. But critics of this military space strategy rejoined, "But the moon didn't fight back," whereas Soviet scientists and engineers were fully capable of adapting their ICBM technologies to evade the defensive characteristics of a missile shield. There seems to be something of the same blind spot in this analysis of ways of reducing social complexity; predation and the common good are in competition with each other, and neither has a decisive advantage.

Complexity Theory and International Relations

Does the theory of complex adaptive systems have implications for the social sciences? Hilton Root offers some very interesting applications of these ideas in *Dynamics among Nations: The Evolution of Legitimacy and Development in Modern States* (Root 2013). Here, he offers an approach to social, political, and economic change through a set of ideas that are not yet strongly integrated into the international relations (IR) theory—the perspective of complexity theory, worked out in a clear and usable form.

The three sources of theoretical argument that he introduces—complexity theory, social network theory, and evolutionary ecology—represent a significant innovation in comparative history. The novel approach Root takes consists of three large ideas: that social systems at all levels display "adaptive complexity"; that the structure of the social networks (governance systems, information systems, economic interdependencies) that are embedded in a specific society have important and unexpected consequences for the behavior of the system; and that complex social developments have much in common with "landscape ecology," by which he means that there are multiple next steps that can be taken at any point leading to an improvement of performance.

His fundamental claim is that communities, states, and international systems need to be understood as dynamic systems with emergent properties. A society is not simply the linear sum of the behaviors of its component systems.

> The system of international relations, like most complex ecosystems, such as the nervous system or a rain forest, is yielding to its rules of complexity. In complex systems, a central administrator rarely guides the collective behaviors that characterize development processes. The system itself has a collective behavior that depends on all its parts. Rather than convergence toward a dominant model, or "global optimum," the interactive dynamics are coevolutionary; their interactions result in reciprocal and evolving change. (2)

One consequence of these ideas is that international relations and economic and political development processes show substantial path dependency and contingency. Another consequence is that some leading metaphors for large-scale historical change are implausible and misleading: in particular, modernization theory, "uniqueness of the West," and "end of history." Finally, Root argues that we should expect substantial variation in the strategies and structures that nations choose, given their own geopolitical environments.

> Competition in highly interdependent global environments produces far greater local variation and diversity of structures and strategies than modernization theory ever anticipated. (3)

The book uses numerous episodes from the political, military, and economic histories of Europe and Asia to illustrate and validate the approach he takes. As a particularly interesting example of this, Root interprets Napoleon's decision to invade Russia, not as folly, but as an intuition of the nodal character of the traditional European state system (126ff.). He also makes repeated use of periods in Chinese imperial history to illustrate his notion that system dynamics and the structure of the governance network create very powerful obstacles to innovation and change.

So, what does Root mean by "complexity"? His central concept is that of a "complex interactive adaptive system" (CIAS) within a heterogeneous environment. Here is a useful description of international relations through the lens of CIAS theory.

> A network is comprised of agents. The agents interact according to shared and evolving rules of behavior that in turn define the larger environment or system. That behavior generates continuous feedback loops that enable agents to learn and to adjust their behaviors to others' actions, thereby re-creating the system in which they operate. Complex adaptive systems are created by interactions and communications of self-adjusting agents. Continuous "feedback" motivates agents to re-evaluate their positions. Because agents are constantly reacting to other agents' behaviors, nothing in the environment is ever fixed or finite. In order to fully understand the impacts of these agents, their behaviors must be understood as they interact with the broader system. (16)

A key analytical idea the author brings forward repeatedly is the notion of "co-evolution." This concept captures one important aspect of a CIAS. CIAS's show two types of unpredictability. First, the mutual interactions of the parts lead to "chaotic" courses of development of the system, as A, B, and C interact to produce unexpected outcome D. But second, the "adaptive" part introduces another kind of indeterminacy, as organisms, actors, and institutions change their characteristics in face of changes in the environment. So, the properties of A, B, and C are not fixed over time; rather, selection and purposive adaptation lead to organisms and actors who respond differently over time to ecological opportunities and threats.

Features of uncertainty, time framing, rule change, and novel behavior all contribute to a set of system characteristics: unpredictability, path dependency, and sensitivity to initial conditions. And, Root believes that these factors have important implications about the feasibility of reducibility or micro- to macro-reconstruction:

> When a state's interactions shift from being locally based to being regionally or nationally based, its behaviors change across the network and the greater system. Thus a general theory of the system cannot be deduced from the properties of its constituent parts, just as the universe cannot be reconstructed from the fundamental laws of physics. (31)

Root's treatment of "New Institutional Economics" is important for several reasons. Most important, he demonstrates the harm that comes from incorporating a questionable theory of change into a comprehensive agenda for policy. The guiding idea of "creating institutions of good governance" as a panacea for slow economic growth and widespread poverty led policy makers to ignore other important causal factors, including locally rational but myopic strategies pursued by sub-actors. Instead of looking for a general theory that can be used by centralized planning ministries to guide their economic and social policies, Root favors a more evolutionary approach: allow for a diversity of development experiments at the middle level of society and then favor those experiments that appear to have the best results.

> Chinese planners never attained the celebrity status of their Indian peers, but by trying multiple paths and starting with smaller interventions from the top, they found a better way to determine what worked. After Deng declared the opening of the Chinese economy, he instituted a multi-level process that facilitated both change and stability, and strengthened social organization and social learning through local experimentation. (108–109)

(Contrast this with the "single experiment" approach associated with land collectivization in the 1950s, resulting in massive agricultural failure and famine during the Great Leap Forward.)

One way of reading Root's book is as a guidebook for administrators in a time of complexity. Root correctly emphasizes the difficulty or impossibility of "solving" a set of social and political problems simultaneously, and the parallel difficulty of making confident predictions about medium- or long-term consequences of various policy interventions. Second best, in his account, is an evolutionary approach: try a diversity of approaches, and cautiously increase the volume of those approaches that seem to work best. But even this approach is uncertain; evolutionary processes lead to dead-ends that are unforeseen in earlier stages of the process.

VERISIMILITUDE IN MODELS AND SIMULATIONS

Modeling always requires abstraction and simplification. We need to arrive at a system for representing the components of a system, the laws of action that describe their evolution and interaction, and a way of aggregating the results of the representation of the components and their interactions. Simplifications are required in order to permit us to arrive at computationally feasible representations of the reality in question; but deciding which simplifications are legitimate is a deeply pragmatic and contextual question. Ignoring air resistance is a reasonable simplification when we are modeling the trajectories of dense, massive projectiles through the atmosphere; it is wholly unreasonable if we are interested in modeling the fall of a leaf or a feather under the influence of gravity.

Modeling the social world is particularly challenging for a number of reasons. Not all social actors are the same; actors interact with each other in ways that are difficult to represent formally; and actors change their propensities for behavior as a result of their interactions. They learn, adapt, and reconfigure; they acquire new preferences and new ways of weighing their circumstances; and they sometimes change the frames within which they deliberate and choose.

Modeling the social world certainly requires the use of simplifying assumptions. There is no such thing as what we might call a Borges-class model—one that represents every feature of the terrain. This means that the scientist needs to balance realism, tractability, and empirical adequacy in arriving at a set of assumptions about the actor and the environment, both natural and social. These judgments are influenced by several factors, including the explanatory and theoretical goals of the analysis. Is the analysis intended to serve as an empirical representation of an actual domain of social action—the effects on habitat of the grazing strategies of a vast number of independent herders, say? Or, is it intended to isolate the central tendency of a few key factors—short-term cost-benefit analysis in a context of a limited horizon of environmental opportunities, say?

If the goal of the simulation is to provide an empirically adequate reconstruction of the complex social situation, permitting adjustment of parameters in order to answer "what-if" questions, then it is reasonable to expect that the baseline model needs to be fairly detailed. We need to build in enough realism about the intentions and modes of reasoning of the actors, and we need a fair amount of detail concerning the natural, social, and policy environments in which they choose.

Comprehensiveness is impossible for social-simulation models. It is plain that all social theories and models disregard some causal factors in order to isolate the workings of specific mechanisms; moreover, there will always be forces that have not been represented within the model. So, judgment of the comprehensiveness of a model depends on a qualitative assessment of the relative importance of various factors in the particular system under analysis. If a given factor seems to be important (e.g. ethnic polarization) but unrepresented within the model, then the model loses points on comprehensiveness.

Chapter 6

Social Causation

CAUSES

To explain an outcome is to demonstrate what conditions combined to bring it about—what caused the outcome in the circumstances, or caused it to be more likely to occur. The most fundamental aspect of an explanation is a hypothesis about what caused the circumstance we want to explain. So, social explanation requires that we provide accounts of the social causes of social outcomes. Consequently, we need to raise two sorts of questions: First, what kind of thing is a social cause—how do social circumstances cause other social circumstances? And, second, what kind of social research can allow us to identify the causes of a social outcome or pattern?

The idea of social causation is a difficult one, as we dig more deeply into it. What does it mean to say that "poor education causes increased risk of delinquency" or "population growth causes technology change" or "the existence of paramilitary organizations contributed to the rise of German fascism"? What sorts of things can function as "social causes"—events, structures, actions, forces, and social opinions? What social interactions extend over time in the social world to establish the links between cause and effect? What kinds of evidence are available to support the claim that "social factor X causes a change in social factor Y"? Social scientists often have a variety of things in mind when they make claims like these. For example: "X is a necessary and/or sufficient condition for Y"; "if X varies, Y can be expected to vary"; "controlling for other factors, more X contributes to more Y." (See Little 1991, chapter 2, for a more extensive discussion of these variations in causal thinking.) However, none of these approaches is sufficiently fundamental, and much of the rest of this chapter will focus on the theories of

183

causal mechanisms and causal powers that have been advanced to permit more adequate accounts of social causation in the past several decades.

THE CAUSAL DYNAMICS OF CATTLE MANAGEMENT SYSTEMS

Let's begin with an intriguing example of a causal approach within new-institutionalist research, Jean Ensminger's account of bridewealth in the cattle-herding culture of Kenya (Ensminger 1992). The study illustrates how it is possible to reason about the causal properties of various institutional arrangements and their microfoundations at the level of the actors who are involved in them.

First, some background. The cattle-herding economic regime of the Orma pastoralists of Kenya underwent substantial changes in the 1970s and 1980s. Commons grazing practices began to give way to restricted pasturage; wage labor among herders came to replace familial and patron-client relations; and a whole series of changes in the property system surrounding the cattle economy transpired as well. This is an excellent example for empirical study from a new-institutionalist perspective. What explained the particular configuration of norms and institutions of the earlier period? And, what social pressures led to the transition toward a more impersonal relationship between owners and herders? These are questions about social causation at multiple levels.

Ensminger examines these questions from the perspective of the new institutionalism. Building on the theoretical frameworks of Douglass North and others, she undertakes to provide an analysis of the workings of traditional Orma cattle management practices and an explanation of the process of change and dissolution that these practices underwent in the decades following 1960. The book puts forward a combination of close ethnographic detail and sophisticated use of theoretical ideas to explain complex local phenomena.

How does the new institutionalism approach help to explain the features of the traditional Orma cattle regime identified by Ensminger's study? The key institutions in the earlier period are the terms of employment of cattle herders in mobile cattle camps. The traditional employment practice takes the pattern of an embroidered patron-client relation. The cattle owner provides a basic wage contract to the herder (food, clothing, and one head of cattle per year). The good herder is treated paternally, with additional "gifts" at the end of the season (additional clothing, an additional animal, and payment of the herder's bridewealth after years of service). The relation between patron and client is multistranded, enduring, and paternal.

Ensminger understands this traditional practice as a solution to an obvious problem associated with mobile cattle camps, which is fundamentally a principal-agent problem. Supervision costs are very high, since the owner does not travel with the camp. The owner must depend on the herder to use his skill and diligence in a variety of difficult circumstances—rescuing stranded cattle, searching out lost animals, and maintaining control of the herd during harsh conditions. There are obvious short-term incentives and opportunities for the herder to cheat the employer—for example, allowing stranded animals to perish, giving up on searches for lost animals, and even selling animals during times of distress. The patron-client relation is one possible solution to this principal-agent problem. An embedded patron-client relation gives the herder a long-term incentive to provide high-quality labor, for the quality of work can be assessed at the end of the season by assessment of the health and size of the herd. The patron has an incentive to cheat the client—for example, by refusing to pay the herder's bridewealth after years of service. But here the patron's interest in reputation comes into play: a cattle owner with a reputation for cheating his clients will find it difficult to recruit high-quality herders.

This account serves to explain the evolution and persistence of the patron-client relation in cattle camps on the basis of transaction costs (costs of supervision). Arrangements will be selected that serve to minimize transaction costs. In the circumstances of traditional cattle-rearing among the Orma, the transaction costs of a straight wage-labor system are substantially greater than those associated with a patron-client system. Therefore, the patron-client system is selected.

This analysis identifies mechanisms at two levels. First, the patron-client relation is the mechanism through which the endemic principal-agent problem facing cattle owners is solved. The normal workings of this relation give both patron and client a set of incentives that leads to a stable labor relation. The higher-level mechanism is somewhat less explicit, but is needed for the explanation to fully satisfy us. This is the mechanism through which the new social relationship (patron-client interdependency) is introduced and sustained. It may be the result of conscious institutional design or it may be a random variation in social space that is emulated when owners and herders notice the advantages it brings. Toward the end of the account, we are led to inquire about another higher-level mechanism, the processes through which the traditional arrangement is eroded and replaced by short-term labor contracts.

This framework also illustrates an important causal-reasoning heuristic, the use of counterfactual reasoning. This account would suggest that if transaction costs change substantially (through improved transportation, for example, or through the creation of fixed grazing areas), then the terms of employment would change as well (in the direction of less costly pure wage-labor contracts). And, in fact, this is what Ensminger finds among the Orma. When villages begin to establish "restricted grazing areas" in the environs of the village, it is feasible for cattle owners to directly supervise the management of their herds; and in these circumstances Ensminger finds an increase in pure wage-labor contracts.

What are the scientific achievements of this account? There are several. First, it takes a complicated and detailed case of collective behavior and it makes sense of the case. It illuminates the factors that influence choices by the various participants. Second, it provides insight into how these social transactions work (the mechanisms that are embodied in the story). Third, it begins to answer—or, at least, to pose in a compelling way—the question of the driving forces in institutional change. This too is a causal mechanism question; it is a question that focuses our attention on the concrete social processes that push one set of social behaviors and norms in the direction of another set of behaviors and norms. Finally, it is an empirically grounded account that gives us a basis for a degree of rational confidence in the findings. The case has the features that we should expect it to have if the mechanisms and processes in fact worked as they are described to do.

A final achievement of this account is very helpful in the context of our efforts to arrive at explanations of features of the social world. This is the fact that the account is logically independent of an effort to arrive at strong generalizations about behavior everywhere. The account that Ensminger provides is contextualized and specific, and it does not depend on the assumption that similar social problems will be solved in the same way in other contexts. There is no underlying assumption that this interesting set of institutional facts should be derivable from a general theory of behavior and institutions. Instead, the explanation is carefully crafted to identify the specific (and perhaps unique) features of the historical setting in which the phenomenon is observed.

Causal Realism for Sociology

Before moving to more specific issues, it is necessary to address the issue of realism. Are social causes "real"? Or, is causal talk just a way of summarizing some of the regularities that we are able to observe in the world around us? The philosophy of social science presented here is committed to the idea that causes and causal relations are real, not merely descriptive.

First, there is such a thing as social causation. Causal realism is a defensible position when it comes to the social world: there are real social relations among social factors (structures, institutions, groups, social movements, organizations, norms, and salient social characteristics like race or gender). We can give a rigorous interpretation to claims like "racial discrimination causes health disparities in the United States" or "rail networks cause changes in patterns of habitation."

Second, it is crucial to recognize that causal relations depend on the existence of real social-causal mechanisms linking cause to effect. Discovery of correlations among factors does not constitute the whole meaning of a causal statement. Rather, it is necessary to have an account of the mechanisms and processes that give rise to the correlation. Moreover, it is defensible to attribute a causal relation to a pair of factors even in the absence of a correlation between them, if we can provide evidence supporting the claim that there are specific mechanisms connecting them. So, mechanisms are more fundamental than regularities.

Third, there is a key intellectual obligation that goes along with postulating real social mechanisms: to provide an account of the ontology or substrate within which these mechanisms operate. This I have attempted to provide through the theory of methodological localism—the idea that the causal nexus of the social world is constituted by the behaviors of socially situated and socially constructed individuals. To put the claim in its simplest form, social mechanisms derive from facts about institutional context, the features of the social construction and development of individuals, and the factors governing purposive agency in specific sorts of settings. And, different research programs target different aspects of this nexus.

Fourth, the discovery of social mechanisms often requires the formulation of mid-level theories and models of these mechanisms and processes—for example, the theory of free-riding. By "mid-level theory" I mean essentially the same thing that Robert Merton meant to convey when he introduced the term (Merton 1967): an account of the real social processes that take place above the level of isolated individual action but below the level of full theories of whole social systems. Marx's theory of capitalism illustrates the latter; Jevons's theory of the individual consumer as a utility maximizer illustrates the former. Coase's theory of transaction costs and the firm is a good example of a mid-level theory (Coase 1988): general enough to apply across a wide range of institutional settings, but modest enough in its claim of comprehensiveness to admit of careful empirical investigation. Significantly, the theory of transaction costs has spawned major new developments in the new institutionalism in sociology (Brinton and Nee 1998).

And, finally, it is important to look at a variety of typical forms of sociological reasoning in detail, in order to see how the postulation and discovery of social mechanisms are carried out within contemporary sociological research. Properly understood, there is no contradiction between the effort to use quantitative tools to chart the empirical outlines of a complex social reality and the use of theory, comparison, case studies, process tracing, and other research approaches aimed at uncovering the salient social mechanisms that hold this empirical reality together. (Critical realist Doug Porpora makes this argument in a chapter titled "Do realists run regressions?" in Porpora 2015).

Social-Causal Ontology

Having a causal theory of a realm requires having an ontology: What kinds of things exist in this realm, how do they work, and how do they interact with each other? In preceding chapters, I have offered a social ontology grounded in the actions and relations of socially constituted actors, which I refer to as methodological localism.

This entails, basically, that we need to understand all higher-level social entities and processes as being composed of the activities and thoughts of individual agents at a local level of social interaction; we need to be attentive to the pathways of aggregation through which these local-level activities aggregate to higher-level structures; and we need to pay attention to the iterative ways in which higher-level structures shape and influence individual agents. Social outcomes are invariably constituted by and brought into being by socially constituted, socially situated individual actors (methodological localism). Both aspects of the view are important. By referring to "social constitution," we are invoking the fact that past social arrangements have created the social actor. By referring to "social situatedness," we invoke the idea that existing social practices and rules constrain and motivate the individual actor. So, this view is not reductionist, in the sense of aiming to reduce social outcomes to pre-social individual activity.

We also want to refer to supra-individual entities—firms, agencies, organizations, social movements, and states. The social sciences are radically incomplete without such constructs. But all such references are bound by a requirement of microfoundations: if we attribute intentionality or causal efficacy to a firm, we need to be able to sketch out an account of how the individuals of the firm are led to act in ways that lead to the postulated decision-making and action by the higher-level entity.

Finally, this approach to causal mechanisms invites an area of study that might be referred to as "aggregation dynamics." It is useful to have theories and tools that permit us to aggregate different micro-level processes over time into meso- and macro outcomes, taking into account the complexity of causal interactions in a dynamic process. The tools of agent-based modeling discussed in chapter 5 are relevant here.

Causal Necessity

What distinguishes non-Humean theories of causation from Humean regularity theories is the assertion that a cause makes the occurrence of its effect necessary in the circumstances. Is this an idea that can be made compelling today?

Here is a fairly intuitive way to talk about causation: our causal judgments rest upon assumptions about *how things work*—what the governing processes and powers are that make up the medium of events in a given domain and provide the connective structure between cause and effect. There is a substrate for any particular domain of causation, and the substrate embodies some features of activity and causal connectedness. It is this causal activity that gives rise to the reality of causal powers attached to things.

So the causal necessity I would like to assert goes something like this:

- Given how domain X works, whenever A happens, it triggers a stream of events that lead to B.

This in turn indicates why the idea of causal mechanisms is such a helpful contribution to the analysis of causation. A causal mechanism is one chunk of this "stream of events" leading from A to B.

All of this looks a little different when we turn from natural causation to social causation. Social causes are the result of constrained and motivated social actions by concrete social actors, and these actors are not subject to anything analogous to laws of nature. (I do not mean this to be an assertion of freewill fundamentalism; just the recognition that there aren't any laws along the lines of "individuals always behave in such-and-so a fashion.") So the idea of natural necessity does not help in the case of social causes. If we wanted to provide a counterpart notion of social necessity, it might go something like this:

- Given a social environment populated with actors something like *this* and embodying rules and institutions something like *that*, change A brings about outcome B through the actions of these ordinary actors.

It is readily observed that this is a substantially weaker foundation for stable causal powers of social structures and entities than we have in the natural world. The constituents of social processes—individuals and institutions—change over time and place. And, the workings of the same institutions and systems of practices and rules will be significantly different if they are populated by actors with significantly different dispositions. (This is one of the central postulates of the idea of "methodological localism," as discussed in chapter 3.)

This does not invalidate the notion of causal necessity sketched above for social causation. The point remains valid that there is a substrate to the social world (socially constituted and situated individuals doing things within specific rules and practices), and this substrate does in fact convey a change at one end of a causal process (*A*—a change in the rules of supervision in an organization, let us say) which leads to a change in the outcome (*B*—less petty corruption within the organization), through a series of events that are systemic enough to allow us to see the "necessity" of the transition from *A* to *B*.

So, the kind of necessity I would like to attach to causal sequences goes something like this:

- Given the underlying nature and constitution of the substrate of the field of action and given the constitution of *A*, we can uncover the active and provoking transitions through which *A* leads to *B* in a non-accidental way.

This conception differs from both apparent alternatives—the unvarnished contingency that Hume asserted for causal linkages and the deterministic "If *A* then *B* necessarily" logic that some theorists would like to see.

CAUSAL MECHANISMS

The most compelling answer to the question, what is social causation, is the theory of causal mechanisms. A causal claim about *A* and *B* always depends on the idea that there is an embodied mechanism or series of mechanisms that leads from *A* to *B* (Hedström and Ylikoski 2010; Hedström 2005). And, in the social realm, causal mechanisms are conveyed through the actions and interactions of individual social actors. The substrate of social causation is the world of social actors enmeshed in institutions, social networks, value systems, and organizations.

So, then, what is involved in asserting that social circumstance *A* causally produces social circumstance *B*? My view is that the best way of understanding a causal claim is in terms of one or more mechanisms leading from cause to effect: *A* caused *B* *if* there is a sequence of causal mechanisms leading from *A* to *B*. This approach is especially suitable for the social realm because, on the one hand, there are few strong statistical regularities among social outcomes, and on the other, it is feasible to identify social mechanisms through a variety of social research methods—comparative analysis, process tracing, case studies, and the like.

This account of causation depends upon something that Hume abhorred: the idea of necessity. For natural causes, we have a suitable candidate in the form of natural necessity deriving from the laws of nature, the idea of natural necessity: "*C* and the laws of nature => necessarily *E*." However, there are no "laws of society" that function ontologically like laws of nature. So, how can there be "social necessity"? Fortunately, the idea of a causal mechanism provides an alternative to law-based necessity. A social mechanism establishes a necessary connection between cause and effect (of some sort). A mechanism is a particular configuration of conditions that always leads from one set of conditions to an outcome. Mechanisms bring about specific effects. For example, "over-grazing of the commons" is a mechanism of resource depletion. And, it is the case that, whenever the conditions of the mechanism are satisfied, the result ensues. Moreover, we can reconstruct precisely why this would be true for rationally self-interested actors in the presence of a public good. So we can properly understand a claim for social causation along these lines: "*C* causes *E*" means "there is a set of causal mechanisms that convey circumstances including *C* to circumstances including *E*."

Where additional work is still needed is at the level of conceptualization of causal mechanisms. There is now a large body of discussion and debate about how to think about social-causal mechanisms, and many observers are persuaded that the move to mechanisms is a very good way of getting a better grip on social explanation and analysis. But how to define a social mechanism is still obscure. My own definition was first offered in Little 1991 and was extended in 2011 along these lines: "What is a causal mechanism? Consider this formulation: A causal mechanism is (i) a particular configuration of conditions and processes that (ii) always or normally leads from one set of conditions to an outcome (iii) through the properties and powers of the events and entities in the domain of concern" (Little 2011: 277). McAdam, Tarrow, and Tilly offer a similar statement (McAdam, Tarrow, and Tilly 2001): a mechanism is "a delimited class of events that alter relations among specified sets of elements in identical or closely similar ways over a variety of situations" (2001: 24).

Various philosophers and scientists have attempted to specify in greater detail the notion of a causal mechanism (Glennan 1996; Hedström and Ylikoski 2010; Kaidesoja 2013b; Machamer, Darden, and Craver 2000; Mayntz 2004; Steel 2004; Ylikoski 2012). James Mahoney (2001) provides an inventory of the main formulations. Mahoney identifies 24 statements, all somewhat different, and Hedström and Ylikoski (2010) provide an excellent review of the current debates.

The general nature of the mechanisms that underlie sociological causation has been very much the subject of debate. Two broad approaches may be identified: agent-based models and social influence models. The former follow the strategy of aggregating the results of individual-level choices into macro-level outcomes; the latter attempt to identify the factors that work behind the backs of agents to influence their choices. (Sørensen refers to these as "pull" and "push" models; Sørensen (1998).) Thomas Schelling's apt title *Micromotives and Macrobehavior* captures the logic of the former approach (Schelling 1978), and his work profoundly illustrates the sometimes highly unpredictable results of the interactions of locally rational behavior. Jon Elster has also shed light on the ways in which the tools of rational choice theory support the construction of large-scale sociological explanations (Elster 1989). The second approach (the "push" approach) attempts to identify socially salient influences such as race, gender, and educational status and to provide detailed accounts of how these factors influence or constrain individual trajectories—thereby affecting sociological outcomes.

Emphasis on causal mechanisms for adequate social explanation has several salutary effects on sociological method. It takes us away from uncritical reliance on uncritical statistical models. But it also may take us away from excessive emphasis on large-scale classification of events into revolutions, democracies, or religions and toward more specific analysis of the processes and features that serve to discriminate among instances of large social categories. Charles Tilly emphasizes this point in his arguments for causal narratives in comparative sociology (Tilly 1995). He writes, "I am arguing that regularities in political life are very broad, indeed transhistorical, but do not operate in the form of recurrent structures and processes at a large scale. They consist of recurrent causes which in different circumstances and sequences compound into highly variable but nonetheless explicable effects" (Tilly 1995: 1601).

Are there any social mechanisms? There are numerous examples. "Collective action problems often cause strikes to fail." "Increasing demand for a good causes prices to rise for the good in a competitive market." "Transportation systems cause shifts of social activity and habitation." Other examples are offered in Table 6.1.

CAUSAL POWERS

Let us turn now to a related theme in current debates about realism, the idea that the notion of a "causal power" is the most fundamental causal concept. In this neo-Aristotelian tradition, things are thought to possess real internal properties that allow them to bring about change in the states of affairs of other things. The idea of a causal power has been appealing to the critical realist tradition within the philosophy of science, and especially so for the philosophy of social science. Leading voices in this tradition are Mumford and Anjum (2011), Groff (2008, 2013); Groff and Greco (2013), Cartwright (1989), and Elder-Vass (2010).

Nancy Cartwright places real causal powers at the center of her account of scientific knowledge. As she and John Dupré put the point, "things and events have causal capacities: in virtue of the properties they possess, they

Table 6.1   Examples of social mechanisms

CONTENTION	SOCIAL COMMUNICATIONS
Escalation	Interpersonal network
Brokerage	Broadcast
Paramilitary organizations	Rumor
Competition for power	Transport networks
Boundary activation	
	ECONOMIC ACTIVITY
COLLECTIVE ACTION	Market
Prisoners' dilemma	Auction
Free rider behavior	Ministry direction
Convention	Contract
Norms	Democratic decision making
Selective benefits	Producers' control
Selective coercion	
	GOVERNMENT
ORGANIZATIONAL ENFORCEMENT	Agenda setting
Audit and accounting	Log rolling
Supervision	Regulatory organizations
Employee training	
Morale building	STATE REPRESSION
Leadership	Secret police
	Informers
NORMS AND VALUES	Spectacular use of force
Altruistic enforcement	Propaganda
Person-to-person transmission	Deception
Imitation	
Subliminal transmission	SYSTEM
Erosion	Flash trading
Charisma	Interlocking mobilization
	Overlapping systems of jurisdiction

have the power to bring about other events or states" (Dupré and Cartwright 1988). Cartwright argues for the natural sciences that the concept of a real causal connection among a set of events is more fundamental than the concept of a law of nature. And, most fundamentally, she argues that identifying causal relations requires substantive theories of the causal powers (capacities, in her language) that govern the entities in question. Causal relations cannot be directly inferred from facts about association among variables. As she puts the point, "No reduction of generic causation to regularities is possible" (Cartwright 1989: 90). The importance of this idea for sociological research is profound; it confirms the notion shared by many researchers that attribution of social causation depends inherently on the formulation of good, middle-level theories about the real causal properties of various social forces and entities.

Dave Elder-Vass provides a succinct description of the role of causal powers within the theory of critical realism:

Bhaskar offers us an alternative way of understanding causality, a causal powers theory. This draws on a different, realist, tradition of thinking about cause, one that goes back at least as far as Aristotle, but one that has been less influential than the covering law model in twentieth-century social science. (Elder-Vass 2010: 43)

Stephen Mumford is also an important contributor to this debate. Here is his summary view from his contribution to *The Oxford Handbook of Causation* (Beebee, Hitchcock, and Menzies 2009):

Where it is most radical, the powers ontology proposes a major reconceptual-ization of causation. Hume, as traditionally interpreted, understood the world to consist of distinct and discrete, unconnected existences. If this is accepted, then the best that can be made of causation is that it is a contingent and external relation between such existences. The powers ontology accepts necessary connections in nature, in which the causal interactions of a thing, in virtue of its properties, can be essential to it. Instead of contingently related cause and effect, we have power and its manifestation, which remain distinct existences but with a necessary connection between. (Mumford 2009: 245)

Advocates of the causal power approach attach a great deal of importance to the metaphysics of causation—the sorts of properties and relations that we attribute to the kinds of things that we want to postulate. The neo-Aristotelian point of view represented by Ruth Groff and others appears to have meta-physical objections to the causal mechanism approach: these theorists believe that the causal mechanism approach postulates the wrong kind of relations among entities. I want to argue that mechanisms and powers are compatible, so I need to take into account the metaphysical arguments. It will be neces-sary to tell a story about the nature of the world that gives a place and mean-ing to the metaphysical premises of each theory.

The primary metaphysical commitment that the causal powers theorists advocate derives from their treatment of powers and essences—two char-acteristic ideas from Aristotle. A power is thought to inhere in a thing in a particularly deep way; it is not an accidental expression of the empirical prop-erties of the thing but rather an essential and active expression of the nature of the thing. The causal power theory comes down to the idea that things and structures have an active capacity to bring about certain kinds of effects. In Groff's terms, things are not passive but rather active.

Particularly interesting are recent writings by Ruth Groff, who represents a wave of contemporary thinking in metaphysics that aims to revitalize portions of Aristotle's views of causation in opposition to Hume's.

Groff's work on causal powers is sustained over a number of recent works (Groff 2013; Groff and Greco 2013; and her contribution to Illari, Russo, and

Williamson 2011). Groff emphasizes a broad clash of perspectives between a Humean theory of causation ("constant conjunction, no necessary relations among things or events") and a neo-Aristotelian theory ("things have powers, powers underlie causal relations among things and events"). Here is how she and Greco put the perspective of the "New Aristotelianism" (Groff and Greco 2013):

> Humeanism is now under serious pressure within analytic metaphysics. In particular, after having been dismissed for generations as so much antiquated animism, the loosely-Aristotelian theorizing of real causal powers has now come to be a major focus of research within the specialty. (Groff and Greco: 1)

Moreover, Groff believes that American social sciences are still largely in the grip of the Humean metaphysics. In "Getting Past Hume" in Illari, Russo, and Williamson (2011), she writes:

> One can't help but wonder what the outcome would actually be, were there to be a floor-fight on the question, i.e., a substantive debate within analytic philosophy and methodology of social science on the merits of Humean anti-realism about causality versus the merits of a powers-based, realist account of causality. (Illari et al. 2011: 298)
>
> . . .
>
> What is significant about all of this for my own argument is not so much that Humeanism continues to be the default ontology of especially American, often positivist, social science; but rather that it can be combined with the idea that it is not—i.e., with the idea that competing versions of regularity theory somehow differ in a deep way, or that it is possible to remain neutral on what causality is, whilst engaging in causal explanation. (Illari et al. 2011: 304)

Putting the point simply, the assertion that an entity has a causal power comes down to a claim about the *nature* of the entity and the strong dispositional properties that this nature gives rise to. Sugar has the causal power to stimulate the taste of sweetness in typical human subjects; this power derives from the chemical structure of the sugar molecule and the micro-organization and functioning of taste receptor neurons. A magnet has a power to attract a piece of iron, in virtue of its microstructure. In each case, we have identified a real feature of the entity, and this feature is a consequence of real properties of its microstructure. This approach makes sense with regard to social structures and institutions as well. If paramilitary organizations have a propensity to create young adherents who are easily mobilized in support of fascist politics (as argued by Michael Mann 2004), then we can make reference to this causal power in our explanation of the rise of Italian fascism. University X's tenure system produces a teaching environment in which students get little attention from their faculty, as a consequence of the incentives and habits it cultivates in young faculty. This means something fairly straightforward: given the specific arrangements associated with this tenure system, the interactions that individuals have within this institution inculcates patterns of behavior that bring about the consequence. On this story, "producing a faculty climate that gives little priority to undergraduate students" is a causal power of this institutional arrangement. Change the internal arrangements and you get different causal properties.

In the case of the social world, however, the fundamental constituents of social powers are the constrained and developed actions of persons who act within the context of a given set of institutions and structures. Unlike the iron magnet, whose powers derive from identical iron atoms arranged in certain geometries, a tenure institution or a safety organization derives its properties from the structured actions of the individuals who compose it.

The rationale for asserting necessity in either the natural or the social realm—the idea that the postulated causal power is a real property of the thing—is the theory of scientific realism: things actually have the causal powers we observe because they have an inner constitution that propels their interactions with other entities. So, the causal relation is a kind of necessary relation, not just a brute fact about regularities. Metals conduct electricity because of the chemical-physical structure of the copper wire. And, universities have the properties they possess because of the institutional arrangements they embody and the actions of individuals within those arrangements.

Why is it useful to use the language of causal powers? Because we can encapsulate a large amount of the pertinent causal properties of an entity into a fairly simple set of expectations. If iron is magnetic (a causal power), we can derive a large number of expectations about its behavior in a variety of circumstances; and we can explain those circumstances based on the powers we have empirically or theoretically established. If a certain kind of regulatory organization is observed to have the causal power of "contributing to an abnormal number of accidents," then one part of an explanation of a particular accident may be the fact that it occurred within the scope of that kind of regulatory organization. (Charles Perrow offers an argument along these lines in *Normal Accidents: Living with High-Risk Technologies*; Perrow (1999).)

Social Powers and Essentialism

A sticking point in the theory of causal powers is its apparent commitment to essentialism: the idea that the powers of a thing derive from its essential nature. Rom Harré expressed this in his early formulations: it is the essential properties of a thing that create its causal powers. Here is how Tuukka Kaidesoja describes Harré and Madden's view in *Causal Powers* (Harré and Madden 1975):

Harré and Madden (1975, 86) analyse the ascription of causal power to a thing as follows: "'X has the power to A' means 'X (will)/(can) do A, in the appropriate conditions, in virtue of its intrinsic nature'." In other words, causal powers are properties of concrete powerful particulars, which they possess in virtue of their natures. (Kaidesoja 2007: 65)

The essentialism of the view is evident. A related point is the idea that the powers of a thing are not reducible to anything more fundamental. Ruth Groff puts the view in these terms: to assert that powers are real is to assert that they are irreducible (introduction, Groff and Greco 2013). But that seems questionable. We may think that feudalism was real, while at the same time thinking that its properties and dynamics derived from more fundamental social relations that compounded to create the distinctive dynamics of feudalism. So, it does not seem that realists have to also accept the idea of irreducibility of the things about which they are realist. Or, to put the point the other way around: the idea that realism about causal powers implies irreducibility appears to also imply a fairly strong thesis about emergence. Groff returns to this set of ideas in *Ontology Revisited*, chapter three (Groff 2013): "An emergent phenomenon (property or entity) is one that is not equivalent, ontologically, to the plurality of its parts." And, here too she emphasizes irreducibility. But, as Poe Yu-ze Wan shows (Wan 2011), philosophers have differed on the question of whether "emergence" implies "irreducibility." The theory of emergence offered by Mario Bunge does not require irreducibility. (These issues are discussed more fully in chapter 4.)

Current powers theorists make similar claims about irreducibility and essential natures. But I do not think things have an essential nature in any rigorous sense. So, we would be better served by a powers theory whose formulation avoids reference to essential characteristics. This is particularly important in the realm of the social world. As I argued in chapter 1, social entities are plastic and heterogeneous, and this view casts strong doubt on the idea that there are social kinds in a strong metaphysical sense. This entails that social entities do not have essential properties. So, if powers theory depends on essentialism, then it seems not to apply in my understanding of the nature of the social world.

Tuukka Kaidesoja (2013a) approaches a view very similar to this in his treatment of Harré and Secord's analysis of individual and collective powers:

I suggest that these views [advanced by Harré and Secord] presuppose that rules and institutions possess causal powers that are ontologically irreducible to those of individuals. (115)

Fortunately, it is possible to formulate an account of the causal powers of a social thing in terms of its contingent and changing properties, so we don't have to hypostatize the essential nature of social things. Orange juice is nutritive. But it is a contingent fact that orange juice does not contain arsenic; if the groves were watered with contaminated water, then orange juice would be toxic. The nutritiveness of orange juice derives from a contingent fact about its current composition and the history of its cultivation. Suppose that criminologists have found that urban police departments have a propensity for excessive use of force. Change the training regime for officers and commanders and this propensity disappears. A propensity for excessive use of force derives from a contingent fact about urban policing, not an essential fact.

Kaidesoja takes up the issue of essentialism and natural kinds within causal power theory, and argues that we need to "naturalize" this issue as well. Whether there are natural kinds in a particular domain is a question for the sciences to answer, not the philosophers. Kaidesoja notes that modern biology does not support the notion that biological things (including species) fall into natural kinds defined by distinctive essential natures.

> Biological variation between and within species (or populations) is thus a normal state of affairs in nature and there is no a priori limit for such variation. . . . This means that it is no longer plausible to conceive biological species as natural kinds in Harré and Madden's (1975) sense. (111–112)

So natural-kind essentialism does not fit into the entities and processes of the biological realm.

> Whether or not the essentialist notion of causal power can be applied to a certain collection of objects studied in a specific discipline should be decided by means of empirical analysis of the scientific research practices, theories and models that are developed in this discipline. (112)

But Kaidesoja does not believe that this invalidates the idea that biological entities have causal powers; and, this entails that there is a separation between essentialism and the attribution of causal powers.

I argued in chapter 1 that the social world is characterized by deep heterogeneity and plasticity. So, Kaidesoja's central insight here applies to the social sciences as well as to biology: causal powers should not be defined in terms of the essential properties of an entity; causal power theory should not be constructed in such a way as to presuppose essentialism.

We can give up the idea of essential causal powers for social entities because we have a good understanding of how the substrate of causal interconnection works in the social world. Social causation always works through the thoughts and actions of socially situated purposive actors. Individuals form representations of the world around them, both social and natural; they form relationships with other actors, and they act accordingly. So, social structures acquire causal powers by shaping and incentivizing the individuals they touch. We can therefore make sense of the fact that a given social entity, with the contingent arrangements that it currently possesses, has the capacity to bring about certain kinds of outcomes in the social world. So, when we say that a certain social entity, structure, or institution has a certain power or capacity, we know what that means: given its configuration, it creates an action environment in which individuals commonly perform a certain kind of action. This is the downward strut in the Coleman's boat diagram (Figure 4.2).

This argument turns out to have a lot to do with the question of whether powers should be thought to be "irreducible" as well. Scientific realists would say they are *not* irreducible; rather, we can eventually arrive at a theory (molecular, genetic, economic, psychological, rational choice, physical) that displays the processes and mechanisms through which the ascribed power flows from the arrangement and properties of the thing.

This analysis has two important consequences: First, powers are not "irreducible"—rather, we can explain how they work by analyzing the specific environment of formation and choice they create. And, second, they are not essential. Change the institution even slightly, and we may find that it has very different causal powers and capacities. Change the rules of liability for open range grazing and you get different patterns of behavior by ranchers and farmers (Ellickson 1991).

So, the theory of causal powers does not have to presuppose an objectionable form of metaphysical essentialism. Instead, it can be a defensible framework for embodying the idea of causal realism: things have the causal properties and dispositions they have in virtue of their micro-composition.

On this standpoint, powers are attributions we make to things when we don't know quite enough about their composition to work out the physics or sociology of the underlying mechanisms. They do attach to the entity or structure in question, surely enough; but they do so in virtue of the physical or sociological composition of the entity, not because of some inherent metaphysical property.

We might try to reconcile the two ideas—the causal powers of a thing and the thing's contingent constitution—with a few simple observations:

- Entities and structures at a range of levels of being have causal powers: active capacities to influence other entities and structures.
- Whenever we identify a causal power of a thing, it is always open to us to ask how this power is embodied; what it is about the inner constitution of the entity that gives it this power.

- When we succeed in arriving at a good scientific answer to this question, we will have shown that the power in question is not irreducible; it is rather the consequence of a set of mechanisms set in play by the constitution of the entity.

So, the discovery of a given causal power of a thing is not a metaphysical fundamental; it is rather an empirical scientific discovery that invites analysis into its underlying composition.

RECONCILING MECHANISMS AND POWERS

Causal power advocates often present their theory as an alternative to causal mechanism theory. Thus Ruth Groff takes up causal mechanism theory in "Getting Past Hume" in *Causality in the Sciences* (Illari, Russo, and Williamson 2011). She concedes that advocates of this approach—in the hands of Jon Elster and in my own writings, for example—claim to be realist and anti-positivist, in that they reject the notion that explanation depends on the discovery of general laws. But Groff is not convinced that the causal mechanism approach actually succeeds in presenting a substantive alternative to the Humean framework on causation: "Upon closer examination, the mainstream mechanism model is more of the same, metaphysically" (306).

The causal power approach to the understanding of causation is sometimes presented as an exclusive alternative to both traditional regularity theories and more recent causal mechanism theories. Groff poses a stark contrast; either you are positivist, antirealist, and Humean or you are anti-positivist, realist, and neo-Aristotelian. Here, I will present a provocative view: that the causal mechanisms and causal powers are complementary rather than contradictory. The causal mechanism theory benefits by being supplemented by a causal powers theory *and* the causal power theory benefits by being supplemented by a causal mechanism theory. In other words, the two theories are not exclusive alternatives to each other, but rather serve to identify different parts of the whole of causation.

It is worth observing that there are at least *two* currents of realist thought that reject Humean causation, not just one: the powers ontology that Groff and others advocate; and the causal mechanism approach that has been advocated by philosophers and sociologists such as Hedström, Elster, and Ylikoski under the broad banner of analytical sociology. One might take the view that the causal mechanism approach ultimately requires something like the powers ontology—"How else are we to account for the fact that sparks cause gasoline to explode?"; but on its face, these are two fairly independent realist responses to Hume.

Generally speaking, advocates of the mechanism approach have not been very interested in the metaphysical issues. These theorists are generally realist, so they postulate that there are real causal interactions. This is indeed a metaphysical position. But this family of thinkers tends to be mid-range realists: they want to understand the necessity of causal relations at one level as deriving from the real workings of the physical or social system a bit lower down; but they generally do not want to pose the ultimate question: How could *any* event or structure exert causal influence on another? So, the causal mechanisms theorists are perhaps better described as *scientific realists* rather than *philosophical or critical realists*. They take the view that the world has the properties (approximately) that our best scientific theories attribute to things.

Fleshing out Groff's argument against the causal mechanism literature, she seems to be arguing that causal mechanism theory can either retreat to constant conjunction (at the level of the linkages of individual causal mechanisms) or press forward to a causal power interpretation; there is no third possibility. "As with the other models, nothing on the mainstream mechanisms model is in a position of actually doing anything, in the sense of actively producing an effect" (Illari et al. 2011: 308). And, it is true that most definitions of causal mechanisms make some kind of reference to regularities and repeatability.

My own formulation of the mechanism theory is one of the targets of Groff's critique. However, my reasons for thinking that mechanisms need to involve some kind of regularities do not imply a collapse onto Humean causation. (At one point, I wanted to call them "pocket regularities," to distinguish them from the grand social or psychological laws that Hempel and Mill seemed to want to discover.) For example, I wanted to assert the following:

- "M [information diffusion] is the mechanism connecting E [police beating] with O [rapid mobilization of an angry crowd]" is a description of a real underlying (perhaps unknown) causal process through which the features of E bring about the occurrence of O.

This is an ontological claim and it is a realist claim. But there is also an epistemic issue: How would we know that M is indeed such an underlying reality? It seems unavoidable that we would need to *either* produce empirical evidence supporting the conclusion that M frequently conveys these kinds of effects in these kinds of circumstances (the approach Tilly takes) *or* have a theory of the mechanism which accounts for how it works to bring about the effect. The first amounts to a discovery of a limited set of regularities in a range of circumstances; the latter is a theoretical demonstration of how it works. So, this way of conceptualizing mechanisms does indeed invoke regularities of some sort. However, it does not agree with the Humean idea that causation is nothing but regularities or constant conjunction. The regularities that are invoked are symptoms of the underlying causal mechanism, not criterial replacements for the mechanism. Moreover, the powers theory seems to be subject to the same possible objection: How do we know that lightning has the causal power of starting barns on fire, unless we have repeatedly observed the chain of events leading from lightning strike to blaze?

So, how can powers and mechanisms be shown to be compatible and mutually supportive? The causal power theory rests on the claim that causation is conveyed from cause to effect through the active *powers and capacities* that inhere in the entities making up the cause. The causal mechanism theory comes down to the idea that cause and effect are mediated by a *series of events or interactions* that lead (typically) from the occurrence of the cause to the occurrence of the effect. In other words, cause and effect are linked by real underlying causal sequences (often repeatable sequences).

My view of the mutual compatibility of powers and mechanisms goes along these lines. If we press down on a putative mechanisms explanation, we are led eventually to postulating a set of causal powers that provide the motive force of the postulated mechanisms. But equally, if we press down on the claim that a certain kind of entity has a specified causal power or disposition, we are led to hypotheses about what mechanisms are set in play be its constituents so as to bring about this disposition.

Begin with a causal mechanism story:

- $C =>$ [x happens bringing about y, bringing about z, bringing about u, which is E] $=> E$

How is it that the sub-links of this chain of mechanism pieces happen to work to bring about their consequent? We seem to have two choices: we can look to discover a further underlying mechanism; or, we can postulate that the sub-link entity or structure has the power to bring about its consequent. So, if we push downward within the terms of a mechanism explanation, one way to close the story is by postulating a causal power at some level.

Now, start with a causal power claim. Suppose we assert that:

- Salt has the causal power of making H_2O electrically conductive when dissolved.

Is this simply an unanalyzable fact about salt (or saline solution)? It is not; instead, we can look downward to identify the physical mechanisms that are brought into play when salt enters solution in H_2O. That mechanism is well understood: the Na⁺ and Cl ions created by the dissolution of salt permit free electrons to pass through the solution.

Whenever we attribute a causal power to a kind of stuff (conductivity to metal, violent volatility to a crowd, propensity to accidents to an organization), it is logical and appropriate to ask what it is about the substrate of the stuff that creates the power in question. What is it about the microstructure of metals that leads them to conduct electricity? What is it about crowds that leads them to be vulnerable to surges of violence? And, what is it about certain kinds of organizations that leads them to be conducive to accidents like Three Mile Island or Bhopal? And, when we answer these questions by detailing the microstructure of the stuff (metal, crowd, organization) and demonstrate how it is that this structure creates the durable power in question, then we have provided a microfoundation for the power. So, powers admit of microfoundations. This response highlights the fact that the quest for microfoundations is really just an illustration of a pervasive explanatory strategy: investigate and measure the micro structure of the thing in question in order to discover why and how it behaves as it does.

So, we can explain the causal power by discovering the causal mechanism that gives rise to it; we explain links in the putative mechanism by alluding to the powers of the entities involved at that stage; and, we can explain other things by referring to the causal powers that we have discovered to be associated with various kinds of things and structures.

If we take this set of possibilities seriously, then powers and mechanisms are answering different questions within the causal nexus. The reference to powers answers the question, "What does *x* do?" while the reference to mechanisms answers the question, "How does *x* work?" Figure 6.1 illustrates this argument.

From a scientific point of view, it is always legitimate to ask how the powers of an entity or structure come to be in the natural world. What is it about

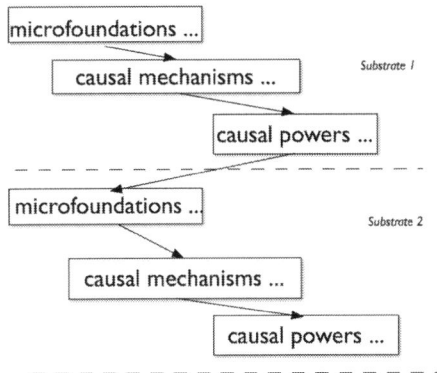

Figure 6.1   Causal powers, causal mechanisms, and microfoundations.

the microstructure of the thing in virtue of which the thing's properties are established? In fact, this is one of the key intellectual challenges of the sciences. And, this is a request for specification of some of the mechanisms that are at work. But likewise, it is always legitimate to ask what gives force to a given mechanism; and here we are eventually driven back to the answer, "some of the components of the mechanism have X, Y, Z powers to affect other entities" without further analysis within that particular explanation.

One might imagine that there are primitive causal powers—powers attached to primitive particles that have no underlying components or mechanisms. We might begin to give a list of primitive causal powers: mechanical interactions among physical objects (transfer of momentum from one particle to another); electromagnetic properties inhering in one object and creating forces affecting other objects; gravitational forces among objects possessing mass; the causal interactions that occur within the central nervous system. And, we might seek to demonstrate that all causal powers depend on combinations of these sorts of "primitive" causal powers—a kind of Hobbesian materialism. But this is needlessly strenuous from a metaphysical point of view. Better is to consider the middle-level range of powers and mechanisms where we are able to move upward and downward in our search for underlying causal mechanisms and supervening causal powers.

This line of thought suggests that questions about the metaphysics of causation are perhaps less pressing than they are sometimes made out to be. A thing's powers are not irreducible attributes of the thing; rather, they are the orderly consequence of the composition of the thing and the causal properties of those components and their interactions. It is hard to see that much turns on whether we think of the world as consisting of entities with powers, or as composites with system properties created by their components. The key question seems to be something like this: What is implied when we make a causal assertion? Both CP and CM agree that the core implication is the idea that one event, structure, or condition *brought about* the occurrence of another event, structure, or condition. And, the languages of both powers and mechanisms do a pretty good job of expressing what we mean in asserting this implication.

(John Dupré takes a similarly ecumenical view about several approaches to the theory of causation in a recent article "Living Causes," where he advocates for what he calls "causal pluralism." He writes: "I believe that causality is a complex and diverse set of phenomena, and most or all of these accounts provide valuable and complementary perspectives on the topic. Such a pluralistic view is quite a common one among contemporary philosophers; however there are significant differences in the form that such pluralisms can take" (Dupre and Woodward 2013: 20). On the mechanisms' side, within the philosophy of biology is William Bechtel who writes: "Beginning in the 1940s an initially small cadre of investigators who were pioneers in the modern discipline of cell biology began to figure out the biochemical mechanisms that enable cells to perform these functions. although miniaturized, the mechanisms they found to be operative in each cell are staggeringly complex" (Bechtel 2006: 1).)

MESO POWERS AND CAUSAL MECHANISMS

So far we have largely focused on social causes that take place at the level of individual actors. Now we turn to a larger question: Do higher-level social entities (structures, normative systems, organizations, institutions) have causal powers that exercise their force autonomously? Is there such a thing as meso-meso social causation?

Of course, meso-level structures have effects—on individuals. The fact that there are laws and enforcement mechanisms governing highway speed has some effect on drivers' behavior. The question here is whether it is legitimate to postulate causal powers for structures whose effects are realized in other meso-level structures. I want to support the affirmative answer to the question: it is legitimate and coherent to assert meso-meso causal interactions, and we sometimes have empirical evidence to support such assertions.

This question is relevant to two groups of sociological theorists, each of whom thinks the answer is trivial and obvious—but in opposite directions. The new methodological individualists, represented by analytical sociology, think the answer is trivially "no," because social causation proceeds always and exclusively through actions and interactions of individuals. This is the fundamental idea underlying Coleman's boat as a model of the relationship between macro and micro (Figure 4.2). And, a range of anti-individualists—Giddens, Elder-Vass, Archer—believe it is self-evident from everyday experience that causal structures do have causal powers, and that it is a waste of time to defend the notion. It is obvious.

So, I have a simple but important question in mind here: Is it ever legitimate to assert something like this:

- Meso structure *X* produced changes in meso structure *Y*,

without being obliged to demonstrate the individual-level pathways through which this effect is thought to have come about? Is a type 4 causal claim on Coleman's boat diagram ever supportable?

A related question is whether there are "mechanisms" that operate at the meso level, or whether all social mechanisms must operate at the individual level (as Hedström and the analytical sociology literature would maintain). I will return to this question.

My defense of meso-level causation is based on four ideas. First, the practice of sociologists justifies this claim, since sociologists do in fact make use of meso-meso claims. They often do not attempt to provide vertical explanations from circumstances of the actor to meso- and macro-level outcomes; instead, they often provide horizontal explanations that explain one set of meso- and macro outcomes on the basis of the causal powers of another set of meso- and macro conditions or structures. Second, sociology is a "special science" analogous to cognitive science, dependent on a set of causally linked entities at a lower level. Arguments offered for the relative explanatory autonomy of the higher-level theories are applicable to sociology as well. The basis for rejecting reductionism is well established here. Third, meso entities (organizations, institutions, normative systems) often have stable characteristics with regular behavioral consequences. This is illustrated with the example of organizations. Fourth, those entities have microfoundations; we must be confident that there are individual behaviors at lower levels that support these macro characteristics. But it is legitimate to draw out the macro-level effects of the macro-circumstance under investigation, without tracing out the way that effect works in detail on the swarms of actors encompassed by the case. The requirement of microfoundations is not a requirement on explanation; it does not require that our explanations proceed through the microfoundational level. It is an ontological principle but not a methodological principle. Rather, it is a condition that must be satisfied on *prima facie* grounds, prior to offering the explanation. (I refer to this as the "weak" requirement of microfoundations.) In short, we are not obliged to trace out the struts of Coleman's boat in order to provide a satisfactory macro- or meso-level explanation or mechanism.

Let's look at these considerations more fully.

First, working sociologists offer explanations that postulate meso-meso causal connections on a regular basis. They identify what they take to be causal properties of social structures and institutions, and then draw out causal chains involving those causal properties. And, often they are able to answer the follow-on question: How does that causal power work, in approximate terms, at the micro level? But answering that question is not an essential part of their argument. They do not in fact attempt to work through the agent-based simulation that would validate their general view about how the processes work at the lower level.

This explanatory framework seems entirely reasonable in the social sciences. It does not seem necessary to disaggregate every claim like "organizational deficiencies at the Bhopal chemical plant caused the devastating chemical spill" onto specific individual-level activities. We understand pretty well, in a generic way, what the microfoundations of organizations are, and it isn't necessary to provide a detailed account in order to have a satisfactory explanation. In other words, we can make careful statements about macro-macro and macro-meso causal relations without proceeding according to the logic of Coleman's boat—up and down the struts. So, one argument for the relative autonomy of meso-level causal claims is precisely the fact that good sociologists do in fact make credible use of such claims.

Second, there is a more general reason within the philosophy of the social sciences for being receptive to the idea of meso-meso social causes. This derives from the arguments against *reductionism* in a range of the special sciences. The idea of relative explanatory autonomy has been invoked by cognitive scientists against the reductionist claims of neuroscientists. Of course, cognitive mechanisms must be grounded in neurophysiological processes. But this doesn't entail that cognitive theories need to be reduced to neurophysiological statements. Jerry Fodor introduced highly influential arguments against reductionism in "special sciences and the disunity of science as a working hypothesis" (Fodor 1974, 1997).

Once we have reason to accept something like the idea of relative explanatory autonomy in the social sciences, we also have a strong basis for rejecting the exclusive validity of one particular approach to social explanation, the reductionist approach associated with methodological individualism, analytical sociology, and Coleman's boat. Rather, social scientists can legitimately use explanations that call upon meso-level causal linkages without needing to reduce these to derivations from facts about individuals. And, this implies the legitimacy of a fairly broad conception of methodological pluralism in the social sciences, constrained always by the requirement of weak microfoundations.

Third, we have good research-based reasons to maintain that meso-level social structures have causal powers. Consider organizations as paradigm examples of meso-level social structures. An organization is a social entity that possesses a degree of stability in functioning that can be studied empirically and theoretically. An organization consists of a structured group of individuals, often hierarchically organized, pursuing a relatively clearly defined set of tasks. In the abstract, it is a set of rules and procedures that regulate and motivate the behavior of the individuals who function within the organization. There are also informal practices within an organization that are not codified that have significant effects on the functioning of the organization (e.g. the coffee room as a medium of informal communication and or the norm of covering for a coworker's absence). Some of those individuals have responsibilities of oversight, which is a primary way in which the abstract rules of the organization are transformed into concrete patterns of activity by other individuals. Another behavioral characteristic of an organization is the set of incentives and rewards that it creates for participants in the organization. Often, the incentives that exist were planned and designed to have specific effects on behavior of participants; by offering rewards for behaviors X, Y, and Z, the organization is expected to produce a lot of X, Y, and Z. Sometimes, though, the incentives are unintended, created perhaps by the intersection of two rules of operation that lead to a perverse incentive leading to W.

Now, we are in a position to address the central question here: Do organizations have causal powers? It seems to me that the answer is yes, in fairly specific ways. The most obvious causal properties of an organization are bound up in the function of the organization. An organization is invented and developed in order to bring about certain social effects: operate and maintain a complex technology, reduce pollution or crime, distribute goods throughout a population, provide services to individuals, seize and hold territory, and disseminate information. But the specifics of an organization also give rise to unintended consequences; these too contribute to the causal powers of the organization. All these effects occur as a result of the coordinated activities of people within the organization. When organizations work correctly, they bring about one set of effects; when they break down, they bring about another set of effects. Here, we can think about organizations in analogy with technology components like amplifiers, thermostats, stabilizers, or surge protectors.

Finally, I too believe that there is a burden of proof that must be met in asserting a causal power or disposition for a social entity—something like, "the entity demonstrates an empirical regularity in behaving in such and such a way" or "we have good theoretical reasons for believing that X social arrangements will have Y effects." And, some macro-concepts (e.g. state, Islam, market economy) are likely cast at too high a level to admit of such regularities. That is why I favor "meso" social entities as the bearers of social powers. As new institutionalists demonstrate all the time, one property regime elicits very different collective behavior from its highly similar cousin. And, this gives the relevant causal stability criterion. Good examples include Robert Ellickson's new-institutionalist treatment of Shasta County and liability norms and Charles Perrow's treatment of the operating characteristics of technology organizations. In each case, the microfoundations are easy to provide. What is more challenging is to show how these social-causal properties interact in cases to create outcomes we want to explain.

So, how does the micro-macro link look when we attempt to provide the idea of meso explanations with microfoundations? The various versions of methodological individualism—microeconomics, analytical sociology, Elster's theories of explanation, and the model of Coleman's boat—presume that explanation needs to invoke the story of the micro-level events as part of the explanation. The perspective offered here requires something quite different. This position requires that we be confident that these micro-level events exist and work to compose the meso level; but it does not require that the causal argument incorporates a reconstruction of the pathway through the individual level in order to have a satisfactory explanation. This account suggests an alternative diagram to Coleman's boat.

This diagram (Figure 6.2) represents each of the causal linkages represented in the Coleman boat (see Figure 4.2). But it also calls out the meso-meso causal connection that Coleman prohibits in his analysis. And, it replaces the idea that causation proceeds through the individual level, with the idea that each meso-level factor has a set of actor-level microfoundations. But this is an ontological fact, not a prescription on explanation.

Consider a familiar social entity, the organization. An organization is a meso-level social structure. It is a structured group of individuals, often hierarchically organized, pursuing a relatively clearly defined set of tasks. In the abstract, it is a set of rules and procedures that regulate and motive the behavior of the individuals who function within the organization. There are also a set of informal practices within an organization that are not codified that have significant effects on the functioning of the organization (e.g., the coffee room as a medium of informal communication). Some of those individuals have responsibilities of oversight, which is a primary way in which the abstract rules of the organization are transformed into concrete patterns of activity by other individuals. Another behavioral characteristic of an

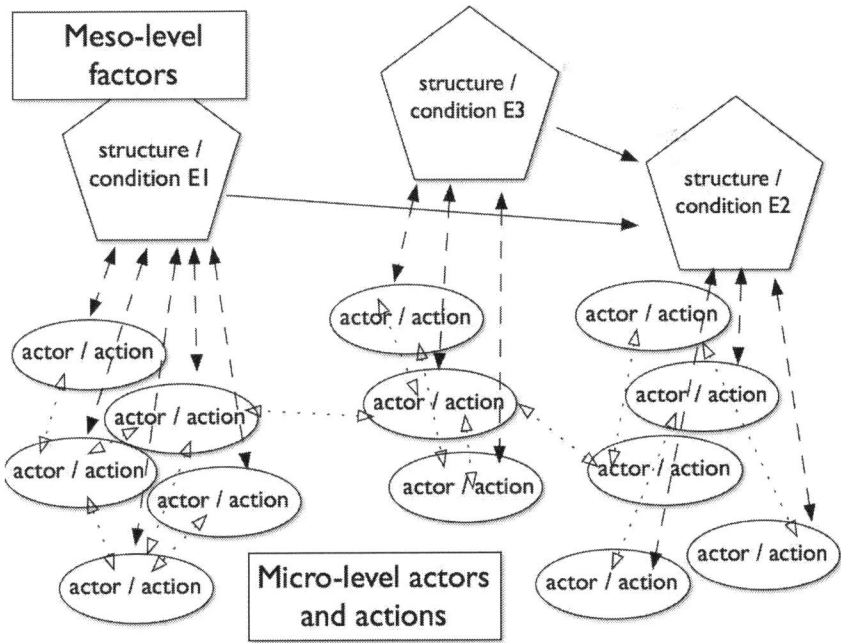

Figure 6.2   Meso-meso causal relations.

organization is the set of incentives and rewards that it creates for participants in the organization. Often, the incentives that exist were planned and designed to have specific effects on behavior of participants; by offering rewards for behaviors X, Y, and Z, the organization is expected to produce a lot of X, Y, and Z. Sometimes, though, the incentives are unintended, created perhaps by the intersection of two rules of operation that lead to a perverse incentive leading to W. For example, a farm supervisor may ask peach pickers to discard the bruised peaches rather than placing them in the basket to be weighed. But if the laborers' wages are determined solely by the weight of the baskets they present for weighing, they will have an incentive to include the bruised peaches (at the bottom!).

Examples of organizations include things like the following:

- The Boston police department
- A collective farm in Sichuan in 1965
- The maintenance and operations routines and staff of a nuclear power plant
- A large investment bank on Wall Street
- Certus Corporation (discoverer of the PCR process)
- The land value assessment process in late Imperial China

The organization consists of a number of things:

- A set of procedures for how to handle specific kinds of tasks
- A set of people with skills and specific roles
- A set of incentives and rewards to induce participants to carry out their roles effectively and diligently
- A set of accountability processes permitting supervision and assessment of performance by individuals within the organization
- An "executive" function with the power to refine, revise, and improve the rules so as to bring about preferred patterns of performance

How do organizations embody causal powers? Let's focus on the nuclear power plant operational procedures as an example. The tasks of the organization are to control the complex technology and its instruments over an extended time; to conduct inspections of the physical infrastructure of the plant to discover failures before they occur; to conduct routine maintenance of machines and other physical systems; to respond quickly to failures, both large and small; and to sometimes conduct major upgrades on the hardware of the system. We may imagine that there are detailed, written procedures for each of these activities, as well as procedures for action during times of malfunction or breakdown. The people of the plant represent a range of specialized skills and specialized tasks. Wainwrights maintain and repair machinery;

computer technicians maintain computer systems; nuclear technicians over-see the measured functioning of the system (pressures, temperatures, power production); safety workers inspect various system; and supervisors assign tasks and monitor performance.

Failures of the system arise for several different kinds of reasons: techni-cal failure (a device fails for unexpected technical reasons, such as a faulty weld); operator failure (an operator disregards or misinterprets a pressure warning, and a pipe explodes before corrective action is taken); training failure (staff are technically or operationally unprepared for performing their tasks routinely or in exceptional circumstances); system failure (two or more subsystems function as designed, but in an unusual circumstance may interact in such a way as to bring about an explosion, a computer crash, or a release of energy or heat); supervisory failure (procedures were good but supervisors permitted deviation from the procedures); and venality failure (individuals in a position to control purchasing decisions authorize bad contracts for faulty materials for their personal profit).

The idea of a principal-agent problem is highly relevant within organiza-tions, at every level. The executive expects the supervisor to faithfully per-form his or her tasks of supervision. But since the executive does not directly monitor the performance of the supervisor, it is possible for the supervisor to shirk his or her duties and permit faulty performance by those he supervises. Likewise, the supervisor expects that the operator will continue to monitor and control the machine throughout the day; but it is possible for the operator to keep a solitaire window open on the screen. Each level of accountability, then, requires both formal expectations and a basis for trust in the good faith of the participants in the organization.

Now, we are in a position to address the central question here: Do organi-zations have causal powers? It seems that the answer is yes, in fairly specific ways. First, the rules and procedures of the organization may themselves have behavioral consequences that lead consistently to a certain kind of outcome. For example, the prescribed cycle of inspections of critical equipment may be too infrequent to have a high probability of detecting failures before they lead to an accident.

Second, different organizational forms may be more or less efficient at per-forming their tasks, leading to consequences for the people and higher-level organizations that are depending on them. For example, two tax collection systems may be designed for the same goal—to collect 10% of the grain pro-duced everywhere in the kingdom. If one system is 75% successful in this task and the other is 50% successful, the state depending on the second system will be starved for resources and will have a propensity toward military weakness.

Third, the discrepancy between what the rules require of participants and what the participants actually do may have consequences for the outputs of the organization. Police department regulations may require that each piece of physical evidence is separately bagged and cataloged with appropriate information about its collection. If police operatives are careless in the cataloging of evidence, it may be more difficult to convict the accused; this may lead to a rising disregard for the likelihood of conviction and a rise in the crime rate. Corruption (venal failure to perform one's tasks faithfully) may lead to large consequences: the company is less profitable, the city is discredited to its citizens, and the church is delegitimized by the self-interested behavior of its clergy.

Fourth, the specific ways in which incentives, sanctions, and supervision are implemented are different across organizations. We may find that organizations with supervision system X are on average more productive or more effective than those with system Y.

Fifth, the organization has causal powers with respect to the behavior of the individuals involved in the organization. By presenting its rules, sanctions, and rewards to its participants, it changes their behavior in specific ways. Google and Apple have organized their internal procedures and rewards in such a way as to encourage creativeness, teamwork, and confidentiality. These organizations look quite different in their functioning and their products from a steel company or a shoe company.

This analysis implies two things. First, we can say with some confidence that the way an organization is structured makes a difference to its performance; this is a causal power all by itself. And, second, we may be able to discover that there are broad characteristics that differentiate organizational types, and it may turn out that these distinct types also have different performance characteristics. We might discover, for example, that one system of oversight and employee motivation is significantly more likely to permit theft and corrupt behavior by its agents than another. In that case, we might say that these two systems differ in their propensities for generating corrupt behavior. (This is an argument that Robert Klitgaard makes in *Controlling Corruption*; Klitgaard (1988).)

So far, we have not mentioned the familiar subject of "microfoundations" at all; we have considered an organization as a complex social entity. It is easy to specify the microfoundations of the causal powers we have identified. The organization's performance is determined by the behaviors of the individuals who fall within it, and the aggregate individual behaviors are explained by the rules and procedures embodied in the organization. So, the causal powers having to do with efficiency, effectiveness, and corruptibility can be disaggregated into the incentives and behaviors of typical individuals. But here is the key point: we don't need to carry out this disaggregation when we want to invoke statements about the causal characteristics of organizations in explanations of more complex social processes.

These observations lay a basis for concluding that meso-level social entities do indeed have causal powers that can legitimately be invoked in social
explanations. Significantly, there are clear and convincing examples of
sociological explanations that take the causal powers of organizations as fundamental to their explanations of important social outcomes—for example,
technology failure (Perrow 1999), corruption (Klitgaard 1988), and the use
of common property resources (Ostrom 1990).

Further, we can often say quite a bit about the lower-level mechanisms
that give rise to a given meso-level power. A meso-level structure S's causal
powers may result from the causal powers of its component systems T_i, and a
set of causal mechanisms that embody the causal powers of S may be found
at the level of mechanisms at the level of T_i. For example, a certain type of
police organization S may have a high level of corruption C among its street
officers. So, S has the causal power to bring about C. The mechanisms that
establish this power may reside at a lower level of organization: the processes
for giving assignments and the processes for checking incident reports. The
diagram might look something like as shown in Figure 6.3.

The dashed line indicates the causal power. The solid arc lines on the left
indicate "composition." The solid arrows indicate meso-meso causal mechanisms. And, the dotted lines indicate the aggregate consequences of "poor
orientation to goals" and "weak incentives for conformance," which is an
elevated level of officer corruption. So, the meso-level power depends on
sub-meso-level mechanisms and actor-level mechanisms. So, the conclusion
I would like to offer is this: meso-level causal powers are created as a consequence of specific causal mechanisms triggered by the properties and changes
of the meso-level structure. Those mechanisms may be at the actor level; they
may be at a sub-meso level; or they may be at the meso level.

This discussion supports the idea that meso-level social entities possess causal powers. Are there meso-level mechanisms as well? Or, are the

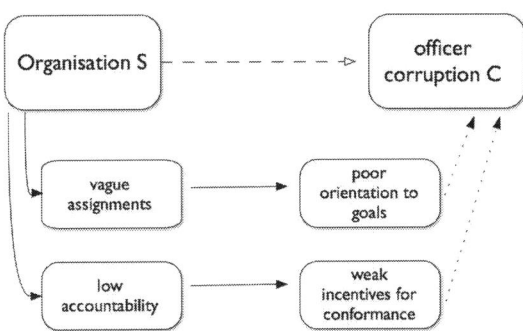

Figure 6.3   Inter-level causal mechanism.

mechanisms that mediate meso causal powers themselves necessarily located at the micro level? It is evident that there are micro-level mechanisms for meso-level causal powers. The mechanisms of a run on the bank or a self-fulfilling prophecy are both micro level; they show how a meso-level event disaggregates onto the beliefs and actions of the individuals involved, leading to collective behavior that results in the meso-level effect. These are exactly the kinds of mechanism that analytical sociologists, including Thomas Schelling, want to be the exclusive kind of causation in the social realm. So, the hard question is this: Are there meso-level causal mechanisms?

Once we have established that entities at a given level have causal powers, it is simple to show that these entities can play a role in causal mechanisms at that level. If S has the power to produce change in T and both S and T are meso-level structures, then $S => T$ is itself a meso-level causal mechanism. And, it is straightforward to identify examples of social causation that satisfy this description; so, it follows that there are simple meso-level causal mechanisms.

Here is a plausible example of a meso-meso causal mechanism. Social isolation is a meso-level characteristic of a population. Alford Young argues that decreasing social isolation causes rising intergroup hostility, another meso-level characteristic of a population (Young 2004). This represents a clear and uncontroversial example of a meso-meso causal link that is also a meso-level causal mechanism. Moreover, this mechanism can be employed in explanations of more complex social events like race rebellions.

In short, it seems that we can make a strong argument for the case that meso-level structures possess some causal powers that do not need to be reduced to the micro level and that can play plausible roles in simple meso-meso causal mechanisms as well.

LARGE CAUSES AND MECHANISM COMPONENTS

So far, we have explored a fairly "micro" approach to explanation and analysis based on the idea of concrete social-causal mechanisms. This approach seeks to understand how a given process works by looking for the causal mechanisms that underlie it. But not all explanatory questions in the social sciences fall at this level of aggregation (Little 2010). Some researchers are less interested in the micro-pathways of particular episodes and more interested in the abiding social forces and arrangements that influence the direction of change in social systems. For example, Marx believed that conflict between the forces and relations of production create a tendency toward crisis within capitalism. And, Michael Mann provides more detailed analysis of world history that understands the development of great civilizations based on a set of large structural factors in *The Sources of Social Power* (1986) He singles out ideological, economic, military, and political forces as fundamental sociological causes.

Large social factors at this level include things like the inequalities of power and opportunity created by various property systems; the logic of a competitive corporate capitalist economy; the large social consequences of climate change—whether in the Little Ice Age or the current day; the strategic and military interests of various nations; and the social and economic consequences of ubiquitous mobile computation and communication abilities. Researchers as diverse as Karl Marx, Manuel Castells, Carl von Clausewitz, and William McNeill have sought out causal hypotheses that attempt to explain large-scale historical change as the consequence, in part, of the particular configurations and variations of macro factors like these. Outcomes like success in war, the ascendancy of one nation or region over others, the configuration of power and advantage across social groups within modern democracies, and the economic rise of one region over another are all large-scale outcomes that researchers have sought to explain as the consequence of other large-scale social, economic, and political factors.

These approaches are not logically incompatible. If we follow along with William McNeill (McNeill 1976) and consider the idea that the modern distribution of national power across the globe is a consequence of the vulnerability of various regions to disease, we are fully engaged in the idea that macro factors have macro consequences. But it is also open to us to ask the question, how do these macro factors work at the more granular level? What are the local mechanisms that underlay the dynamics of disease in Southeast Asia, West Africa, or South America? So we can always shift focus upward and downward, and we can always look for more granular explanations for any form of social-causal influence. And, in fact, some historical sociologists succeed in combining both approaches; for example, Michael Mann in his study of fascism (2004), who gives attention both to large-scale regional factors (the effects of demobilization following World War I) and local, individual-level factors (the class and occupational identities of fascist recruits).

That said, the pragmatics of the two approaches are quite different. Moreover, the logic of causal research appears to differ as well. The causal mechanism theory of explanation suggests close comparative study of individual cases—particular rebellions, particular episodes of population change, and particular moments of change of government. The "large social factor" approach to explanation suggests a different level of research, a research method that permits comparison of large outcomes and the co-variance of putative causal factors. Mill's methods of causal reasoning appear to be more relevant to this type of causal hypothesis. Theda Skocpol's study of social revolution in *States and Social Revolutions* is a case in point (Skocpol 1979).

The harder question is this: Are the large social factors mentioned here legitimate "causes," or are they simply placeholders for more granular study of particular mechanisms and pathways? Should reference to "capitalism," "world trading system," or "modern European reproductive regime" be expected to disappear in the ideal historical sociology of the future? Or, is this "large structure" vocabulary an altogether justified and stable level of social analysis on the basis of which to construct historical and social explanations? I am inclined to believe that the latter position is correct, and that it is legitimate to conceive of social research at a range of levels of aggregation. The impulse toward disaggregation is a scientifically respectable one, but it should not be understood as replacing analysis at a higher level.

CAUSAL PROCESSES UNDERLYING
INTELLECTUAL MOVEMENTS

Let us consider another example of sophisticated causal analysis in sociology. How do intellectual movements (SIMs; e.g. logical positivism, post-structuralism, string theory, the New Historicism) take hold in an academic field? Frickel and Gross's "General Theory of Scientific/Intellectual Movements" (Frickel and Gross 2005) offers a theory of how intellectual movements take hold in a field. They put their goal in this article in this way:

> The theory seeks to answer the question, under what social conditions is any particular scientific/intellectual movement, or SIM (whose nature we clarify shortly), most likely to emerge, gain adherents, win intellectual prestige, and ultimately acquire some level of institutional stability? (205)

This description evokes an explanatory goal with a causal perspective— "conditions" that make "emergence of the intellectual movement" likely. They emphasize the importance of identifying common features of SIMs in order to "mark them as objects for sociological study" (208), which implies that a precondition of sociological study is that we need to identify a social kind of entities with reasonably similar properties. This too suggests an underlying causal perspective that looks to regularities and common properties rather than causal mechanisms or causal powers.

They define SIMs as collective efforts to pursue research programs or projects for thought in the face of resistance from others in the scientific or intellectual community (206). Frickel and Gross are quite explicit in looking for a "general theory" of the factors that promote the growth of an intellectual movement. What they mean by this is an account of a limited set of social conditions whose presence or absence "explains" the success or failure of a candidate SIM at a point in time. In other words, their analysis is guided by the idea that causal relationships work through necessary and sufficient conditions which can be discovered through comparative research. Mechanisms come into the story fairly quickly: "Our general theory insists that the precise mechanisms whereby a field's external environment shapes a SIM must be specified" (209). The four premises of the general theory are as follows:

- Proposition 1: A SIM is more likely to emerge when high-status intellectual actors harbor complaints against what they understand to be the central intellectual tendencies of the day. (209)
- Proposition 2: SIMs are more likely to be successful when structural conditions provide access to key resources. (213)
- Proposition 3: The greater a SIM's access to various micro mobilization contexts, the more likely it is to be successful. (219)
- Proposition 4: The success of a SIM is contingent upon the work done by movement participants to frame movement ideas in ways that resonate with the concerns of those who inhabit an intellectual field or fields. (221)

For each of these theoretical propositions, they offer the sketch of an idea about what the mechanisms are that might support this factor. For example, concerning proposition 1, they maintain that "grievance" is a necessary condition for the emergence of a SIM because it puts potential adherents in a state of psychological readiness for mobilization. Another mechanism they cite for the emergence and mobilization of a SIM is the sudden entry into a field of nontraditional practitioners—for example, women or African American scholars entering the field of urban studies in the 1960s who found that prevailing wisdom failed to do justice to their own experiences. And, on the resources point, Frickel and Gross refer to the job market, academic organizations, and funding sources and sketch out how favorable conditions with regard to these structural features can facilitate the success of a SIM. This is, at least in sketch, a mechanisms analysis.

The mechanisms associated with proposition 3 are encapsulated in the notion of "micromobilization". Frickel and Gross hold that the success of a SIM is influenced by the strength or weakness of the various organizations and networks through which it is able to spread its message and its mobilization efforts at the grassroots level. They mention laboratories, conferences, research retreats, and academic departments (219). Once one or more advocates of the given SIM has a position of influence in one of these centers, he or she is enabled to influence and mobilize other scholars to the SIM.

The mechanisms associated with proposition 4 pick up on the rhetorical side of intellectual work. This might be described as the marketing campaign it pursues. In order to influence prospective adherents to an intellectual movement, it is necessary to provide "messages" that resonate with them. This factor has to do with effective framing of issues and research questions.

BUSINESS ETHICS AS AN INTELLECTUAL MOVEMENT

Gabriel Abend's *The Moral Background: An Inquiry into the History of Business Ethics* (2014) is a remarkable book on the history of the academic field of business ethics. Abend's goal is to understand the actual history of the field of business ethics. He is not trying to discover the patterns of behavior that are found among businessmen, or the ethical ideas they embrace. Rather, he wants to tease out the material and ideological content expressed by professional "business ethicists," largely found in schools of business. What has been the public expert discourse on business ethics over the past century, and what framing assumptions about the ethical field does this discourse presuppose?

> The book scrutinizes the content of business ethicists' understandings and prescriptions—taking into account their context, the audiences they were addressed to, and the cultural repertoires they drew upon. . . . Much like sociologists and anthropologists of science, I am interested in the tools, devices, technologies, methods, and tactics business ethicists came up with and avail themselves of. Manuals of proper behavior, success manuals, pamphlets, biographies, obituaries, typologies, illustrations, and codes of ethics are not neutral, interchangeable containers of information. They are social things, with particular causal histories and social functions, and whose particular modes of operation, modes of existence, and materiality must be analyzed as well. (11)

He correctly observes that there are three levels of ethics that can be considered from a sociological point of view:

> First, there is the level of behavior or practices. . . . Second, there is the level of people's moral judgments in the least, and societies' and social groups' moral norms and institutions. . . . In this book I introduce a third level, which up to now has not been recognized as a distant object inquiry: the moral background. (17)

His interest throughout the book is with the third level, the moral background. This refers, essentially, to the frameworks, concepts, and principles of reasoning that people have in mind when they think ethically or normatively.

> Moral background elements do not belong to the level or realm of first-order morality. Rather, they facilitate, support, or enable first-order moral claims, norms, actions, practices, and institutions. (53)

He compares the moral background with the meta-scientific beliefs that scientists bring to the study of nature or society.

> What is it that members of a scientific community share, exactly? For one, they likely share many social and demographic characteristics. That helps account sociologically for their having become members of that community in the first place. More important, they have common epistemological and ontological intuitions, dispositions, or assumptions. They agree on how you go about answering a scientific question, and what kind of evidence and how much of it you need to corroborate a hypothesis. (28)

This focus is particularly interesting because it provides additional leverage on the problem of offering a vocabulary for the background conceptual resources that are a necessary part of all social cognition. There is an important body of conceptual and factual presuppositions that human beings unavoidably use when they try to make sense of the world around them. And, the framework itself is only rarely available for inspection. So, it is a valuable contribution when sociologists like Abend, Gross, or Lamont are able to pinpoint the content and structure of such systems of tacit cognitive framework in action.

Abend's discussion of conceptual repertoires is particularly detailed and helpful. Abend defines conceptual repertoires as "the set of concepts that are available to any given group or society, in a given time and place" (37). He makes the valid and important point that conceptual schemes are culturally specific and historically variable; "this repertoire enables and constrains their thought and speech, their laws and institutions, and, importantly, the actions they may undertake" (37). He offers as examples of moral concepts ideas: "dignity, decency, integrity, piety, responsibility, tolerance, moderation, fanaticism, extremism, despotism, chauvinism, rudeness . . ." (38) and makes the correct point that ideas like these show up in some cultural and historical settings and not in others. So, the realities that can be "seen" and experienced by historically situated people depend on the schemes or repertoires they have available to them in those settings.

Abend finds two thematic sets of beliefs and concepts that largely serve to characterize most approaches to business ethics, which he refers to as "standards of practice" and "the Christian merchant." The first approach works on the assumption that ethical standards like honesty are good for business, all things considered, and that the function of business ethics writings and teaching is to help businesspeople come to see that their interests dictate that they should conform, even when there are strong incentives to do otherwise. The second principle argues that there are higher moral standards that govern behavior, and that prudent adherence to rules of honesty does not get to the heart of business ethics. Broadly speaking, the first approach is scientific and consequentialist (JS Mill), while the second is theological and deontological (Kant).

Abend demonstrates that the field of business ethics is substantially older than it is usually thought to be, extending back at least a century. To demonstrate this point, he makes interesting use of Google's Ngram tool, a research tool based on Google's massive collection of scanned books, and finds that the phrase "business ethics" begins to take off around 1900, passing "commercial morality" in 1912 and "business morality" in 1917. All the other phrases go into a sustained decline in books from 1920 forward, while "business ethics" takes off.

Chapter 7

Social Realism

SCIENTIFIC REALISM FOR THE SOCIAL SCIENCES

Scientific realism is the idea that scientific theories provide descriptions of the world that are approximately true. Realists in a particular domain of science postulate that the realm under consideration consists of entities, forces, and structures that are real and independent from our observations. Realism involves the view that at least *some* of the assertions of a field of knowledge make true statements about the properties of unobservable things, processes, and states in the domain of study. This view presupposes a correspondence theory of truth—the idea that the world is separate from the concepts that we use to describe it. And, it implies some sort of theory of scientific rationality— a theory of the grounds that we have for believing or accepting the findings of a given area of science. Realism, objectivity, and facts go together. We can interpret a theory realistically just in case we believe that there is a fact of the matter concerning the assertions contained in the theory.

Several major philosophers of science have taken up this issue in the past three decades, including Hilary Putnam, Richard Boyd, Rom Harré (Harré and Madden 1975), Roy Bhaskar (1975), and Peter Manicas (2006). Ilkka Niiniluoto's *Critical Scientific Realism* provides an excellent contemporary analysis of the premises and varieties of scientific realism (Niiniluoto 1999). Richard Boyd's arguments for scientific realism are particularly compelling (1990, 2002): various areas of the natural sciences are highly successful in predicting and controlling natural phenomena; their accounts are based on hypothetical theories of the unobservable mechanisms of nature; and, the best explanation of that success is the assumption that those theories are approximately true. Here is a good statement of Boyd's view:

Scientific realists hold that the characteristic product of successful scientific research is knowledge of largely theory-independent phenomena and that such knowledge is possible (indeed actual) even in those cases in which the relevant phenomena are not, in any non-question-begging sense, observable. The characteristic philosophical arguments for scientific realism embody the claim that certain central principles of scientific methodology require a realist explication. In its most completely developed form, this sort of abductive argument embodies the claim that a realist conception of scientific inquiry is required in order to justify, or to explain the reliability with respect to instrumental knowledge of, all of the basic methodological principles of mature scientific inquiry. (1990: 355)

Boyd also argues for the approximate continuity that exists within the natural sciences:

The historical progress of the mature sciences is largely a matter of successively more accurate approximations to the truth about both observable and unobservable phenomena. Later theories typically build upon the (observational and theoretical) knowledge embodied in previous theories. (1984)

Realism raises all kinds of interesting questions when we consider applying it to the social sciences. For one thing, it requires a usable distinction between the world and the knower. This raises the question: Is there an objective social world independent from the perceptions and concepts of observers? And, this also is a complicated question in the case of the social sciences, because the persons who make up social processes at the micro level are themselves "knowers" of the social world. So, there is a question about the objectivity of the social world and a corresponding question about social construction of social reality. If all social phenomena are socially constructed, then how can it be the case that some statements about social phenomena are objective and independent from the conceptual schemes of the observer?

Much of the discussion of scientific realism has depended upon examples drawn from the natural sciences. What is the relevance of scientific realism in the social sciences? Are there differences between the natural realm and the social world that make scientific realism a different proposition for the social world? Here is one important difference: the social sciences are barely "theoretical" at all in the sense associated with the natural sciences. The concepts that play central roles in social theories—charisma, bureaucratic state, class, power, habitus—are not exactly "theoretical" in the sense of being non-observational. And, social concepts are not defined implicitly, in terms of the role that they play in an extended formal theoretical structure. Rather, we can give a pretty good definition of social concepts in terms of behavior and commonsense attributes of social entities. Social entities are abstract but not obscure. In the social sciences, we do not find the conceptual holism that

Duhem (1906; 1977) and Quine (1960) attributed to the natural sciences. Instead, both meaning and confirmation can proceed piecemeal. So, if realism were primarily a doctrine about the interpretation of theoretical terms, there wouldn't be much need for it in the social sciences.

In fact, the situation in sociology and political science is quite different from astronomy, atomic theory, and mechanics. First, it seems fairly clear that there are no areas of research in the social sciences that have the predictive and explanatory success of the physical sciences. Second, the social world is more like the heterogeneous and contingent scenario described in chapter 1 than it is an icy surface with frictionless surfaces and predictable mechanics. The social world embodies multiple heterogeneous causal and structural influences that aggregate in contingent and surprising ways. Third, sociologists and political scientists sometimes make hypotheses about unobservable or hypothetical social entities. But these hypotheses do not play the logical role of that played by hypotheses in the natural sciences. Hypothetical social entities may be unobservable in a fairly ordinary sense—no one can directly observe or measure a social class. But in fact, these concepts do not depend on holistic confirmation in the way that hypotheses in the natural sciences do. Rather, it is perfectly possible to further refine our ideas about "social class," "prisoners' dilemma," or "bipolar security field" and then investigate the manifold aspects of these concepts through direct social research. Sociology and political science do not consist of unified deductive systems whose empirical success depends upon a derivation of distant observational consequences; instead, it is possible to investigate essentially every sociological or political concept through various direct methods of research and inquiry.

In short, the social sciences do not possess the remarkable coherence and predictive accuracy of physics, so confidence in realism is not grounded in the high level of success of the enterprise. Sociology is not like physics. But equally, the concepts of the social sciences are not "hypothetical constructs" that depend upon their role in a developed theoretical system for application. It is therefore possible to be piecemeal realists. Again, social science is not like physics.

So, it seems that two specific ideas follow. First, the inference to the best explanation argument for realism offered by Boyd and others does not work at all in sociology or political science. We simply do not have the extraordinary predictive successes of a theoretical system that would constitute the ground of such an argument. Social science theories and models remain heuristic and suggestive, but rarely strongly indicative of the reality of the social factors they highlight.

But second, there is a very different kind of argument for social realism that is not available in the natural sciences: the piecemeal investigation of claims and theories about social entities, properties, and forces. If we believe that class conflict is a key factor in explaining political outcomes, we can do sociological research to further articulate what we mean by class and class conflict, and we can investigate specific social and political processes to piece together the presence or absence of these kinds of factors. These investigations may give us confidence that "class" exists.

So, it seems that we can justify being realists about class, field, habitus, market, coalition, ideology, organization, value system, ethnic identity, institution, and charisma, without relying at all on the hypothetico-deductive (H-D) model of scientific knowledge upon which the "inference to the best explanation" argument depends. We can look at sociology and political science as loose ensembles of empirically informed theories and models of meso-level social processes and mechanisms, each of which is to a large degree independently verifiable. And, this implies that social realism should be focused on mid-level social mechanisms and processes that can be identified in the domains of social phenomena that we have studied rather than sweeping concepts of social structures and entities.

Here are several specific ways in which scientific realism is useful in the social sciences. And, they all have to do with the kinds of statements in the social sciences that we think can be interpreted as expressing facts about the world, independent of our theories and concepts.

Causal realism. We can be realist about statements about causation, causal mechanisms, and causal powers of social facts and entities. We can take the position that there is a fact of the matter as to whether X caused Y in the circumstances, and we can assert the objective reality of social causal mechanisms and powers. On the realist interpretation, social causal mechanisms exist in the social world—they are not simply constructs of the observer's conceptual scheme. And, the statement that "Q is the process through which X causes Y" makes a purportedly objective and observer-independent claim about Q; it is an objective social process, and it conveys causation from X to Y. Q is the causal mechanism underlying the causal relationship between X and Y.

Structure realism. We can be realist about the existence of extended social entities and structures—for example, "the working class," "the American Congress," and "the movement for racial equality." These social entities and structures have some curious ontological characteristics—it is difficult to draw boundaries between members of the working class and the artisan class, so the distinctness of the respective classes is at risk; institutions like the Congress change over time; a social movement may be characterized in multiple and sometimes incompatible ways; and social entities don't fall into "kinds" that are uniform across settings. But surely it is compelling to judge that the Civil Rights movement was an objective fact in the 1960s or that the Congress exists and is a partisan environment. And, this is a version of social realism.

Social relations realism. If we say that "Pierre is actively involved in a social network of retired French military officers," we refer to a set of social relations encapsulated under the concept of a social network and composed of many pairwise social relations. Here, too, we can take the perspective of social realism. It seems unproblematic to postulate the objective reality of both the pairwise social relations and the aggregate network that these constitute. Each level of social relationship can be investigated empirically (we can discover that Pierre has regular interactions with Jean but not with Claude), and it seems unproblematic to judge that there is a fact of the matter about the existence and properties of the network—independent of the assumptions and concepts of the observer.

Meaning realism. Now, how about the hardest case: meanings and the objectivity of interpretation. Can we say that there is ever a fact of the matter about the interpretation of an action or thought? When Thaksin offends Charat by exposing the bottoms of his feet to him—can we say, "Charat's angry reaction is the result of the meaning of this insulting gesture in Thai culture"? Even here, it is credible to me that there is a basis for saying that this judgment expresses an objective fact (even if it is a fact about subjective experience); and therefore, we can interpret this sentence along realist lines: "Thaksin's gesture was objectively offensive in the setting of Thai culture." It is evident that many of our interpretations of behavior and action are substantially underdetermined by context and evidence; so it may be that much interpretation of meaning does not constitute a "fact of the matter." But this seems to be a fact about particular judgments rather than a universal feature of the interpretation of meanings.

So, it seems that it is feasible and useful to take a social realist perspective on many of the assertions and theories of the social sciences; and, this implies that we can interpret social science statements as being approximately true of a domain of social phenomena that have objective properties (i.e. properties that are independent from our conceptualization of them).

These considerations should perhaps lead us to conclude that the topic of realism is just as legitimate in sociology, political science, and economics as it is in the natural sciences. Social scientists have every reason to be realist about the actions, relations, and interactions of individuals. They are justified in thinking that the practices of education and socialization that bring children to adulthood are "real" and can be empirically investigated. And, they are justified in observing that there are higher-order configurations of action, power, and social relationship that are "real," insofar as they are present in the activities of the individuals who constitute them and they possess some stable characteristics over time. In other words, social scientists are justified in postulating the social reality of the social processes and institutions that they postulate and investigate.

POSITIVISM AND ANTI-POSITIVISM

Realism has been a central and contested part of the philosophy of social science for at least forty years. One reason for its prominence is the fundamental fault line that exists within the philosophy of science between positivism and anti-positivism. Positivists draw much of their conception of science from Hume; all knowledge is based on the evidence of the senses, and the only general statements in which we can have scientific confidence are statements of regularities. As Hume insisted, there is no such thing as causal necessity; there are only regularities of association between observable events. The anti-positivist approach maintains that nature (and society) possesses an unobservable structure that is more fundamental than the scattered observations we are able to make; that there are real causal connections among events that are determined by unobservable structures and properties; and that it is the task of science to arrive at theories about those underlying structures and properties.

Carl Hempel represented the fruition of positivist philosophy of science in the 1950s and 1960s, with his H-D model of confirmation, his deductive-nomological model of explanation, and his covering law model of historical explanation (Hempel 1965). These all amount to the same idea, of course: that scientific knowledge takes the form of a set of general theoretical principles or laws, a set of empirical statements about existing conditions, and a set of deductions from the laws and statements of consequences for the observable phenomena. There was a strong reaction in the 1960s to the orthodoxies of logical positivism and Hempelian philosophy of science by philosophers such as Norwood Hanson, Paul Feyerabend, and Thomas Kuhn. Compelling criticisms were offered of the strict distinction between observation and theory, concerns were raised about the putative coincidence of explanation and derivation from general laws, and more nuanced theories of scientific rationality than the H-D method were offered.

Richard Rudner was the American philosopher who made concerted efforts to apply the neopositivist philosophy of science to the social sciences (Rudner 1966). Several core assumptions about the social sciences are advanced in Rudner's book.

- Unity of science and naturalism; all sciences should resemble physics
- Emphasis on the distinction between the context of discovery and context of justification
- Insistence on the symmetry of explanation and prediction

- Insistence on the essential role of lawlike generalizations in explanation
- Fundamental reliance on a strict distinction between observation and theory
- Advancement of "formalizability" as a desirable characteristic of a theory

Perhaps the key philosophical assumption that Rudner defends is the idea that the logic of science is everywhere the same. Concept formation, deduction, confirmation, and explanation all involve the same formalizable operations. A theory should be formalized as a first-order deductive system with primitive terms and defined terms; some of its terms should have criteria of application to observable outcomes; explanation proceeds by deriving a description of the explanandum from the theory; and the theory should be tested by evaluating the truth or falsity of its observational consequences.

What is the logic of scientific explanation in the social sciences, according to Rudner? His answer is straight from Hempel's covering law theory:

> The formal structure of a scientific explanation of some particular event has three parts: first, a statement E describing the specific event to be explained; second, a set of statements C_1 to C_n describing specific relevant circumstances that are antecedent to, or otherwise causally correlated with, the event described by E; third, a set of lawlike statements L_1 to L_n, universal generalizations whose import is roughly "Whenever events of the kind described by C_1 through C_n take place, then an event of the kind described by E takes place." (Rudner 1966: 60)

What are the strengths and weaknesses of this approach to the philosophy of the social sciences? It is an exceptionally clear exposition and development of the central ideas of logical positivism in application to social science theorizing. Unfortunately, this approach proves to be singularly unhelpful when it comes to understanding the social sciences as they actually exist. It has the effect of attempting to force a style and form of reasoning onto social researchers that deforms the ways in which they attempt to theorize and explain the social world.

Rudner's work pays virtually no attention to the actual content and methods of existing social science disciplines. The foundational premise is that all sciences have the same fundamental logic. So, it isn't necessary to examine sociology, political science, or economics in detail in order to trace out the particular characteristics of inquiry, explanation, and theory in these disciplines. Either the social science disciplines conform to the received view or they do not and for that reason show themselves to be defective as science. So, the philosophy of a special science is simply the special case of the more general theory of scientific knowledge represented by the received view. This is a bad way of beginning the philosophical study of any science, whether the social sciences or the biological sciences.

Second, by highlighting the issues that are central to the exposition of the received view—for example, the observation-theoretic distinction—the neopositivist philosopher of social science is drawn away from consideration of other, more substantive problems to which philosophers could make a useful contribution. For example, the assumptions of purposive rationality underlie many explanations in areas of political science and economics; and, it turns out to be very productive to examine the intricacies that arise when we try to give a careful explanation of the concept of rationality and to link this assumption to particular areas of social explanation. The intellectual disposition created by the neopositivist view is to reduce this question to a simple matter of "concept formation." "Rationality" becomes simply another theoretical construct to be introduced into scientific theories. But as Sen, Harsanyi, Margolis, and dozens of other philosophers and social scientists have demonstrated, we need to spend quite a bit of intellectual energy to the task of unpacking the theory of rationality if it is to be of use in the social sciences.

Finally, this approach imposes an inappropriate simplification on the social sciences when it comes to empirical evaluation of social science hypotheses. It presupposes the comprehensive generality of the H-D model of confirmation theory. Once again, the key error derives from the assumption that the logic of scientific reasoning must be the same in every area of science. The social sciences sometimes involve the sorts of theoretical systems that are found in the natural sciences; but, more commonly, a social science analysis comprises a number of relatively independent models and mechanisms—theories of the middle range—that are amenable to piecemeal evaluation. Social science analyses are not generally unified theoretical systems along the lines of the theory of thermodynamics or genetics. And, there are other ways of providing empirical evaluation and support for these sorts of analysis—for example, process tracing, piecemeal empirical evaluation, and applying the logic of comparative causal analysis.

In short, logical positivist philosophy of science was conspicuously unhelpful as a contribution to the task of better understanding the nature of social science research and explanation.

A particular sticking point within the logical positivist theory of science was its common adherence to a Humean theory of the meaning of causation as constant conjunction. Hume derided the idea of "causal necessity" and sought to replace this notion with the idea of conformance to a strong regularity. Rom Harré and Edward Madden undertook a strong critique of this assumption in *Causal Powers: Theory of Natural Necessity* (1975). And, this anti-positivist strand of thinking about causation was more important to the emergence of critical realism than any other influence.

Several gifted sociologists joined this debate in the 1990s. Especially astute were contributions by George Steinmetz and Margaret Somers, both sociologists at the University of Michigan, and Philip Gorski at Yale. In a review article in *Society for Comparative Study of Society and History* (1998), Steinmetz provides a careful review of the intellectual background and the central ideas that Roy Bhaskar introduces in his writings on naturalism and realism. Steinmetz reviews the mainstream assumptions that defined positivist philosophy of social science through the 1960s and the echo of these assumptions in mainstream sociology; and, he provides a fairly detailed description of Bhaskar's alternative. He emphasizes several central ideas: Bhaskar's propensity for transcendental reasoning; his distinctions among the real, the actual, and the empirical; the scientific importance of "open systems"—systems lacking causal closure and displaying contingency; and a specific idea about emergence (176ff.). Steinmetz concludes with these observations:

> Critical realism is especially "liberating" for historical sociology. It provides a rebuttal to the positivist and theoretical realist insistence on the dogmas of empirical invariance, prediction, and parsimony (see Bhaskar 1989:184). Critical realism guards against any slide into empiricism by showing why theoretical mechanisms are central to all explanation. At the same time, critical realism suggests that contingent, conjunctural causality is the norm in open systems like society. Yet critical realism's epistemological relativism allows it to accept the results of much of the recent history and sociology of science in a relaxed way without giving in to judgmental relativism. Historical social researchers are reassured of the acceptability of their scientific practice, even if it does not match what the mainstream misconstrues as science. Critical realism allows us to safely steer between the Scylla of constricting definitions of science and the Charybdis of solipsistic relativism. (184)

Phillip Gorski is another talented historical sociologist who has advocated for the importance of critical realism for sociology (Gorski 2013). Gorski made the important point that sociological research needs to be pluralistic when it comes to methodology. Interpretation requires contextualization (662); causal hypotheses are often supported by statistical evidence; it is reasonable for realists about structures to look for the constitutive actions of lower-level powers that make them up. There isn't a primary method of inquiry or empirical reasoning that works best for all social research; instead, sociologists need to define significant research topics and then craft methods of inquiry and inference that are best suited to those topics. Quantitative, interpretive, comparative, deductive, inductive, abductive, descriptive, and explanatory approaches are all appropriate methods for some problems of social research. So, it is important for sociologists to "unlearn" some of the dogmas of positivist methodology that have often thought to be constitutive of the scientific warrant of sociology.

Against the dominant philosophies of social science of positivism, inter-pretivism, and constructivism, Gorski argues that there is only one credible alternative, the philosophical theory of critical realism. And, this means, largely, the writings of Roy Bhaskar. So, the bulk of this piece is an exposition of Bhaskar's central ideas. And, he argues that the ontological framework embodied in these aspects of a specific philosophy of science—realism about underlying structures, powers, and processes—is the best available as a general starting point for the sciences. Other philosophies of social science place epistemology or methodology at the center of what a philosophy of the sciences should resolve. Gorski, on the other hand, emphasizes the importance of the ontology of critical realism—what critical realism conveys about the nature and stratification of the social world.

Steinmetz and Gorski make it plain that one important reason for the recent appeal of realism within the social sciences is precisely the fact that there was a felt need to have a systematic reply to Humean positivism within debates about methodology in the social sciences. Sociology was dominated during the decades of the 1950s through 1980s by a positivist orthodoxy of quantitative-statistical research methodology. Leading scholars, departments, granting agencies, and journals took the view that "scientific" sociology needed to be conducted within this orthodoxy. The methodology that Steinmetz commends is one that highlights social contingency and conjuncture, while at the same time discovering explanatory relations among circumstances based on the causal mechanisms we can identify that connect them. These are all important aspects of sociological research, and we should indeed seek out philosophies of social science that make room for them. However, comparative, historical, and ethnographic research efforts were given less value by the neopositivist orthodoxy.

The disputes between these methodological frameworks continued to create large, fractious divides within graduate sociology departments, with advocates for one method or the other claiming virtually exclusive legitimacy. And, this struggle for methodological primacy appears to extend to the editorial practices of major sociology journals, association programs, and tenure deliberations. Until fairly recently—the 1990s, let us say—the quantitative-statistical faction held sway as the hegemonic methodological doctrine. Inspired by positivism and the example of the natural sciences and perhaps guided by governmental and foundation funding priorities, quantitative studies were considered most scientific, most rigorous, most objective, and most explanatory. Historical and interpretive studies were treated as "ideographic" or anecdotal—not well suited to discovering important social regularities.

But beginning in the 1970s a number of critical voices within the disciplines of the social sciences began to express dissatisfaction with this orthodoxy. A defense of comparative historical social science, small-N research, and ethnographic research began to gather steam through writings of sociologists such as Abbott (2001), Adams, Clemens, and Orloff (2005), Gouldner (1970), Steinmetz (2005), Tilly (1984), and Wallerstein (1999). Moreover, critical voices began to emerge from within the quantitative orthodoxy as well, including acute quantitative sociologists such as Stanley Lieberson (1987). (It is interesting to note that political science experienced a similar upheaval, the Perestroika debate, at roughly the same time (Monroe 2005).)

How should such a fundamental debate about methods be resolved? The fundamental issue here is understanding the world, not method per se. Methodology is a tool for helping us to arrive at knowledge. For any given empirical question, there will be a variety of methods on the basis of which to investigate this problem. And, ideally, we should select a set of tools that are well suited to the particular characteristics of the problem at hand.

In other words, analysis of the situation of scientific research into the unknown would suggest methodological pluralism. We should be open to a variety of tools and methods and should design research in a way that is closely tailored to the nature of the empirical problem. And, therefore, young sociologists—graduate students—should be encouraged to be eclectic in their reading and thinking; they should be exposed to many of the approaches, perspectives, and methods through which imaginative sociologists have addressed their problems of research and explanation.

This general recommendation in favor of pluralism in sociology is strengthened when we consider the fact of the inherent heterogeneity of the social world. There is not one single kind of social process for which there might conceivably be a uniquely best kind of method of inquiry. Rather, the social world consists of a deeply heterogeneous mix of processes, some of which are better suited to an ethnographic or comparative approach, just as other processes may be best studied quantitatively. If one is interested in the topic of corruption, for example—he or she will need to be informed about institutions, culture, principal-agent problems, social psychology, and many other potentially relevant sociological factors. And, these researches may well require a combination of statistical analysis, comparison across a select group of cases, and ethnographic investigation in a small number of specific cases and individuals.

In other words, there are very deep arguments supporting the value and epistemic suitability of methodological pluralism. And, this in turn suggests that sociology departments are well advised to incorporate a variety of methods and frameworks into their doctoral programs.

These are general considerations, however, and are not strongly persuasive to social scientists inclined toward the philosophical compactness of the Humean approach to knowledge. Therefore, it is important to provide an alternative philosophical perspective on the elements of social-scientific knowledge. A systematic treatment of scientific realism was needed to provide a systematic and philosophical encompassing response to Humean fundamentalism. Such a treatment proved to be very attractive to social scientists looking for a different basis for their methods and arguments. Critics of positivist social science ask us to consider a broader space of possibilities for research and theory formation in the social sciences. What is a "post-positivist realism" for the social sciences? Here are several important principles that such a position ought to embrace.

- It is realist about causation; it affirms the scientific validity of seeking for real social mechanisms.
- It advocates for a conception of scientific explanation that hinges on the discovery of real causal connections among features of the social world.
- It is pluralistic about method; it acknowledges that there are multiple rationally supportable methods of inquiry in the social sciences and multiple forms that social science knowledge can take.
- It is evenhanded among quantitative, qualitative, comparative, and narrative approaches to social inquiry and social explanation.
- It is antireductionist and anti-naturalistic: it does not presuppose that various areas of the social sciences should be reducible to some other, more fundamental scientific theory; and it does not presuppose that the social sciences should resemble the natural sciences.
- And, finally, it is fully committed to the positive features of rationality that were mentioned above: the scientific virtues of conceptual clarity and empirical-rational justification for scientific beliefs.

This set of alternatives opens up the space of the social sciences quite dramatically; it permits a wide and pluralistic range of inquiries to proceed, without the requirement of theoretical or methodological unity. And, this frees researchers to arrive at accounts of their domains of research that are well suited to the particulars of these domains.

CRITICAL REALISM

The philosophical system that emerged in the 1970s that undertook to respond to this set of concerns was critical realism, developed with rigor and persistence by Roy Bhaskar. Bhaskar's theory of critical realism has become a very important topic within sociological theory in recent years. As a point of reference for this ongoing discussion, consider a few key statements by Bhaskar about transcendental (critical) realism in *A Realist Theory of Science* (1975). (Sayer (2000) and Collier (1994) provide useful efforts to reformulate and summarize the doctrines of critical realism.) Here is a simple and clear definition of Bhaskar's theory of realism:

> The third position, which is advanced here, may be characterized as transcendental realism. It regards the objects of knowledge as the structures and mechanisms that generate phenomena; and the knowledge as produced in the social activity of science. These objects are neither phenomena (empiricism) nor human constructs imposed upon the phenomena (idealism), but real structures which endure and operate independently of our knowledge, our experience and the conditions which allow us access to them. Against empiricism, the objects of knowledge are structures, not events; against idealism, they are intransitive (in the sense defined). (Bhaskar 1975:15)

Against Humean inductivism, Bhaskar advocates for a neo-Kantian approach to scientific knowledge. He makes use of transcendental arguments to probe the necessary conditions that must exist in order for scientific knowledge to be possible. Here is Bhaskar's statement of how he views the cognitive status of the theory of transcendental realism:

> It is not necessary that science occurs. But given that it does, it is necessary that the world is a certain way. It is contingent that the world is such that science is possible. And, given that it is possible, it is contingent upon the satisfaction of certain social conditions that science in fact occurs. But given that science does or could occur, the world must be a certain way. Thus, the transcendental realist asserts, that the world is structured and differentiated can be established by philosophical argument; though the particular structures it contains and the ways in which it is differentiated are matters for substantive scientific investigation. (1975: 19)

This passage makes it clear that Bhaskar believes the statements of ontology are philosophical statements, and they are established with a kind of necessity that differentiates them from ordinary empirical statements. This indicates Bhaskar's adherence to a philosophical method of discovery, inquiry, and justification.

Essentially, Bhaskar makes a classic Kantian transcendental argument in his philosophy of science: he argues that we cannot make intellectual sense of a scientist's use of experiment without presupposing that there are underlying objects and causal laws governing them which are the subject of the experiment. The passage identifies the necessary presupposition of the experiment:

the presence of objective, theory-independent causal laws governing the objects of the experiment. And, as the subsequent sentence in the text makes clear, the causal laws in question are of a different ontological order than the events that manifest them. Bhaskar postulates that things (objects) possess real causal powers, and we explain the behavior of objects (and ensembles) as a consequence of the operation of their powers, as discussed in chapter 6. And, powers and causal laws are linked; powers generate laws.

Bhaskar adopts what he refers to as a "laminar" view of the social world, with higher levels of social organization resting upon lower levels. But he also believes that social properties are "emergent." That is, he believes that higher-level social things (structures) have properties not possessed by the lower-level things of which they are composed. And, as we saw in chapter 4, he believes that these emergent causal properties can affect the behavior of entities at the lower level.

> Emergence is defined as the relationship between two levels such that one arises diachronically (or perhaps synchronically) out of the other but is capable of reacting back on the lower level and is causally irreducible to it. (1993:73)

Various particulars of Bhaskar's system have been criticized and extended in recent debates, in ways that are very relevant to the philosophy of social science being developed here. (Recall the discussion of Bhaskar's theory of emergence in chapter 4.) Most persistent are concerns about the fairly specific philosophical methodology through which Bhaskar develops his theories. It is a method that derives from Kant's transcendental metaphysics. And, Bhaskar seems to be confident in arriving at definite and assertoric conclusions based on this method. Ontology is not an empirical discipline, according to Bhaskar; instead, it is a philosophical reflection on the preconditions of science, and it is grounded in philosophical arguments rather than empirical, scientific, or experimental arguments.

This feature of Bhaskar's method lays him open to the kind of criticism that is offered by Tuukka Kaidesoja, Justin Cruickshank (Cruickshank 2003a, 2003b), and others, on the ground that his construction is unacceptably aprioristic. Kaidesoja argues against this aprioristic strategy and puts forward an alternative: "naturalized critical realist social ontology" (2013a). Here is his preliminary description of this alternative:

> In very rough terms, naturalists contend that theories in social ontology should be built by studying (1) the ontological assumptions and presuppositions of the epistemically successful practices of empirical social research (including well-confirmed theories produced in them); and (2) the well-established ontological assumptions advanced in other sciences, including natural sciences.

> This procedure is needed because naturalists hold that ontological theories cannot be justified by means of philosophical arguments that rely on a priori forms of conceptual analysis and reasoning. (2013a: 2)

So, the heart of Kaidesoja's approach is the idea that the activity of formulating and evaluating scientific theories through empirical research is the only avenue we have for arriving at justified ideas about the world, including our most basic ontological beliefs. We might refer to this as a "boot-strapping" approach to ontology: we discover the more fundamental aspects of the world by constructing and evaluating scientific theories in various areas of phenomena, and then extracting the "ontological assumptions" these theories make.

Kaidesoja's naturalistic alternative permits a very straightforward respecification of the status and content of critical realism. Instead of arriving at conclusions that have philosophical certainty (philosophical transcendental ontology), we arrive at potentially the same conclusions based on reasoning to the best explanation. This is Richard Boyd's best argument for realism, and it provides a philosophically modest way of giving rational credibility to the ontological conclusions critical realism wants to reach without presupposing the validity of philosophical transcendental arguments.

HETEROGENEITY AND CRITICAL REALISM

In chapter 1, it was argued that the social world is highly heterogeneous and plastic. Is the ontology of critical realism compatible with this view? Is Bhaskar's version of realism consistent with this treatment of heterogeneous social entities and heterogeneous social causes, or does Bhaskar presuppose *social essences* and *universal causes* in ways that are inconsistent with heterogeneity?

There are elements in Bhaskar's theory that point in both directions on this question.

His emphasis on the logic of experimentation is key to his transcendental argument for realism. But this approach cuts against the premise of heterogeneity because it emphasizes exceptionless causal factors. He emphasizes the necessity of postulating underlying causal laws, which are themselves supported by generative causal mechanisms, and the implication is that the natural world unfolds as the expression of these generative mechanisms. Here is a clear statement from *The Possibility of Naturalism* (Bhaskar 1989):

> Once made, however, the ontological distinction between causal laws and patterns of events allows us to sustain the universality of the former in the face of the non-invariance of the latter. Moreover, the actualist analysis of laws now

loses all plausibility. For the non-invariance of conjunctions is a condition of an empirical science and the non-empirical nature of laws a condition of an applied one. (1989: 11)

And, his account sometimes seems to rest upon a kind of "mechanism fundamentalism"—the idea that there is a finite set of non-reducible mechanisms with essential properties:

> On the transcendental realist system a sequence A, B is necessary if and only if there is a natural mechanism M such that when stimulated by A, B tends to be produced. (1989: 11)

Concerns about mechanism fundamentalism are allayed, however, because Bhaskar notes that it is always open to the scientist to ask the new question: How does this mechanism work (Bhaskar 1989: 13)? So, mechanisms are not irreducible.

These are a few indications that Bhaskar's realism might be uncongenial to the idea of social heterogeneity.

However, a strong case can be made on the other side of the issue as well. First, Bhaskar's introduction of the idea of the social world as an "open" system of causation leaves space for causal heterogeneity. Here is a relevant passage from *A Realist Theory of Science* (1975), deriving from an example of historical explanation:

> In general as a complex event it will require a degree of what might be called "causal analysis," i.e. the resolution of the event into its components (as in the case above). (1975: 116)
>
> For the different levels that mesh together in the generation of an event need not, and will not normally, be typologically locatable within the structures of a single theory. In general the normic statements of several distinct sciences, speaking perhaps of radically different kinds of generative mechanism, may be involved in the explanation of the event. This does not reflect any failure of science, but the complexity of things and the multiplicity of forms of determination found in the world. (1975: 116)

Here is how Bhaskar conceives of social and historical things in *The Possibility of Naturalism*:

> From this perspective, then, things are viewed as individuals possessing powers (and as agents as well as patients). And actions are the realization of their potentialities. Historical things are structured and differentiated (more or less unique) ensembles of tendencies, liabilities and powers; and historical events are their transformations. (1989: 20)

The phrase "more or less unique" is crucial. It implies the kind of heterogeneity postulated here, reflecting the ideas of contingency and heterogeneity mentioned above.

Another reason for thinking Bhaskar is open to heterogeneity in the social realm is his position on reductionism.

> But, it might be objected, is not the universe in the end nothing but a giant machine with inexorable laws of motion governing everything that happens within it? I want to say three things: First, that the various sciences treat the world as a network of "machines," of various shapes and sizes and degrees of complexity, whose proper principles of explanation are not all of the same kind as, let alone reducible to, those of classical mechanics. Secondly, that the behaviour of "machines," including classical mechanical ones, cannot be adequately described, let alone understood, in terms of the "whenever x, then y" formula of regularity determinism. Thirdly, that even if the world were a single "machine" this would still provide no grounds for the constant conjunction idea, or a fortiori any of the theories of science that depend upon it. Regularity determinism is a mistake, which has been disastrous for our understanding of science. (1975: 58)

Here, Bhaskar is explicit in referring to multiple kinds of causal processes ("machines"). And, indeed, Bhaskar affirms the conjunctural nature of social causation:

> Now most social phenomena, like most natural events, are conjuncturally determined. And as such in general have to be explained in terms of a multiplicity of causes. (1989: 54)

Similar ideas are expressed in *Scientific Realism and Human Emancipation* (Bhaskar 1982):

> Social phenomena must be seen, in general, as the product of a multiplicity of causes, i.e. social events as "conjunctures" and social things as (metaphysically) "compounds." (1982: 107)

Finally, his discussion of social structures in *The Possibility of Naturalism* (PON) as the social equivalent of natural mechanisms also implies heterogeneity over time:

> (3) Social structures, unlike natural structures, may be only relatively enduring (so that the tendencies they ground may not be universal in the sense of space-time invariant). (1989: 49)

So, on balance, I am inclined to think that Bhaskar's philosophy of social science is indeed receptive to social heterogeneity. And, this in turn allows it to make a substantially more compelling contribution to the philosophy of social science than it would otherwise do, and superior to many of the positivist variants of philosophy of science that he criticizes.

MORPHOGENESIS AND SOCIAL REALITY

Critical realism has progressed far since Roy Bhaskar's early writings on the subject in *A Realist Theory of Science*. One of the most important thinkers to have introduced new ideas into the debate is Margaret Archer. Several books in the mid-1990s represented genuinely original contributions to issues about the nature of social ontology and methodology, including especially *Realist Social Theory: The Morphogenetic Approach* (Archer 1995) and *Culture and Agency: The Place of Culture in Social Theory* (Archer 1996). Archer's contribution to critical realism has been an important part of the recent progress of the field, and her theory of *morphogenesis* is key to this progress. She has created a productive research group whose efforts have resulted in three volumes of research to date, including Archer (2013, 2014, 2015).

Archer's work addresses several topics of interest here, including especially the agent-structure dichotomy. This is key to the twin concerns highlighted here involving "actor-centered social science" and "autonomous meso-level explanations." Archer argues for a form of methodological dualism about agents and structures—that each pole needs to be treated separately and in its own terms. So, neither methodological individualism nor methodological holism is correct. She acknowledges, of course, that social structures depend on the individuals who make them up; but she does not believe that this basic fact tells us anything about how to analyze or explain facts about either agents or structures.

Archer argues that the two primary approaches that theorists have taken—methodological individualism and methodological holism—are fundamentally inadequate. They represent what she calls upward and downward *conflation*. In the first case, "society" disappears and is replaced by some notion of aggregated individual action; in the second case "agents" disappear and the human individuals do no more than act out the imperatives of social norms and structures. She associates the first view with J. S. Mill and Max Weber and the second view with Durkheim. On her view, agents and structures are distinct, and neither is primary over the other.

She refers to her view as the "morphogenetic" approach. Here is how she explains this concept:

> The "morpho" element is an acknowledgement that society has no pre-set form or preferred state: the "genetic" part is a recognition that it takes its shape from,

and is formed by, agents, originating from the intended and unintended consequences of their activities. (Archer 1995: 5)

So, what is Archer's central notion, the idea of *morphogenesis*? It is the idea that processes of change occur for agents and social structures in interlocking and temporally complex ways. Agents are formed within a set of social structures—norms, language communities, and power relationships. The genesis of the agent occurs within the context of these structures. On a larger time scale, the structures themselves change as a result of the activities and choices of the historically situated individuals who make them up. She summarizes this ontology as a set of cycles with different time frames: structural conditioning => social interaction => structural elaboration (Archer 1995: 16). This notion leads Archer to a conception of the social and the actor that reflects a fundamentally historical understanding of social processes. Formation and transformation are the central metaphors (Archer 1995: 154).

Morphogenesis applies at all levels, from "the capitalist system" to "the firm" to "the actor" to personal identity and motivation. And, she believes that properties at various levels—micro and macro—have a degree of autonomy from each other.

Autonomy is also temporal (and temporary) in the joint senses that such structural properties were neither the creation of contemporary actors nor are ontologically reducible to "material existents" (raw resources) and dependent upon current acts of human instantiation (rule governed) for all their current effects. (Archer 1995: 138)

These basic ideas are developed further by Archer and her collaborators in the recent series (Archer 2013, 2014, 2015). The first volume of this series, *Social Morphogenesis* (Archer 2013), represents a rigorous and serious step forward in the project of articulating this theory as both a meta-theory for the social sciences and a substantial contribution to sociological theory within the general framework of critical realism. The central themes are profound social change and the generative mechanisms that produce it.

Archer's theory of morphogenesis refers to three "moments" of the morphogenesis and morphostasis sequences—that is, the sequences through which social arrangements are stimulated to change and are brought into a temporary stability (Archer 2014: 2), which she breaks into three phases T1, T2–T3, and T4:

- T1 structural and cultural conditioning →
- T2–T3 social interaction →
- T4 structural and cultural elaboration or stasis

At the risk of over-simplifying, we might summarize her view in these terms. Her view is that each phase involves constraints on action and interaction. T1 involves the large structural and cultural contexts in which individuals take shape and act. T2–T3 involves the interactions of individuals who bear interests and group identities and who strive to bring about outcomes that favor those interests and identities. And, T4 represents a new formation (elaboration) of a complex of structural and cultural constraints. (It is striking how closely this summary resembles the theory of strategic action fields put forward by Fligstein and McAdam (2012).)

An important line of criticism that comes through *Late Modernity* (2014) is a persistent critique of unanalyzed ideas about speed and acceleration, a common theme of social commentary. "The modern world changes rapidly"; what does that tell us if we haven't specified the dimensions and clocks according to which we measure the speed of a process? So, the language of speed is simply uninformative, according to Archer and her collaborators. More specifically, Archer and her colleagues take issue with the metaphor of "liquid modernity" as a way of understanding the contemporary world (Bauman 2000). Archer takes aim at the intuition that the contemporary social world is contingent and plastic without limit. She criticizes "liquid modernity" in these terms:

> Labile "flows" comprehensively displaced and replaced the determinate (not deterministic) influences of social structure and cultural systems on tendential change or stability. As structure and culture were pulverised under the tidal bore of liquidity, so was agency condemned to serial self-reinvention. (Archer 2014: 1)

Archer's complaint against liquid modernity, then, is what she takes to be its extreme version of plasticity on the part of structures, cultures, and actors. Bauman views the individual as a form shifter, pursuing fleeting purposes and impulses within fast-changing circumstances, with the result of a form of chaotic Brownian motion in the social world.

Archer prefers substantive analysis of the social world organized around the poles of morphostasis (the mechanisms that preserve the properties of a social structure or cultural feature) and morphogenesis (the generative mechanisms of change that work to disrupt and change the existing structure and cultural elements). Both are critical and persistent features of the social world, and it is absurd (she believes) to imagine that modernity consists exclusively of morphogenesis unbound (Archer 2014: 7).

Archer emphasizes that morphogenesis leads to processes of social change that defy some of the presuppositions of fixity that come along with a settled conceptual scheme. The fact that the names and concepts we use remain the same does not imply that the underlying social realities are unchanged (Archer

2014: 6). This point supports the arguments offered in chapter 1 against ι̣. temptation of reifying an established system of social concepts and assuming that the social entities to which these concepts refer are unchanging. At the same time, if social change were continuous and unlimited, then it would be impossible to apply language at all. So, a degree of stability is required if we are to be able to study and understand the world around us. If there were *no* continuing stability in the social world from one hour to the next, then planning and action would be impossible. The harder question is this: How much stability is necessary for intelligible thought and action within the social world?

An important complexity in Archer's account of stability is the fact that she believes that the processes of change (morphogenesis) can create their own conditions of stability and continuity that transcend the traditional forms inherited from the morphogenetic past. So, the opposition is not between morphostasis and morphogenesis, but between activity and various forms of stability, both morphostasis and morphogenesis. "The alternative—not always recognized—is that there are forms of 'stabilization' produced by morphogenesis itself that furnish an equally adequate (and more consonant) basis for planning activities" (2014: 14). And, this turns out to be a point to which Archer attaches a great deal of importance (19).

Archer's research collaboration on topics concerning the theory of morphogenesis continues with the publication of the third volume in the *Social Morphogenesis* series, *Generative Mechanisms Transforming the Social Order* (Archer 2015). Like the earlier volumes, this volume offers a highly stimulating treatment of issues that are prominent in the branch of the critical realism research community that Archer has defined. The focus here is upon the idea of "generative mechanisms," which allows for a very interesting set of connections to other segments of the philosophy of social science field.

Archer's realist theory of morphogenesis is highly complementary to the ideas about methodological localism and social heterogeneity that have been argued for here. The idea that actors are socially constituted and socially situated (methodological localism) is a different way of expressing her point that actors are constituted by surrounding social structures. The idea that structures are themselves adapted and changed by active individuals doing things within them corresponds to her "social interaction" and "structural elaboration" phases of morphogenesis. The methodological insight that seems to come along with morphogenesis—the idea that it is valuable to move both *upward* toward more comprehensive social structures and *downward* toward more refined understanding of action and interaction—is certainly a part of the view associated with methodological localism and actor-centered sociology. Her view of the inherent "transformability" of society (Archer 1995: 1) parallels my own view of the heterogeneity and contingency of social arrangements. In short, Archer's research program around the theories and historical applications of morphogenesis represents an important, dense, and worthwhile body of thought that has the potential for shedding real light on the social world we inhabit. And, given the emphasis she and her associates place on understanding the dynamics of change, it is a philosophy of society that is especially relevant to the social conditions we face in the twenty-first century.

METHODS OF SOCIAL RESEARCH

It was mentioned above that a line of disagreement between logical positivist philosophy of science and realist philosophy of science has to do with the idea of methodological pluralism. Positivist philosophers emphasize the unity of method, whereas anti-positivist social scientists are generally attuned to the fact that the social world is heterogeneous, and that different aspects of the social world are amenable to investigation through varied methodologies. It is sometimes held that there is a dichotomy in social science methodologies, between quantitative research and interpretive or ethnographic research. But, in fact, the differentiation of methodologies in the social sciences is broader than this dichotomy would allow. Instead of "either-or," we are better off thinking of research methodologies as a family of different ways of investigating the social world and validating the findings at which we arrive. Here, we will examine several different families of research methods in the social sciences. Figure 7.1 provides a preliminary attempt to map out the primary research methodologies in use in the social sciences today.

What are the frameworks that generally come to mind in discussions of methodology in the social sciences? Several families of methodological frameworks are indicated in Figure 7.1. These are deliberately presented as a wheel, with no sense of priority among them.

(A) Quantitative methodology—what Andrew Abbott refers to as the variables paradigm. This is the approach that analyzes the social world as a set of individuals, groups, and properties, and simply sorts through to find correlations, associations, and possible causal relationships using a range of statistical tools. This is an inductivist approach. In this approach, the role of the social sciences is to accurately observe the facts and to build up systems of regularities among them. This seems like an assumption-free framework, but there is an underlying ontology here no less than the other frameworks mentioned here—the idea that the social world is governed by some system of underlying laws or regularities.

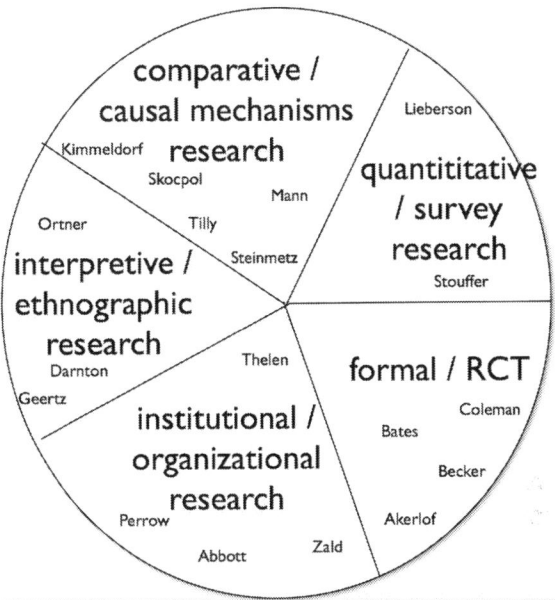

Figure 7.1   Taxonomy of social science methods.

(B) Interpretive methods. Clifford Geertz recommends an approach to social
research within a generally interpretive worldview. He maintains that
the most important feature of the social world is the fact of meaning.
He urges us to consider as most important the meanings individuals and
groups attach to behaviors and performances. So, the research task is to
reconstruct those meanings by observing and interacting with the social
actors in a particular setting. The observer should observe the patterns of
action and interaction he or she finds and carefully investigate the patterns of meaning the participants weave around their worlds.

A related framework is ethnomethodology, the approach taken by
qualitative sociologists like Goffman and Garfinkel. This is the idea that
one important function of the social sciences is to figure out the underlying grammar of the assumptions and rules that individuals are following
as they interact with each other. The ontological assumption here is that
individuals are basic in the social world, and individuals are complex.
On this approach, the methodology is to observe ordinary behavior
and try to discover the underlying rules and expectations that indicate
something like a grammar or normative frame that drives or generates
interpersonal behavior.

(C) A family of approaches we might call realist methodology. These
approaches begin with the premise that the social world consists of

certain kinds of entities, forces, and processes and then guides the researcher to attempt to discover the characteristics of those structures. This is a process of hypothesis formation and theory development and of testing out theories—large or small—of things like class, charisma, or bureaucratic state apparatus.

(D) A number of methods of analysis developed in the comparative social sciences, including causal methods associated with comparative historical sociology. That includes the methods of paired comparisons, Mill's methods, and methods of similarity and difference. The researcher attempts to work out which factors are necessary or sufficient and enhancing or inhibiting, for various social outcomes of interest. We can call this comparative methodology.

(E) Causal mechanisms methodology. This framework is a variety of realist methodology. On this approach, we work on the assumption that there are social causes and that causes take the form of concrete causal mechanisms. The task of research is to gain enough empirical detail about selected cases to be able to piece together assumptions about the mechanisms at work. Ideas associated with the notion of process tracing have a natural fit here.

(F) Methods emphasizing techniques of formal modeling. This methodology is especially prominent in political science and economics. Here, the goal of the research is to arrive at elegant, simple mathematical models of the phenomena. On this approach, the evaluation of the model is not so much empirical but rather mathematical and formal. This approach is commonly faulted exactly because it is not sufficiently responsive to empirical constraints do standards. Its empirical relevance is not so clear. If we believe the social sciences are empirical, then a formal model that is a valued for its abstract elegance is unsatisfactory. It needs to contribute to an understanding of real empirical phenomena. At the least, this means that we should be able to tie the model to some real behavioral characteristics. In the best case—for example, with agent-based models or computable-general-equilibrium models—we should be able to begin to reproduce important features of real empirical cases by calibrating the model to empirical circumstances.

There are two other aspects of methodology that need to be called out. One has to do with the methods of data collection which are recommended, which differ substantially from domain to domain. The other is methods of empirical evaluation of the theories we advance. Social sciences differ substantially in both these ways—what kind of data is needed, how it should be collected (e.g. survey methodology), and how we should validate the results. These are often discipline specific and substantially more concrete than prescriptions in the philosophy of science. The ways in which we should evaluate a social science construction also varies significantly by national research tradition. Gabriel Abend (2006) points out that schemes of evaluation vary substantially across the sociological traditions of Mexico and the United States in terms of the standards in play about what constitutes rigor, empirical argument and theoretical argument.

Each of these is a methodology in the loose sense I favor. It is a guide for the researcher, indicating what kinds of factors he or she should be looking for by postulating a social ontology, which is an indication of what an explanatory account ought to look like and what counts as warrant for such explanations.

We might observe that if we favor a pluralistic social ontology, according to which there are properties, individuals, relationships, structures, networks, meanings, and values, then the method we use to acquire knowledge about these things should be pluralistic as well. Our methods should allow us to pose research questions about all these kinds of things.

MEANINGS AND MECHANISMS

There are two large categories of factors that are fundamental to understanding social processes—meanings and mechanisms. Throughout this book, I have given a preponderance of attention to the importance of social causal mechanisms within historical and social explanation. We explain a social outcome when we identify the social mechanisms that brought it about.

It is crucial to bear in mind always, however, that there is a complementary dimension to social life and social process—the pervasive fact that people act within frames of meanings and interpretations that they bring to their social relationships and their social worlds. Human action is meaningful action, and we cannot make sense of action without attributing meanings, intentions, and frameworks of understanding and desire to the individuals who constitute a social encounter. This is part and parcel of the ideas that underlie the notion of "actor-centered social science."

In fact, the causal mechanism approach to social explanation is often thought to stand in broad opposition to another important approach, the *interpretivist* approach. On the interpretive approach, the task of the human sciences is to understand human activities, actions, and social formations as unique historical expressions of human meaning and intention. Individuals are unique, and there are profound differences of mentality across historical settings. This "hermeneutic" approach is not interested in discovering causes of social outcomes, but instead in piecing together an interpretation of the meanings of a social outcome or production. This contrast between causal explanation and hermeneutic interpretation ultimately constitutes a major divide between styles of social thinking.

On this approach, all social action is framed by a meaningful social world. To understand, explain, or predict patterns of human behavior, we must first penetrate the social world of the individual in historical concreteness: the meanings he or she attributes to her environment (social and natural); the values and goals she possesses; the choices she perceives; and the way she interprets other individuals' social action. Only then will we be able to analyze, interpret, and explain her behavior. But now the individual's action is thickly described in terms of the meanings, values, assumptions, and interpretive principles she employs in her own understanding of her world.

This is not a new insight, of course; it was fundamental to the hermeneutic approach to social life, including the influential thinking of Wilhelm Dilthey in books like *Introduction to the Human Sciences* (Dilthey 1989). But the classical hermeneutic approach tended to undervalue the importance of causation and mechanisms in the social world, whereas it is clear today that both mechanisms and meanings are inseparably embedded within the social world.

The interpretivist approach has been of interest to several major philosophers of the human sciences within the Anglo-American tradition. Consider first Alasdair MacIntyre's discussion of the possibility of comparative theories of politics ("Is a science of comparative politics possible?" (1973)). MacIntyre poses the problem in these terms: "I shall be solely interested in the project of a political science, of the formulation of cross cultural, law-like causal generalizations which may in turn be explained by theories" (172). And, roughly, MacIntyre's answer is that a science of comparative politics is not possible, because actions, structures, and practices are not directly comparable across historical settings. An automobile strike in an Italian Fiat plant is similar in some ways to a strike against General Motors or Land Rover in different times and places; but the political cultures, symbolic understandings, and modes of behavior of Italian, American, and British auto workers are profoundly different.

MacIntyre places great emphasis on the densely interlinked quality of local concepts, social practices, norms, and self-ascriptions, with the implication that each practice or attitude is inextricably dependent on an ensemble of practices, beliefs, norms, concepts, and the like that are culturally specific and, in their aggregate, unique. Thus, MacIntyre holds that as simple a question as, "Do Britons and Italians differ in the level of pride they take in civic institutions?" is unanswerable because of cultural differences in the concept of pride (172–173).

These points pertain to difficulties in identifying political attitudes cross-culturally. Could it be said, though, that political institutions and practices are less problematic? MacIntyre argues that political institutions and practices are themselves very much dependent on local political attitudes, so it isn't possible to provide an a-historical specification of a set of practices and institutions:

So, interpretation is mandatory—for institutions no less than for individual behavior. So, MacIntyre's position is disjunctive. Now, turn to Charles Taylor in another pivotal essay, "Interpretation and the sciences of man" (1985). Taylor's central point is that the subject matter of the human sciences—human actions and social arrangements—always require interpretation. It is necessary for the observer to attribute meaning and intention to the action—features that cannot be directly observed. He asks whether there are "brute data" in the human sciences—facts that are wholly observational and require no "interpretation" on the part of the scientist (19). Taylor thinks not; and, therefore, the human sciences require interpretation from the most basic description of data to the fullest historical description.

> To be a full human agent, to be a person or a self in the ordinary meaning, is to exist in a space defined by distinctions of worth. . . . My claim is that this is not just a contingent fact about human agents, but is essential to what we would understand and recognize as full, normal human agency. (3)
>
> Thus, human behaviour seen as action of agents who desire and are moved, who have goals and aspirations, necessarily offers a purchase for descriptions in terms of meaning what I have called "experiential meaning." (27)

One way of putting Taylor's critique of "brute data" is the idea that human actions must be characterized intensionally (34ff.) in terms of the intentions and self-understanding of the agent and that such factors can only be interpreted, not directly observed.

Both MacIntyre and Taylor are highlighting an important point: human actions reflect meanings, purposes, beliefs, emotions, and solidarities that cannot be directly observed. And, human practices are composed of the actions and thoughts of individual human actors—with exactly this range of hermeneutic possibilities and indeterminacies. So, the explanation of human action and practice presupposes some level of interpretation. There is no formula, and no universal key to human agency, that permits us to "code" human behavior without the trouble of interpretation.

Arguments like these have been taken to show that there are two fundamentally different approaches to the study of the social world—causal and interpretive. However, it is in fact misleading to portray mechanisms and meanings as complementary "dimensions" of social change. Rather, we might say that mechanisms depend upon meanings, for the simple reason that mechanisms depend upon actions, and actions presuppose meanings. This is the thrust of my emphasis on "actor-centered" approaches to sociology, as presented in chapter 2. The actor-centered perspective takes seriously the meanings, values, and cognitive and practical frameworks that individuals bring to their interactions in the social world, and it urges social scientists and historians to improve upon their current theories of the actor.

Institutions and organizations are often invoked as causal factors or mechanisms in the production of important social outcomes. But institutions always work by influencing the behavior of the individual actors whom they touch; so, either explicitly or implicitly we need to have a theory of the actor's mental frameworks if we are to understand the causal power of institutions to influence outcomes.

If we want to know why there is grade inflation in universities, we need to refer to some of the institutional mechanisms that influence grading practices (causal influences!), but we also need to refer to the goals and meanings that participants bring to the interaction between students, professors, and appeals committees. Sometimes those mental frameworks are trivial and manifest—students want higher grades for reasons of career success as well as personal validation and faculty want to function in accordance with their responsibilities as neutral assessors of academic performance while at the same time demonstrating empathy for the needs of their students. These interlocking intentions and desires lead to a dynamic movement of average grades over time—sometimes higher, and once in a while lower. But sometimes the underlying mental frameworks that drive important social outcomes are more obscure—for example, the disaffection and doubt that lead inner-city minority students to despise high school.

Think for a moment about how meanings and intentional actions give rise to a common social mechanism, hate-based nationalist mobilization. A few strident leaders formulate a message of hate against a group—currently, Middle East and North Africa (MENA) immigrants in various European countries; they find means of gaining access to national media (through provocative demonstrations); and they extend their influence from the tiny percentage of racist extremists *ex ante* to a sizable percentage of the more moderate population. How does this work? Why do ordinary non-racist citizens fall prey to the hateful messages of the extreme right? Presumably a convincing answer will depend on the specifics of the communications strategies and messages conveyed by the nationalist party, interlocking with an astute reading of the fears and suppressed prejudices of the majority population. In other words, the mechanism of racist mobilization depends on a substratum of political emotion and belief that can be adroitly manipulated by the racist group and its leaders.

Philosophers sometimes distinguish meanings and causes as subjective and objective. (This is implied in Georg Henrik von Wright's classic book *Explanation and Understanding* (von Wright 1971).) But this is not a useful way of thinking about the two categories. Meanings are often fully objective—in the sense that we can investigate them empirically and they can be demonstrated to have stable and enduring effects in the world. And, social causes have an element of subjectivity built into them, for the simple reason that social causes always invoke the subjective states of mind of the actors who make them up. It is not even accurate to say that meanings exist solely within the actor, whereas causes exist outside the actor. As we saw in chapter 3, systems of norms, values, and meanings have a social reality outside the consciousness of the actor, and these systems themselves have causal powers. The meanings that Weber identified in the notion of the Protestant Ethic are indeed embodied in a population of individuals (inward); but they are pervasive and influential on those same individuals (outward). So, the Protestant Ethic is both an inner state of mind and an external and coercive set of values and beliefs.

These points underline the importance of the arguments for methodological pluralism advanced in the preceding section. The research methods of the ethnographer and the qualitative sociologist are critical for arriving at empirically justified representations of the meanings and norms that exist within specific cultures at specific points in time, and the findings from these types of research can complement the effort to arrive at causal and institutional explanations for patterns of change and persistence in those social settings.

SCIENTIFIC OBJECTIVITY?

What is objectivity in social science? What might be meant by the claim that a given theory represents an objective scientific analysis of a range of social phenomena? Debate over the objectivity of social science has often combined a variety of separate theses:

1. There are social facts that are independent of the concepts and theories of the scientist which the theory is intended to uncover—that is, there is an objective social world (ontological objectivity).
2. It is possible for a theory of a given range of social facts to be well grounded on the basis of the right sorts of reasons (empirical and theoretical adequacy) (epistemic objectivity).
3. Social facts are independent of the states of consciousness of participants.
4. Scientific inquiry can be value free and interest neutral.
5. Scientific inquiry tends to converge around a consensus among all researchers over the properties of the world as a result of further empirical and theoretical research.

Thesis (1) contradicts conceptual relativism. Thesis (2) contradicts a family of underdetermination arguments within the philosophy of science. Thesis (3) divides materialist social science from interpretation theory and *verstehen* sociology. Thesis (4) upholds the position that it is possible to exclude value commitments from the conduct of science. And, thesis (5) asserts that science progresses toward a higher degree of agreement among researchers.

We may dispense quickly with (4). It is unquestionably true that scientific research is interest relative: what particular features of the social system, what aspects of action, and what causal processes are selected for scrutiny and explanation and are dependent on the interests—both intellectual and moral—of the investigator. Further, it is plain that scientific reasoning presupposes a set of normative commitments—for example, to the primacy of empirical evidence over religious authority. But Weber's treatment of this issue is convincing; these points do not diminish the objectivity of science in "'Objectivity' in Social Science" (1949). Once having defined the program of research, it is still possible to arrive at an objective analysis of the subject matter.

Thesis (1) represents a general metaphysical view of the social world, in that it asserts the mind independence of various kinds of social processes, structures, etc. This is the fundamental ontological premise of realism. Scientific research attempts to identify underlying processes, structures, mechanisms, and the like, whose properties explain the observable data. This goal presupposes that social phenomena are the result of a set of causally ordered, objective social processes that the social scientist can discover and map out. (Call this the realism component.)

Thesis (2) represents the view that scientific theories are put forward as being justified on the basis of a "scientific method" and not simply personal advocacy, political bias, or one's value perspective. There need to be objective procedures in terms of which to compare competing theories and to provide empirical and logical arguments favoring one such theory over its competitors. (Call this the justification component.)

Thesis (5) represents the view that scientific inquiry progresses toward consensus among members of a given research community, and that this consensus is best explained on the hypothesis that the consensus theory is true and has been arrived at through reliable procedures of scientific inquiry. (This is one of the ideas that underlies Richard Boyd's arguments for realism, as discussed above.)

Various combinations of these components of objectivity in social science are possible. For example, Weber appears to affirm (1) and hold that there are social facts; he denies (3) asserting that these facts are "subjective" in the sense that they depend essentially on the states of mind of the persons whose meaningful behavior constitutes them; and he accepts (2) holding that it is possible to offer theoretically and empirically well-grounded descriptions of these facts (Weber 1949, chapter 2). Nelson Goodman appears to contradict (1), maintaining that there are as many social worlds as there are schemes of concepts in terms of which to organize and describe experience (*Ways of Worldmaking* (Goodman 1978)). Such a view is forced to reject (2) as well, since it maintains that there is no uniquely best theory of the world. It would be possible to reject (1) while maintaining (2)—that is, to hold that there is a best social-scientific theory of a given range of social phenomena, but deny that such a theory describes an independently existing set of social facts.

The form of objectivity of social science that I want to defend affirms (1) and (2). Concerning thesis (3), I hold that there is no need to choose between "material" and "subjective" features of the social world. Some social facts may be constituted by the meanings attributed to them by participants, while others may be meaning independent. And, finally, I maintain that the procedures internal to various social science disciplines are sufficient to produce the sort of convergence of theoretical beliefs described in thesis (5) in most concrete historical and social science debates.

REALISM AND CONFIRMATION

How should a realist think about confirmation of hypotheses and theories about real social structures and properties?

The philosophy of science devotes a large fraction of its attention to this question: What is the logic of empirical confirmation for scientific beliefs? In the natural sciences, this question became entangled with the parochial fact about the natural sciences that scientific theories postulated unobservable entities and processes and that the individual statements or axioms of a theory could not be separately confirmed or tested. So, a logic of confirmation was developed according to which theories are empirically evaluated as wholes; we need to draw out a set of deductive or probabilistic consequences of the theory; observe the truth or falsity of these consequences based on experiment or observation; and then assign a degree of empirical credibility to the theory based on the success of the observational consequences. This could be put as a slogan: "No piecemeal confirmation of scientific beliefs!"

This is the familiar H-D model of confirmation, articulated most rigorously by Carl Hempel and criticized and amended by philosophers such as Karl Popper, Israel Scheffler, Norwood Hanson, and Imre Lakatos. These debates constituted most of the content of the evolution of positivist philosophy of science into post-positivist philosophy of science throughout the 1960s and 1970s.

I do not want to go deeply into this set of debates, because I am interested in knowledge in the *social* sciences; and I don't think that the theoretical-holism that this train of thought depends upon actually has much relevance for the social sciences. The H-D model of confirmation is approximately well suited to certain of the natural sciences—but not to the social sciences. The reason is that the social sciences are not theoretical in the relevant sense. Social science "theories" are mid-level formulations about social mechanisms and structures; they are "theories of the middle range" (Robert Merton, *On Theoretical Sociology* (1967)). They often depend on formulations of ideal types of social entities or organizations of interest—and then concrete empirical investigation of specific organizations to determine the degree to which they conform or diverge from the ideal-typical features specified by the theory. And, these mid-level theories and hypotheses can usually be empirically investigated fairly directly through chains of observations and inferences.

This is not a trivial task, of course, and there are all sorts of challenging methodological and conceptual issues that must be addressed as the researcher undertakes to consider whether the world actually conforms to the statements he or she makes about it. But it is logically very different from the holistic empirical evaluation that is required of the special theory of relativity or the string theory of fundamental physics. The language of hypothesis testing is not quite right for most of the social sciences. Instead, the slogan for social science epistemology ought to be, "Piecemeal empirical evaluation!"

I want to argue, further, that this *epistemological* feature of social knowledge is a derivative of some basic facts about *social ontology*: social processes, entities, and structures lack the rigidity and law governedness that is characteristic of natural processes, entities, and structures. So, general, universal theories of social entities that cover all instances are unlikely. But second, it is a feature of the accessibility of social things: we interact with social entities in a fairly direct manner, and these interactions permit us to engage in scientific observation of these entities in a way that permits the piecemeal empirical investigation that is highlighted here. And, we can construct chains of observations and inferences from primary observations (entries in an archival source) to empirical estimates of a more abstract fact (the level of crop productivity in the Lower Yangzi in 1800).

Let's say that we were considering a theory that social unrest was gradually rising in a region of China in the nineteenth century because of a gradual shift in the sex ratios found in rural society. The connection between sex ratios and social unrest isn't directly visible; but we can observe features of both ends of the equation. So, we can gather population and family data from registries and family histories; we can gather information about social unrest from gazettes and other local sources; and we can formulate subsidiary theories about the social mechanisms that might connect a rising male-female ratio to the incidence of social unrest. In other words—we can directly investigate each aspect of the hypothesis (cause, effect, mechanism), and we can put forward an empirical argument in favor of the hypothesis (or critical of the hypothesis).

This is an example of what I mean by "piecemeal empirical investigation." And, the specific methodologies of the various social and historical sciences are largely devoted to the concrete tasks of formulating and gathering empirical data in the particular domain. Every discipline is concerned to develop methods of empirical inquiry and evaluation; but, I hold, the basic logic of inquiry and evaluation is similar across all disciplines. The common logic is piecemeal inquiry and evaluation.

Now let's see how confirmation seems to work within critical realism. Here is what Roy Bhaskar has to say about the object of scientific knowledge in his approach in *A Realist Theory of Science* (1975):

[CR] regards the objects of knowledge as the structures and mechanisms that generate phenomena; and the knowledge as produced in the social activity of science. These objects are neither phenomena (empiricism) nor human constructs imposed upon the phenomena (idealism), but real structures which endure and operate independently of our knowledge, our experience and the conditions which allow us access to them. (1975: 14)

So, how would a realist confirm or justify the claims he or she wants to make about these real underlying structures and mechanisms? What kinds of evidence and modes of reasoning are available to allow us to conclude that a given statement is true (or false)?

This is an important question, and it poses difficulties for critical realists. The problem arises from the rhetoric of critical realism (CR) and its staunch anti-positivism. The most obvious answer to the question takes us to the logic of observation, experiment, and testing through derivation of indirect implications of hypotheses. We are led to think immediately of Mill's methods and the logic of causal inference as primary modes of scientific reasoning. And, this begins to sound a lot like the H-D model of confirmation—a key premise of neo-positivism. But critical realists are allergic to this answer.

So, how can we sort out the reasonable and uncontroversial core of our ordinary intuitions about scientific reasoning from the full baggage of logical empiricism? One crucial difference is the neopositivist presumption that scientific knowledge must take the form of general statements of lawlike regularities. CR focuses instead on singular statements about causal powers and mechanisms. And, testing of singular causal statements has important differences from testing comprehensive unified theories. If we believe that vitamin C has the causal capacity to inhibit infection by the rhinovirus, it is fairly straightforward to design an experiment or observational study that helps to evaluate this belief.

Another important difference is the centrality of the observation-theoretic distinction for the neopositivist theory of science. Positivist and neopositivist philosophers of science often accepted the Duhem thesis about the nature of scientific knowledge (1906)—the idea that scientific knowledge takes the form of a unified body of theory that can only be evaluated as a whole, and that this system unavoidably includes the use of theoretical concepts that are inherently unobservable. The CR approach, on the other hand, rejects a strict distinction between social reality and social observation. There is nothing in social reality that is in principle unobservable.

Bhaskar places the idea of a scientific experiment at the core of his justification of the theory of transcendental realism. But surprisingly, he does not discuss the epistemic importance of experimentation. What does a successful experiment contribute to knowledge? The intuitive answer is fairly obvious: an experiment allows us to assign particular causal effects to particular interventions. **C** in the absence of **I** leads to **O**; **C** in the presence of **I** leads to **P**. Therefore, **I** causes **P**. The successful experiment gives us empirical and logical grounds for believing that "**I** causes **P**." But perhaps, surprisingly, Bhaskar does not pay any attention to the epistemic value of experimentation, or the role this method plays in inferences about real causes of changes in our world. Bhaskar prefers to argue that experimentation contributes to the ontology rather than the epistemology of science.

So, once again—how should a critical realist offer an empirical justification for a claim like this: structure **S** has causal powers **P** and tends to bring about outcomes **O**?

It seems to me that the answer is not esoteric. There is no better way of establishing the credibility of a social hypothesis than we can find through the familiar modes of causal inquiry, detailed sociological investigation, and an accumulation of knowledge about concrete aspects of the social world. A realist researcher is advised to pursue familiar approaches to the problem of assessing the truth or falsity of hypotheses about causal properties of social entities. Do we believe that a certain kind of industrial organization has the tendency to produce a higher-than-average level of industrial accidents? Then collect observational data about how this organizational form functions; how it is internally regulated; and how its internal composition gives rise to a propensity for industrial accidents. This is the kind of research that Charles Perrow carries out in books such as *Normal Accidents: Living with High-Risk Technologies* (1999) and *The Next Catastrophe: Reducing Our Vulnerabilities to Natural, Industrial, and Terrorist Disasters* (Perrow 2011). Hypotheses about social structures and their powers can be investigated piecemeal, and we can tease out the causal properties that they possess through familiar methods along the lines of Mill's methods.

Take two ideas about social structures in particular: the idea of an economic structure and the idea of a business corporation. Both these ideas can be articulated in reasonable detail and then investigated through piecemeal empirical inquiry. Consider the economic structure: What are the property relations through which labor and other resources are managed and controlled in specific instances of capitalist economies? How do these relations work in concrete detail? What variations exist? What failures do these relations experience? This is the kind of materialist historical research that is conducted by Charles Sabel and his colleagues and which they offer in *World of Possibilities: Flexibility and Mass Production in Western Industrialization* (Sabel and Zeitlin 1997).

Or, take a specific corporation—the IBM corporation, for example. Here, again, it is unproblematic to identify many independent avenues of research through which the relations, properties, norms, and patterns of behavior that make up the corporation. There is nothing occult about the corporation. Do we think that the power of management distorts the decision-making of the corporation by favoring executives over shareholders and employees? It is straightforward to think of numerous independent ways of empirically investigating this hypothesis. Do we believe there are significant principal-agent problems among employees and corresponding solutions in the relations and roles embodied in the organization? Likewise, these hypotheses can be empirically investigated.

So, it seems most reasonable to argue that empirical reasoning looks the same for critical realists as it does for any other empirical scientist. There is no distinctive critical-realist model of empirical reasoning.

WHAT KIND OF REALIST?

Scientific realism is almost self-evidently true. Scientific theories and hypotheses put forward ideas that go beyond the evidence of direct experience. They postulate the existence of entities and forces that cannot be directly observed but whose effects can be teased out through the assumptions we have made about their characteristics. And, when we have a theory that "succeeds" in explaining a domain of observation and experimentation, we have reason to believe that its hypothetical entities and forces actually exist. The existence of the hypothetical entities is the "best explanation" for the success of the theory or hypothesis.

This is not, of course, a deductively certain inference from the success of the theory to the reality of the unseen entities. There may be other explanations for the observational and experimental success of the theory. And, the history of science in fact offers plenty of examples where this has turned out to be the case. Reality sometimes turns out to be more complicated, and structured differently, than our theories postulate.

This is the position that I would describe as "scientific realism." It represents a garden variety ontology; it simply holds that the entities postulated by successful scientific theories are likely to exist in approximately the form they are postulated to possess.

There are coherent alternatives to scientific realism. Phenomenalism and instrumentalism are coherent interpretations of the success of scientific theories that do not postulate the real existence of unseen entities. Milton Friedman's instrumentalist treatment of economic theory is a case in point (Friedman 1953). However, instrumentalists have a hard time accounting for the success of scientific theories in the absence of a realist interpretation of the theoretical premises. Why should cloud chambers show the specific arcs and tracks that are predicted by theory if the underlying model of the mechanisms is not correct?

So, how does all of this play out for the social sciences? In my view, the social sciences are substantially different from physics when it comes to hypothetical entities and theoretical hypotheses. The entities and forces to which we want to refer in the social world are *not* highly theoretical; rather, we can probe our concrete assumptions about these social entities and forces fairly directly. We don't need to turn to the Duhemian deductivism and theoretical holism that physics largely forces us into. Instead, we can devise strategies for probing them piecemeal.

So, when we postulate that "class" is an important entity or structure in the modern world, our evidence for this claim is not largely based on inference to the best explanation and the overall success of class theory; it is instead the bundle of concrete researches that have been performed to identify, specify, and investigate the workings of class. Conceptual specification is more important that theoretical articulation and deduction: we need to know what a given researcher means to encompass in his or her use of the term "class structure." To take the photo above of Eton boys as an example—what inferences can we draw about class from the photo? And, what do we mean when we say that it illustrates an important social reality in the Britain of the 1930s, the reality of class? Is it a fact about attitudes, about the mechanisms of opportunity and selection, about the differential assignment of privilege, and about modes of speech and thought?

If this is the approach we take, then our claims about what is "real" in the social realm will be more modest that some have thought. We will understand that there are real social processes, mechanisms, and powers, that they derive from the actions and agency of actors, and that these processes can be traced out through fairly direct sociological and historical research. And, we will understand too that claims about the reality of "capitalism," the world financial system, or fascism are to be understood less weightily than they first appear. Capitalism exists in a time and place; but it is understood to be an ensemble of relations and actions by the people of the time. It is not a "thing" in the way that deoxyribonucleic acid is a thing.

These thoughts should perhaps lead us to consider that the topic of realism is less important in sociology, political science, and economics than it might appear to be. Social scientists have every reason to be realist about the actions, relations, and interactions of individuals. They are justified in thinking that the practices of education and socialization that bring children to adulthood are "real" and can be empirically investigated. And, they are justified in observing that there are higher-order configurations of action, power, and social relationship that are "real," insofar as they are present in the activities of the individuals who constitute them and they possess some stable characteristics over time. In other words, social scientists are justified in postulating the social reality of the social processes and institutions that they postulate and investigate. But this is a weak and qualified conception of realism, and it suggests a fairly weak social ontology.

These commitments add up to a form of realism; but it isn't *critical* realism in the technical or substantive senses. It is a realism of a different stripe—a pragmatic realism, a galilean realism, and a scientific realism. "Critical realism" is a term of art; it refers to a very specific bundle of philosophical and ontological ideas that have been developed by Roy Bhaskar and his followers. It makes substantive philosophical assumptions about how the social world works, and it depends resolutely on a philosophical method of discovery and justification. And, this means that the reasons we have for embracing realism of a more general kind do not necessarily extend to support for critical realism. One can be realist about the social world without accepting the assumptions and doctrines of critical realism.

So, here is a moderate form of scientific realism that is well suited to the nature of the social world: be realist about social mechanisms but not about social kinds. Be realist in metaphysics and empiricist in epistemology: we can arrive at rationally justified beliefs about social mechanisms. And, be a skeptic or nominalist about social kinds. There are no macro- or molar-level social kinds.

Conclusion

The philosophy of social science offered here is fundamentally opposed to naturalism—the idea that the social and behavioral sciences should have the same structure and logical characteristics as the natural sciences. Chemistry and physics—especially the classical versions of these sciences—have a unified H-D structure; they discover laws of nature; and they derive the observable features of the domains of phenomena they encompass. Naturalism postulates, therefore, that sociology, economics, or psychology should have the same logical structure, because that is what "science" requires. John Stuart Mill clearly presupposed this assumption in his discussion of the "moral sciences" (Mill 1988).

We can provide an alternative social ontology—a better grounding for sociological research. The social sciences could have begun with a greater degree of agnosticism about the orderliness of social phenomena. We could have started with the following observations:

- Social phenomena are created by human beings (deliberately, intentionally, or unknowingly).
- Human beings behave as a result of their socially constructed beliefs, values, goals, attitudes, modes of reasoning, emotions, . . .
- There is a wide range of variation that is visible among social arrangements and institutions, across cultures, across space, and across time (long duration and short duration).
- Social institutions, organizations, and structures have a degree of observable stability across cohorts and generations of the human beings who make them up.
- There are social causes, and they are ordinary, observable, and mundane. They are variants of the agent-structure nexus.

These initial ontological observations would have led us to some framing expectations about the social and about the likely results of social science inquiry:

• Contingency of social outcomes
• Variation of social trajectory
• Plasticity of social institutions
• Heterogeneity among instances of a "type" of social thing
• No "laws of motion" for development or modernization

And, we might have set several research objectives for the social sciences:

• To study in some detail how various institutions work in different social settings (empirical, fact-driven observation and analysis)
• To study human behavior, motivation, and action—again, with sensibility to variation, without the assumption that there is one ultimate human nature or governing mode of behavior
• To be as aware of variation and plasticity as we are attentive to the discovery of social regularities
• To discover and theorize some of the causal mechanisms that can be observed within social processes
• To identify weak regularities of behavior and institution through observation
• To theorize these regularities in terms of agent-structure dynamics, aggregation of features of decision-making, and unintended consequences; for example, free-rider phenomena (economists) and self-regulating commons (common-property resource institutions)

We then might have arrived at a different conception of what a "mature" social science would involve: not a deductive theory with a few high-level generalizations and laws, but rather an eclectic ensemble of theories of mid-level processes and mechanisms that embodies as many of the characteristics and varieties of behavior as possible into the simulation, and then projects different possible scenarios.

This set of observations suggests a different way of ranking the importance of various subdisciplines of the social sciences. Currently, the disciplines and topics with the highest level of respect and recognition are the areas of quantitative research that continue to dominate the institutions of the social sciences. This status derives from the ascendancy of positivist and Humean ideas about "good" science. But if we take seriously the points made throughout this book and summarized above, then it becomes apparent that subdisciplines that aim to provide a more granular level of study of the social world are in fact more insightful and a better basis for building an understanding of the processes of change we are experiencing. This means social research that looks carefully for underlying causal mechanisms of large-scale social processes; that pays attention to the diversity and heterogeneity of social phenomena; that takes history seriously; and that makes a fuller attempt to do justice to the states of mentality through which social actors make their choices in various social settings. The study of concrete social institutions and arrangements sheds more light on the social world than large-N studies of interstate war, the properties of democracies, or the characteristics of welfare states. And, this implies that the research broadly classified as comparative historical sociology should have much greater primacy in the disciplines of the social sciences than the professions currently assign to these research paradigms.

These observations perhaps give urgency as well to research in the philosophy of social science. Philosophers can contribute to better methods and research strategies by working social scientists by understanding the problems they are attempting to understand and by helping to refine methods of inquiry and theoretical constructions that are well designed to shed light on a heterogeneous and dynamic social world.

So, indeed, it makes good sense for social researchers to engage with philosophers in considering how to formulate a better philosophy of social science. This is because the nature of the current discussions in the philosophy of social science parallels constructively the process of theory formation and development that we need to see take place in sociology and political science. We would like to see greater exercise of intellectual imagination by social researchers, unconstrained by the dogmas of methodology or ontology that a discipline is all too ready to provide. The social world is strikingly and permanently surprising, with novel conjunctions of processes and causes leading to unexpected outcomes. We need new ways of thinking about the social world and the social sciences, and philosophy of social science can help stimulate some of that thinking.

References

Abbott, Andrew. 1988. *The system of professions: An essay on the division of expert labor*. Chicago: University of Chicago Press.
———. 1998. "The causal devolution." *Sociological Methods and Research* no. 27 (2): 148–181.
———. 2001. *Chaos of disciplines*. Chicago: University of Chicago Press.
———. 2005. "The historicality of individuals." *Social Science History* no. 29 (1): 1–13.
———. 2007. "Mechanisms and relations." *Sociologica* no. 2: 1–22.
Abend, Gabriel. 2006. "Styles of sociological thought: Sociologies, Epistemologies, and the Mexican and U.S. Quests for Truth." *Sociological Theory* no. 24 (1):1–40.
———. 2014. *The moral background: An inquiry into the history of business ethics, Princeton studies in cultural sociology*. Princeton: Princeton University Press.
Adams, Julia, Elisabeth Stephanie Clemens, and Ann Shola Orloff. 2005. *Remaking modernity: Politics, history, and sociology, Politics, history, and culture*. Durham: Duke University Press.
Anderson, Elijah. 1999. *Code of the street: Decency, violence, and the moral life of the inner city*. 1st ed. New York, NY: W. W. Norton.
Archer, Margaret Scotford. 1995. *Realist social theory: The morphogenetic approach*. Cambridge; New York, NY: Cambridge University Press.
———. 1996. *Culture and agency: The place of culture in social theory*. Rev. ed. Cambridge England; New York, NY, USA: Cambridge Unviersity Press.
———. 2013. *Social morphogenesis*. New York, NY: Springer.
———. 2014. *Late modernity: Trajectories towards morphogenic society, social morphogenesis*. Cham; New York, NY: Springer.
———. 2015. *Generative mechanisms transforming the social order*. New York, NY: Springer Berlin Heidelberg.
Aristotle. 1987. *The Nicomachean ethics*. Buffalo, NY: Prometheus Books.
Axelrod, Robert, and Michael D. Cohen. 2000. *Harnessing complexity: Organizational implications of a scientific frontier*. New York, NY: Simon and Schuster.

Axelrod, Robert M. 1984. *The evolution of cooperation*. New York, NY: Basic Books.

Axelrod, Robert M., and Michael D. Cohen. 1999. *Harnessing complexity: Organizational implications of a scientific frontier*. New York, NY: Free Press.

Bauman, Zygmunt. 2000. *Liquid modernity*. Cambridge, UK; Malden, MA: Polity Press; Blackwell.

Bearman, Peter S. 2005. *Doormen, Fieldwork encounters and discoveries*. Chicago: University of Chicago Press.

Bechtel, William. 2006. *Discovering cell mechanisms: The creation of modern cell biology, Cambridge studies in philosophy and biology*. New York, NY: Cambridge University Press.

Beebee, Helen, Christopher Hitchcock, and Peter Charles Menzies. 2009. *The Oxford handbook of causation, Oxford handbooks in philosophy*. Oxford: Oxford University Press.

Bem, Sacha. 2011. "The explanatory autonomy of psychology: Why a mind is not a brain." *Theory & Psychology* no. 11 (6): 785–795.

Bhaskar, Roy. 1975. *A realist theory of science*. Leeds: Leeds Books.

———. 1982. "Emergence, explanation, and emancipation." In *Explaining human behaviour: Consciousness, human action, and social structure*, edited by P. F. Secord. Beverly Hills, London and New Delhi: Sage.

———. 1989. *The possibility of naturalism: A philosophical critique of the human sciences*. 2nd ed. London: Harvester Wheatsheaf.

Bianchi, Federico, and Flaminio Squazzoni. 2015. "Agent-based models in sociology." *Wiley Interdisciplinary Reviews: Computational Statistics* no. 7 (4): 284–306.

Bianco, Lucien. 2001. *Peasants without the party: Grass-root movements in twentieth-century China*. Armonk, NY: M. E. Sharpe.

Block, Ned. 2003. "Do causal powers drain away?" *Philosophy and Phenomenological Research* no. 67 (1): 133–150. doi: 10.2307/20140585.

Bourdieu, Pierre. 1977. *Outline of a theory of practice*. Cambridge: Cambridge University Press.

Boyd, Richard. 1990. "Realism, approximate truth, and philosophical method." In *Scientific theories*, edited by C. Wade Savage. Minneapolis: University of Minnesota Press.

———. 2002. Scientific realism. *Stanford Encyclopedia of Philosophy*, http://plato.stanford.edu/entries/scientific-realism/.

Boyd, Richard N. 1984. "The current status of scientific realism." In *Scientific realism*, edited by Jarrett Leplin, pp. 192–222.

Bridge, Gary, and Sophie Watson. 2011. *The new Blackwell companion to the city, Wiley-Blackwell companions to geography*. Malden, MA: Wiley-Blackwell.

Brinton, Mary C., and Victor Nee. 1998. *New institutionalism in sociology*. New York, NY: Russell Sage Foundation.

Bunge, Mario. 2003. *Emergence and convergence: Qualitative novelty and the unity of knowledge, Toronto studies in philosophy*. Toronto; Buffalo: University of Toronto Press.

Cartwright, Nancy. 1989. *Nature's capacities and their measurement*. Oxford: Oxford University Press.

———. 1999. *The dappled world: A study of the boundaries of science*. Cambridge; New York, NY: Cambridge University Press.

Coase, R. H. 1988. *The firm, the market, and the law*. Chicago: University of Chicago Press.

Cohn, Alain, Ernst Fehr, and Michel Andre Marechal. 2014. "Business culture and dishonesty in the banking industry." *Nature*. doi: 10.1038/nature13977.

Crozier, Michel, and Erhard Friedberg. 1980. *Actors and systems: The politics of collective action*. Chicago: University of Chicago Press.

Cruickshank, Justin. 2003a. *Critical realism: The difference in makes, Routledge studies in critical realism*. London; New York, NY: Routledge.

———. 2003b. *Realism and sociology: Anti-foundationalism, ontology, and social research, Routledge studies in critical realism*. London; New York, NY: Routledge.

Darnton, Robert. 1984. *The great cat massacre and other episodes in French cultural history*. New York, NY: Basic Books.

Davidson, Donald. 1974. "On the very idea of a conceptual scheme." *Proceedings and Addresses of the American Philosophical Association* no. 47: 5–20.

De Landa, Manuel. 2006. *A new philosophy of society: Assemblage theory and social complexity*. London; New York, NY: Continuum International Publishing Group.

Deleuze, Gilles, and Félix Guattari. 1987. *A thousand plateaus: Capitalism and schizophrenia*. Minneapolis: University of Minnesota Press.

Diani, Mario, and Doug McAdam. 2003. *Social movements and networks: relational approaches to collective action, comparative politics*. Oxford; New York, NY: Oxford University Press.

Dilthey, Wilhelm. 1989. *Introduction to the human sciences*. Edited by Rudolf A. Makkreel and Frithjof Rodi. Princeton, NJ: Princeton University Press.

Dobbin, Frank. 1994. *Forging industrial policy: The United States, Britain, and France in the railway age*. Cambridge [England]; New york, NY, USA: Cambridge University Press.

Duhem, Pierre Maurice Marie. 1906; 1977. *The aim and structure of physical theory, Atheneum paperbacks; 13*. New York, NY: Atheneum.

Dupré, John, and Nancy Cartwright. 1988. "Probability and causality: Why Hume and Indeterminism don't mix." *Nous* no. 22: 521–536.

Dupre, John, and James Woodward. 2013. "Mechanism and causation in biology." *Proceedings of the Aristotelian Society Supplementary Volume* no. LXXXVII. doi: 10.1111/j.1467-8349.2013.00218.x.

Elder-Vass, David. 2010. *The causal power of social structures: Emergence, structure and agency*. Cambridge, MA: Cambridge University Press.

Elias, Norbert, and Michael Schröter. 1991. *The society of individuals*. Oxford, UK; Cambridge, MA, USA: Basil Blackwell.

Ellickson, Robert C. 1991. *Order without law: How neighbors settle disputes*. Cambridge, MA: Harvard University Press.

Elster, Jon. 1989. *The cement of society: A study of social order*. Cambridge, MA: Cambridge University Press.

Ensminger, Jean. 1992. *Making a market: The institutional transformation of an African society, The Political economy of institutions and decisions*. Cambridge [England]; New York, NY: Cambridge University Press.

Epstein, Brian. 2007. "Ontological individualism reconsidered." *Synthese* no. 166 (1): 187–213.

———. 2015. *The ant trap: Rebuilding the foundations of the social sciences*, Oxford studies in philosophy of science. New York, NY: Oxford University Press.

Epstein, Joshua M. 2002. "Modeling civil violence: An agent-based computational approach." *Proceedings of the National Academy of Sciences* no. 99 (suppl. 3): 7243–7250.

———. 2006. *Generative social science: Studies in agent-based computational modeling*, Princeton studies in complexity. Princeton: Princeton University Press.

———. 2013. *Agent zero: Toward neurocognitive foundations for generative social science*, Princeton studies in complexity. Princeton, NJ: Princeton University Press.

Epstein, Joshua M., and Robert Axtell. 1996. *Growing artificial societies: Social science from the bottom up, complex adaptive systems*. Washington, DC: Brookings Institution Press.

Fehr, Ernst, and Klaus M. Schmidt. 1999. "A theory of fairness, competition, and cooperation." *The Quarterly Journal of Economics* no. August.

Fink, Carole. 1989. *Marc Bloch: A life in history*. Cambridge; New York, NY: Cambridge University Press.

Fligstein, Neil, and Doug McAdam. 2011. "Toward a general theory of strategic action fields." *Sociological Theory* no. 29 (1): 1–26. doi: 10.1111/j.1467-9558.2010.01385.x.

———. 2012. *A theory of fields*. New York, NY: Oxford University Press.

Fodor, Jerry. 1974. "Special sciences and the disunity of science as a working hypothesis." *Synthese* no. 28 (2): 97–115.

———. 1997. "Special sciences: Still autonomous after all these years." *Philosophical Perspectives 11, Mind, Causation, and World* no. 11: 149–163.

Frank, Thomas. 2005. *What's the matter with Kansas?: How conservatives won the heart of America*. 1st Owl Books ed. New York, NY: Henry Holt.

Frickel, Scott, and Neil Gross. 2005. "A general theory of scientific/intellectual movements." *American Sociological Review* no. 70: 204–232.

Friedman, Milton. 1953. *Essays in Positive Economics*. Chicago: University of Chicago Press.

Gambetta, Diego. 2009. *Codes of the underworld: How criminals communicate*. Princeton: Princeton University Press.

Geertz, Clifford. 1968. *Islam observed; religious development in Morocco and Indonesia*, The Terry lectures, v. 37. New Haven: Yale University Press.

———. 1971. *The interpretation of cultures; selected essays*. New York, NY: Basic Books.

Gibbard, Allan. 1990. *Wise choices, apt feelings: A theory of normative judgment*. Cambridge: Harvard University Press.

Giddens, Anthony. 1979. *Central problems in social theory: Action, structure and contradiction in social analysis*. Berkeley: University of California Press.

Gilbert, Margaret. 1989. *On social facts*. Princeton: Princeton University Press.

Glaeser, Andreas. 2011. *Political epistemics: The secret police, the opposition, and the end of East German socialism*, Chicago studies in practices of meaning. Chicago; London: The University of Chicago Press.

Glennan, Stuart. 1996. "Mechanisms and the nature of causation." *Erkenntnis* no. 44: 49–71.

Goffman, Erving. 1963. *Behavior in public places; notes on the social organization of gatherings.* New York, NY: Free Press of Glencoe.

———. 1967. *Interaction ritual; essays in face-to-face behavior.* Chicago: Aldine Pub. Co.

Goodman, Nelson. 1978. *Ways of Worldmaking.* Indianapolis, IN: Hackett Publishing.

Gorski, Philip. 2013. "What is critical realism? And why should you care?" *Contemporary Sociology* no. 42 (5): 658–670.

Gouldner, Alvin Ward. 1970. *The coming crisis of Western sociology.* New York, NY: Basic Books.

Granovetter, Mark. 1985. "Economic action and social structure: The problem of embeddedness." *American Journal of Sociology* no. 91 (3): 481–510.

Green, Donald P., and Ian Shapiro. 1994. *Pathologies of rational choice theory: A critique of applications in political science.* New Haven: Yale University Press.

Griswold, Wendy. 2013. *Cultures and societies in a changing world.* 4th ed. *Sociology for a new century series.* Thousand Oaks, CA: SAGE Publications.

Groff, Ruth. 2008. *Revitalizing causality: Realism about causality in philosophy and social science, Routledge studies in critical realism.* London; New York, NY: Routledge.

———. 2013. *Ontology revisited: Metaphysics in social and political philosophy, Ontological explorations.* London; New York, NY: Routledge.

Groff, Ruth, and John Greco. 2013. *Powers and capacities in philosophy: The new Aristotelianism.* New York, NY: Routledge.

Gross, Neil. 2009. "A pragmatist theory of social mechanisms." *American Sociological Review* no. 74 (3): 358–379.

Hacking, Ian. 1991. "A tradition of natural kinds." *Philosophical Studies: An International Journal for Philosophy in the Analytic Tradition* no. 61 (1/2): 109–126.

Harré, Rom, and E. H. Madden. 1975. *Causal powers: A theory of natural necessity.* Oxford: Basil Blackwell.

Hedström, Peter. 2005. *Dissecting the social: On the principles of analytical sociology.* Cambridge, UK; New York, NY: Cambridge University Press.

Hedström, Peter, and Petri Ylikoski. 2010. "Causal mechanisms in the social sciences." *Annual Review of Sociology* no. 36: 49–67.

Hellman, Geoffrey. 2011. Reduction, Determination, Explanation. *unpublished,* http://www.tc.umn.edu/~hellm001/Publications/ReductionDeterminationExplanation.pdf.

Hempel, Carl Gustav. 1965. *Aspects of scientific explanation, and other essays in the philosophy of science.* New York, NY: Free Press.

Heppenstall, Alison J., Andrew T. Crooks, Linda M. See, and Michael Batty. 2011. *Agent-based models of geographical systems.* New York, NY: Springer.

Holland, John. 2014. *Complexity: A very short introduction.* Oxford: Oxford University Press.

Holland, John H. 1997. "Emergence." *Philosopohica* no. 59 (1): 11–40.

Illari, Phyllis McKay, Federica Russo, and Jon Williamson. 2011. *Causality in the sciences.* Oxford: Oxford University Press.

Johnson, Mark. 1994. *Moral imagination: Implications of cognitive science for ethics*. Chicago: University of Chicago Press.

Kaidesoja, Tuukka. 2007. "Exploring the concept of causal power in a critical realist tradition." *Journal for the Theory of Social Behaviour* no. 37 (1): 63–87.

———. 2013a. *Naturalizing critical realist social ontology, Ontological explorations*. London: Routledge.

———. 2013b. "Overcoming the biases of microfoundationalism: Social mechanisms and collective agents." *Philosophy of the Social Sciences* no. 43 (3): 301–322.

Kiel, L. Douglas, and Euel W. Elliott. 1996. *Chaos theory in the social sciences: foundations and applications*. Ann Arbor, MI: University of Michigan Press.

Kim, Jaegwon. 1993. *Supervenience and mind: Selected philosophical essays*. Cambridge, MA: Cambridge University Press.

———. 2005. *Physicalism, or something near enough, Princeton monographs in philosophy*. Princeton, NJ: Princeton University Press.

Klitgaard, Robert E. 1988. *Controlling corruption*. Berkeley: University of California Press.

Lamont, Michèle. 1992. *Money, morals, and manners: The culture of the French and American upper-middle class, Morality and society*. Chicago: University of Chicago Press.

Lee, Ching Kwan. 2007. *Against the law: Labor protests in China's rustbelt and sunbelt*. Berkeley: University of California Press.

Lewis, David K. 1969. *Convention: A philosophical study*. Cambridge: Harvard University Press.

Lieberson, Stanley. 1987. *Making it count: The improvement of social research and theory*. Berkeley, CA: University of California Press.

Little, Daniel. 1991. *Varieties of social explanation: An introduction to the philosophy of social science*. Boulder, CO: Westview Press.

———. 1998. *Microfoundations, method and causation: On the philosophy of the social sciences*. New Brunswick, NJ: Transaction Publishers.

———. 2000. "Explaining large-scale historical change." *Philosophy of the Social Sciences* no. 30 (1): 89–112.

———. 2006. "Levels of the social." In *Handbook for philosophy of anthropology and sociology*, edited by Stephen Turner and Mark Risjord, 343–371. Amsterdam; New York, NY: Elsevier Publishing.

———. 2010. *New Directions in the Philosophy of History, Methodos*. Dordrecht: Springer Science.

———. 2011. "Causal mechanisms in the social realm." In *Causality in the sciences*, edited by Phyllis Illari, Federica Russo, and Jon Williamson. Oxford: Oxford University Press.

Luhmann, Niklas, Dirk Baecker, and Peter Gilgen. 2013. *Introduction to systems theory*. Cambridge, UK; Malden, MA: Polity.

Machamer, Peter, Lindley Darden, and Carl F. Craver. 2000. "Thinking about mechanisms." *Philosophy of Science* no. 67 (1): 1–25.

MacIntyre, Alasdair. 1973. "Is a science of comparative politics possible?" In *The philosophy of social explanation*, edited by Alan Ryan.

Mahoney, James. 2001. "Beyond correlational analysis: Recent innovations in theory and method" *Sociological Forum* no. 16 (3): 575–593.

Mahoney, James, and Kathleen Ann Thelen. 2010. *Explaining institutional change: Ambiguity, agency, and power*. Cambridge; New York, NY: Cambridge University Press.

Manicas, Peter T. 2006. *A realist philosophy of social science: Explanation and understanding*. Cambridge, UK; New York, NY: Cambridge University Press.

Mann, Michael. 1986. *The sources of social power. A history of power from the beginning to A.D. 1760*. Vol. 1. Cambridge, MA: Cambridge University Press.

———. 2004. *Fascists*. New York, NY: Cambridge University Press.

Manzo, Gianluca. 2014. *Analytical sociology: Actions and networks, Wiley series in computational and quantitative social science*. Hoboken: Wiley.

Martin, John Levi. 2009. *Social structures*. Princeton, NJ: Princeton University Press.

Mayntz, Renate. 2004. "Mechanisms in the analysis of social macro-phenomena." *Philosophy of the Social Sciences* no. 34 (2): 237–259.

McAdam, Doug. 1999. *Political process and the development of Black insurgency, 1930–1970*. 2nd ed. Chicago: University of Chicago Press.

McAdam, Doug, Sidney G. Tarrow, and Charles Tilly. 2001. *Dynamics of contention, Cambridge studies in contentious politics*. New York, NY: Cambridge University Press.

McNeill, William. 1976. *Plagues and peoples*. Garden City: Doubleday.

Merton, Robert King. 1967. *On theoretical sociology; five essays, old and new, Free Press paperback*. New York, NY: Free Press.

Mill, John Stuart. 1988. *The logic of the moral sciences*. La Salle, IL: Open Court.

Miller, John H., and Scott E. Page. 2007. *Complex adaptive systems: An introduction to computational models of social life, Princeton studies in complexity*. Princeton, NJ: Princeton University Press.

Monroe, Kristen R. 2005. *Perestroika!: The raucous rebellion in political science*. New Haven: Yale University Press.

Moya, Paula M. L., and Michael Roy Hames-Garcia. 2000. *Reclaiming identity: Realist theory and the predicament of postmodernism*. Berkeley, CA: University of California Press.

Mumford, Stephen. 2009. "Causal powers and capacities." In *The Oxford handbook of causation*, edited by Helen Beebee, Christopher Hitchcock, and Peter Charles Menzies. Oxford: Oxford University Press.

Mumford, Stephen, and Rani Lill Anjum. 2011. *Getting causes from powers*. Oxford; New York, NY: Oxford University Press.

Niiniluoto, Ilkka. 1999. *Critical scientific realism, Clarendon library of logic and philosophy*. Oxford; New York, NY: Oxford University Press.

Ollman, Bertell. 1971. *Alienation: Marx's conception of man in capitalist society, Cambridge studies in the history and theory of politics*. Cambridge [England]: University Press.

Olson, Mancur. 1965. *The logic of collective action: Public goods and the theory of groups*. Cambridge, MA: Harvard University Press.

Ostrom, Elinor. 1990. *Governing the commons: The evolution of institutions for collective action*. Cambridge [England]; New York, NY: Cambridge University Press.

Perrow, Charles. 1999. *Normal accidents: Living with high-risk technologies: With a new afterword and a postscript on the Y2K problem.* Princeton, NJ: Princeton University Press.

———. 2011. *The Next Catastrophe: Reducing Our Vulnerabilities to Natural, Industrial, and Terrorist Disasters.* Princeton: Princeton University Press.

Pierson, Paul. 2004. *Politics in time: History, institutions, and social analysis.* Princeton: Princeton University Press.

Polanyi, Karl. 1957. *The Great Transformation.* Boston: Beacon Press.

Popkin, Samuel L. 1979. *The rational peasant: The political economy of rural society in Vietnam.* Berkeley: University of California Press.

Porpora, Douglas V. 1989. "Four concepts of social structure" *Journal for the Theory of Social Behaviour* no. 19 (2): 195–211. doi: 10.1111/j.1468-5914.1989. tb00144.x.

———. 2015. *Reconstructing sociology: The critical realist approach.* Cambridge, United Kingdom: Cambridge University Press.

Quine, W. V. 1960. *Word and object, studies in communication.* [Cambridge]: Technology Press of the Massachusetts Institute of Technology.

Resnicow, Kenneth, and Scott E. Page. 2008. "Embracing chaos and complexity: A quantum change for public health." *Framing Health Matters* no. 98 (9): 1382–1389.

Root, Hilton L. 2013. *Dynamics among nations: The evolution of legitimacy and development in modern states.* Cambridge, MA: The MIT Press.

Rudner, Richard S. 1966. *Philosophy of social science, Prentice-Hall foundations of philosophy series.* Englewood Cliffs, NJ: Prentice-Hall.

Sabel, Charles F., and Jonathan Zeitlin. 1997. *Worlds of possibility: Flexibility and mass production in western industrialization, Studies in modern capitalism = Etudes sur le capitalisme moderne.* Cambridge [England]; New York, NY: Maison des sciences de l'homme; Cambridge University Press.

Sassen, Saskia. 2001. *The global city: New York, London, Tokyo.* 2nd ed. Princeton, NJ: Princeton University Press.

Sawyer, R. Keith. 2005. *Social emergence: Societies as complex systems.* Cambridge; New York, NY: Cambridge University Press.

Schelling, Thomas C. 1971. "Dynamic models of segregation." *Journal of Mathematical Sociology* no. 1: 143–186.

———. 1978. *Micromotives and macrobehavior.* New York, NY: Norton.

Schultz, Theodore W. 1964. *Transforming traditional agriculture.* New Haven: Yale University Press.

Scott, James C. 1976. *The moral economy of the peasant: Rebellion and subsistence in Southeast Asia.* New Haven: Yale University Press.

Searle, John R. 2010. *Making the social world: The structure of human civilization.* Oxford; New York, NY: Oxford University Press.

Sen, Amartya. 1987. *On ethics & economics.* New York, NY: Basil Blackwell.

Sewell, William Hamilton. 1980. *Work and revolution in France: The language of labor from the Old Regime to 1848.* Cambridge; New York, NY: Cambridge University Press.

Simon, Herbert. 1962. "The architecture of complexity." *Proceedings of the American Philosophical Society* no. 106 (6): 467–482. http://ecoplexity.org/files/uploads/ Simon.pdf.

Simon, Herbert A. 1996 [1969]. *The sciences of the artificial*. 3rd ed. Cambridge, MA: MIT Press.

Sklar, Lawrence. 2006. Varieties of explanatory autonomy. In *Robert and Sarah Boote conference in reductionism and anti-reductionism in Physics*. Center for Philosophy of Science, University of Pittsburgh, Pittsburgh, PA.

Skocpol, Theda. 1979. *States and social revolutions: A comparative analysis of France, Russia, and China*. Cambridge; New York, NY: Cambridge University Press.

Somers, Margaret. 1998. "We're no angels: Realism, rational cohice, and relationality in social science." *American Journal of Sociology* no. 104 (3): 722–84.

Sørensen, Aage B. 1998. "Theoretical mechanisms and the empirical study of social processes." In *Social mechanisms: An analytical approach to social theory*, edited by P. Hedström and R. Swedberg.

Srbljinovic, Armano, Drazen Penzar, Petra Rodik, and Kruno Kardov. 2003. An agent-based model of ethnic mobilisation. http://jasss.soc.surrey.ac.uk/6/1/1.html.

Steel, Daniel. 2004. "Social Mechanisms and Causal Inference." *Philosophy of the Social Sciences* no. 34 (1): 55–78. file://C:%5CMy%20Documents%5Carchive%20 discussions%20of%20my%20work%5Csteel%20social%20mechanisms%20msu. pdf.

Steinmetz, George. 1998. "Critical realism and historical sociology: A review article." *Comparative Studies in Society and History* no. 40 (1): 170–186.

———. 2004. "Odious comparisons: Incommensurability, the case study, and 'small N's' in sociology." *Sociological Theory* no. 22 (3).

———. 2005. *The politics of method in the human sciences: Positivism and its epistemological others, politics, history, and culture*. Durham: Duke University Press.

———. 2007. *The devil's handwriting: Precoloniality and the German colonial state in Qingdao, Samoa, and Southwest Africa*. Chicago: University of Chicago Press.

Strawson, P. F. 1963. *Individuals, an essay in descriptive metaphysics*. Garden City, NY: Doubleday.

Strevens, Michael. 2011. Explanatory Autonomy and Explanatory Irreducibility. *unpublished*, http://www.strevens.org/research/expln/Autonomia.pdf.

Taylor, Charles. 1985. "Interpretation and the sciences of man." In *Philosophy and the Human Sciences: Philosophical Papers 2*, edited by Charles Taylor. Cambridge, MA: Cambridge University Press.

Taylor, Michael. 1982. *Community, anarchy and liberty*. Cambridge, MA: Cambridge University Press.

Thelen, Kathleen Ann. 2004. *How institutions evolve: The political economy of skills in Germany, Britain, the United States, and Japan, Cambridge studies in comparative politics*. Cambridge; New York, NY: Cambridge University Press.

Thompson, E. P. 1966. *The making of the English working class, Vintage books, V-322*. New York, NY: Vintage Books.

Thunen, Johann Heinrich von. 1826. *Der isolierte Staat*: Berlin.

Tilly, Charles. 1970. *La Vendée. Révolution et contre-Révolution*. Paris: Fayard.

———. 1984. *Big structures, large processes, huge comparisons*. New York, NY: Russell Sage Foundation.

———. 1986. *The contentious French: Four centuries of popular struggle*. Cambridge: Harvard University Press.

———. 1995. "To explain political processes." *American Journal of Sociology* no. 100: 1594–610.

———. 2005. *Trust and rule, Cambridge studies in comparative politics*. New York, NY: Cambridge University Press.

Tomasello, Michael. 2009. *Why we cooperate, A Boston review book*. Cambridge, MA: MIT Press.

Tuomela, Raimo. 2002. *The philosophy of social practices: A collective acceptance view*. Cambridge, New York, NY: Cambridge University Press.

Turner, Stephen, and Mark Risjord. 2006. *Handbook for Philosophy of Anthropology and Sociology*. Edited by Dov Gabbay, Paul Thagard, and John Woods. Vol. 15, *Handbook of the Philosophy of Science*. Amsterdam; New York, NY: Elsevier Science.

Udehn, Lars. 2001. *Methodological individualism: Background, history and meaning*. London: Routledge.

von Wright, G. H. 1971. *Explanation and understanding, contemporary philosophy*. Ithaca, NY: Cornell University Press.

Wallerstein, Immanuel Maurice. 1999. *The end of the world as we know it: Social science for the twenty-first century*. Minneapolis: University of Minnesota Press.

Wan, Poe Yu-ze. 2011. "Emergence a la systems theory: epistemological totalausschluss or ontological novelty?" *Philosophy of the Social Sciences* no. 41 (2): 178–210.

Watkins, J. W. N. 1968. "Methodological individualism and social tendencies." In *Readings in the philosophy of the social sciences*, edited by May Brodbeck. New York, NY: Macmillan.

Weber, Max. 1930. *The Protestant ethic and the spirit of capitalism*. Edited by Talcott Parsons and R. H. Tawney. London: G. Allen & Unwin Ltd.

———. 1949. *The methodology of the social sciences*. New York, NY: Free Press.

Wendt, Alexander. 2015. *Quantum mind and social science: unifying physical and social ontology*. Cambridge, United Kingdom; New York, NY: Cambridge University Press.

Wilensky, U. 2015. *NetLogo*. Center for Connected Learning and Computer-Based Modeling, Northwestern University 19992015. Available from http://ccl.northwestern.edu/netlogo/.

Wilensky, Uri. *EpiDEM Basic*. Northwestern University 2011a. Available from http://ccl.northwestern.edu/netlogo/models/epiDEMBasic.

———. *EpiDEM Rebellion*. Northwestern University 2011b. Available from http://ccl.northwestern.edu/netlogo/models/Rebellion.

Wimsatt, William C. 2006. "Reductionism and its heuristics: Making methodological reductionism honest." *Synthese*. doi: 10.1007/s11229-006-9017-0.

Wong, R. Bin. 1997. *China transformed: Historical change and the limits of european experience*. Ithaca, New York, NY: Cornell University Press.

Woodward, James. 2003. *Making things happen: A theory of causal explanation, Oxford studies in philosophy of science*. New York, NY: Oxford University Press.

Ylikoski, Petri. 2012. "Micro, Macro, and Mechanisms." In *The Oxford Handbook of Philosophy of Social Science*, edited by Harold Kincaid. New York, NY: Oxford University Press.

Young, Alford A. 2004. *The minds of marginalized black men: Making sense of mobility, opportunity, and future life chances, Princeton studies in cultural sociology*. Princeton, NJ: Princeton University Press.

Zahle, Julie, and Finn Collin. 2014. *Rethinking the Individualism-Holism Debate: Essays in the philosophy of social science*. Dordrecht; London: Springer.

Index

Abbott, Andrew, 2, 41, 50, 62, 72, 242
Abend, Gabriel, 218–20, 245
actor-centered sociology, xvii–xviii,
    20, 24, 37–72, 86, 91, 110, 132,
    164–65, 238, 241, 245, 247
agent-based modeling (ABM), 71,
    148–66
aggregation, 38, 73, 143, 147, 167–68,
    173, 188, 214, 216, 260
analytical sociology, xviii–xxi, 70–72,
    152, 200, 205–208
Archer, Margaret, xix, 40, 146, 205,
    238–41
Aristotle, 46–47, 194
assemblage theory, xviii–xxi, 10–13,
    92, 99

Bhaskar, Roy, xix, xx, 10, 94, 137–42,
    194, 221, 229–38, 253–54, 257.
    See also critical realism
Bourdieu, Pierre, 23–24, 49, 53
Boyd, Richard, 221–23, 235, 250
Bunge, Mario, 141, 197

Cartwright, Nancy, 8, 192–93
causal:
    explanation, xviii, 195, 246;
    mechanism. *See* mechanism, causal;
    necessity, 189, 226, 228;

powers. *See* powers, causal;
    realism, xviii, 199. *See also* realism
causation, xvii–xxi, 6, 16, 54, 81, 91,
    93, 116, 119, 125–26, 143, 146,
    175, 183, 184, 186, 188–95,
    198–209, 214, 224, 228, 232,
    236, 237, 246;
    conjunctural, 6, 13, 229, 237;
    meso-level, xvii, 66, 79, 82, 91–92,
    98, 126, 143–46, 205–209,
    213–14, 224, 238
China, xiv–xvi, 45, 136, 210, 252
city, xiv, 9–10, 32–35, 95–96, 108–109,
    151, 170, 212, 217, 248
civil violence, 3, 155, 157
Coleman, James, xx, 38, 70, 72, 93,
    101–103, 119, 129, 145, 147,
    199–209
Coleman's boat, xx, 38, 70, 72, 102,
    119, 129, 145, 147, 199, 205–209
collective actors, 103–106
complex adaptive system, 148, 171–79
complexity, xiii–xix, 9–12, 30, 91, 115,
    137–40, 147–48, 166–80, 188,
    236, 237
conceptual frameworks, xviii, 7, 15,
    24, 25–30, 37, 40–44, 54, 61–66,
    76–77, 94, 164–66, 219, 222,
    224, 245, 248

conceptual scheme, 27–31
confirmation, 4, 82, 223, 227, 251–53.
  See also piecemeal confirmation
constant conjunction, xvii, 195,
  201–202, 228, 237
contingency, xv–xvi, 1–2, 4, 9, 35, 77,
  100, 112, 178, 190, 229–30, 237,
  241, 260
cooperation, 24, 51, 56, 58, 76, 98, 100,
  107, 134, 152, 177
critical realism, xviii–xxi, 94, 137–39,
  193, 228–35, 238–39, 241,
  253, 257

DeLanda, Manuel, xix, 10–13.
  See also assemblage theory
Dobbin, Frank, 111–12

Elder-Vass, Dave, 93–94, 139–41,
  193, 205
embeddedness, 49–51
emergence, xiv–xvii, xx, 34, 89, 112,
  115–19, 137–42, 144, 146,
  148–49, 152, 155, 167–74, 197,
  228–29, 234
Ensminger, Jean 184–86
equilibrium, 17–20, 72, 157, 159,
  176, 244
essentialism, 11, 196–99
explanatory strategy, 7, 122, 203

fascism, 5, 25–34, 38, 75, 183, 195,
  215, 257
field:
  Bourdieu's concept of, xviii,
    23–24, 27;
  Strategic action field, 21, 89, 97–99,
    100–101, 240
Fligstein, Neil, 20, 21, 97–99, 101, 240
functionalism, 18, 177

generativity, xvii, 115, 118, 121,
  147–49, 153
Giddens, Anthony, 86, 93–94, 205
Goffman, Erving, 38, 51–53, 63–64,
  68–70, 243

Gorski, Philip, 229, 230
Granovetter, Mark, 49–51, 155
Groff, Ruth, 192–97, 200–201
Gross, Neil, 41, 50, 216–19

habitus, 49, 53, 222, 224
Harré, Rom, 196–98, 221
heterogeneity, x, xv–xvi, xxi, 1, 4,
  5–24, 30, 33, 35, 105, 128, 150,
  154, 158, 165, 174, 198, 231,
  235–38, 241, 260
historical sociology, 13, 30, 38, 112,
  216, 229, 244, 261
holism, 3, 127
Holland, John, 171–72
Hume, David, 190, 194–95, 200,
  226, 228
hypothetico-deductive model of
  confirmation (H-D), 224, 226,
  228, 251, 253

identity, 14, 15, 48, 61–62, 66–67, 76,
  105, 110, 157, 224, 239
incommensurability, 28
institutions, x, xiv–xv, xvii, 1–2, 6–8,
  14–22, 29, 31, 34, 40, 41, 45,
  50–51, 56–57, 62, 75–79, 83–84,
  89–92, 95, 98–101, 109, 111–12,
  116, 128–29, 133, 135–36,
  154, 179–80, 184–90, 195–99,
  205–206, 218–19, 224, 226, 231,
  246–48, 257–59
Interpretive methods, xviii, 229–30,
  242–43, 245–49

Kaidesoja, Tuukka, xix, 138–39,
  196–98, 234–35

law-governed processes, 1–2, 5, 252
Lee, C. K., xv
liquid modernity, 21–22, 240

McAdam, Doug, 7, 20–21, 47, 84–87,
  97–101, 105, 158, 191, 240
mechanisms, causal, xvi–xxi, 2, 5, 7,
  12, 14–26, 31, 34, 38–39, 44, 55,

58, 66–67, 72, 74, 76, 79–87,
93–96, 110–13, 120, 132, 144,
152, 170, 181, 184–261
methodological individualism, xvii, xx,
79, 86, 90, 93, 122, 126, 129,
141–42, 145–46, 207–208, 238
methodological localism, xxi, 2, 75–79,
100, 106, 132, 146, 187–89, 241
microfoundations, 3, 5, 7, 24, 37–38,
60, 72, 76–82, 91–98, 103, 105,
108–11, 115–19, 126, 128, 136,
144–46, 149, 184, 188, 203,
206–209, 212
morphogenesis, xix, 4, 40, 146, 238–42

natural kind, 27, 31, 34
NetLogo, 159–60
norms, xvii, 15, 21, 42, 44, 50, 53–59,
63, 68, 70, 74–80, 84, 92, 94,
102, 106–10, 127–28, 133–35,
146, 184, 186, 208, 218, 238–39,
246, 249, 255

objectivity, xviii, 221–22, 225, 249–51
ontological individualism, 3, 78–83,
126–29, 136, 148
ontology, x, xvi, xix–xxi, 1, 2, 8–14,
28, 30, 37, 41, 43, 54, 73–99,
102–104, 116–18, 124, 131–32,
136, 142, 147, 187–88, 194–95,
200, 230, 233–35, 238–39, 242,
245, 252–60
organizations, x, xvii, 2, 5, 14–15,
19–20, 31, 35, 38, 59, 63, 74–78,
82–101, 110, 112, 146, 158–59,
163–64, 174, 177, 183, 186, 188,
190, 193, 195, 203, 205–13, 217,
248, 252, 259

piecemeal confirmation, 20, 99, 223,
228, 251–56
plasticity, x, xvi, xxi, 1, 2, 14–22, 31,
34–35, 100, 128, 142, 197–98,
235, 240, 260
positivism, xx, 2, 6, 195, 200, 216,
226–32, 238, 242, 251, 253, 260

power, political, 19, 29–30, 58, 84–85
powers, causal, xvii–xxi, 79, 82, 90–95,
116, 120, 125–26, 138, 142–46,
168, 184, 189, 192–216, 224,
234, 249, 253–54
principal-agent problem, 185, 211,
231, 255

race, x, 9, 16, 40, 67, 86, 95–96, 108,
155, 186, 192, 214
rational choice theory, 7–8, 13, 44, 46,
48–51, 56–57, 70–72, 86, 126,
152, 176, 192, 199
rationality, 2, 25, 43–50, 56, 72, 110,
150, 157, 176, 221, 226, 228,
232
realism, xviii, xx–xxi, 84, 153, 163,
181, 186, 192, 195–97, 221–25,
229–36, 250, 254–57.
See also critical realism, scientific
realism
reductionism, xvii, xx–xxi, 3, 78,
82, 90–93, 103, 115, 119–29,
139–45, 167–68, 188, 193,
206–207, 232, 237
regularities, 2–6, 31, 38, 53, 60, 121,
124, 126, 146, 151, 186–87, 190,
192–93, 196, 201, 208, 216, 226,
230, 242, 253, 260
relative explanatory autonomy, xxi,
115, 118, 125, 132, 138, 142–45,
168, 206–207
relativism, 28, 229, 250

Schelling, Thomas, xix, 79, 122, 147,
150, 155, 191, 214
scientific realism, 4, 221, 255.
See also critical realism, realism
Scott, James, 47, 57, 148
Searle, John, 3, 81, 131–37
Sen, Amartya, 47, 228
Simon, Herbert, 118, 140, 166–71
simulation, 117, 147–52, 156–64, 175,
181, 206, 260
social capital, 24–27
social kinds, xxi, 27, 31–34, 197, 257

social network, 86–87, 92, 156, 178, 225

Steinmetz, George, 2, 13, 23–24, 38, 229–30

structures, social, xvi–xxi, 2–8, 12–16, 22–23, 26, 28–34, 37, 39–40, 48–49, 51, 53, 72–75, 77–103, 110–17, 119, 123, 128–29, 137–46, 152, 154, 168–70, 176–79, 183, 186, 188–89, 192, 194–99, 201–209, 213–27, 226–59

supervenience, 94, 115–32, 139–40, 144–45, 149, 168

technological change, 111–12

Tilly, Charles, 7, 31, 41, 44, 58–60, 84, 105, 156, 158, 177, 191–92, 201

trust, 51, 54, 58–62, 177, 211

variables paradigm, 2, 242

Wan, Poe Yue-ze, 141, 197

About the Author

Daniel Little is a philosopher who has written broadly on the foundations of the social sciences, the philosophy of history, and global justice. Recent books include *New Contributions to the Philosophy of History* (2010) and *The Paradox of Wealth and Poverty: Mapping the Ethical Dilemmas of Global Development* (2003). He also has a substantial interest in the history and politics of China. Little received his PhD in philosophy from Harvard University. Since 2000 he has served as chancellor of the University of Michigan–Dearborn.

Printed in Great Britain
by Amazon